YOUNGER

THAN THAT

NOW

Younger Than That Now

The Collected Interviews with Bob Dylan

THUNDER'S MOUTH PRESS • NEW YORK

YOUNGER THAN THAT NOW
THE COLLECTED INTERVIEWS WITH BOB DYLAN

Published in the United States by
Thunder's Mouth Press
An Imprint of Avalon Publishing Group Incorporated
245 W. 17th St. • 11th Floor
New York, NY 10011

AVALON
publishing group incorporated

Library of Congress Cataloging-in-Publication Data is available.

ISBN: 1-56025-590-0

9 8 7 6 5 4 3 2 1

Designed by Paul Paddock

Printed in the United States of America
Distributed by Publishers Group West

I can't provide for you no easy answers,
Who are you that I should have to lie?

Bob Dylan, "When the Night Comes Falling from the Sky"

MADEMOISELLE, AUGUST 1964

Prologue
Baez and Dylan:
A Generation Singing Out

Richard Fariña

WHEN BOB DYLAN DROVE ACROSS the Berkeley campus with his songs in a hip pocket and a station wagon full of friends, it was as if the undergraduates had been whispering of his imminent arrival for months. They seemed, occasionally, to believe he might not actually come, that some malevolent force or organization would get in the way. From north into Oregon and as far south as Fort Ord. near Monterey, college-age listeners had found time to make the trip, secure tickets, and locate seats in the mammoth Berkeley Community Theatre. They had come with a sense of collective expectancy, some attracted by already implausible legend, some critical of an idiom that seemed too maverick to be substantial, but most with an eye to taking part in a passing event that promised more than usual significance for their generation.

Each of Dylan's concerts this past year had had a way of arousing the same feeling. There was no sensation of his having performed somewhere the previous night or of a schedule that would take him away once the inevitable postconcert party was over. There was, instead, the familiar comparison with James Dean, at times explicit, at times unspoken, an impulsive awareness of his physical perishability. Catch him now, was the idea. Next week he might be mangled on a motorcycle.

The Berkeley performance did little to set anyone at ease. It often looked as if it were calculated to do the opposite, as a result both of its haphazard form and the provocative nature of its content. There were songs about the shooting of Medgar Evers, the Mississippi drowning of Emmett Till, the corporate tactics of munitions executives, even a fiercely cynical review of American war history called "With God on Our Side." Dylan appeared as usual in well-worn clothes. said whatever occurred to him at the time and sang his songs in no particular order. When he surprised everyone by introducing Joan Baez from the wings, the students were electrified. Their applause was potent, overwhelming, unmitigated. Had a literary audience been confronted by Dylan Thomas and Edna St. Vincent Millay the mood of aesthetic anxiety might have been the same.

To professional observers—and I talked to a good many—this mood threatened to overreach the abilities of the unassisted performers. They spoke of the fragility of the two people onstage, the lack of props and dramatic lighting, the absence of accompanying musicians, the banality of costume. A writer from one of the new folk magazines told me, "They can't be that confident, man; sooner or later they're going to play a wrong chord." But he was talking in terms of show-business proficiency, while the performers themselves were concerned with more durable values. They never doubted their capacity to equal the ovation and, if anything, they felt applause was a dubious reward for their efforts.

They claimed to be there not as virtuosos in the field of concretized folk music but as purveyors of an enjoined social consciousness and responsibility. They felt the intolerability of bigoted opposition to Civil Rights, the absurdity of life under a polluted atmosphere, and they were confident that a majority of their listeners felt the same way. "I don't know how they do it," said a San Francisco columnist, "but they certainly do it." When they left the stage to a whirlwind of enthusiastic cheers, it seemed that the previously unspoken word of protest, like the torch of President Kennedy's inaugural address, had most certainly been passed.

Significantly, when Joan and Dylan are together and away from the crush of admirers and hangers-on, the protest is seldom discussed. They are far more likely to putter with the harmonies of a rock-'n'-roll tune or run through the vital scenes of a recent movie than consider the tactics of civil disobedience. Like many another person in his early twenties, they derive a sense of political indignation from the totality of everyday conversation and the media that surround them—a process more akin to osmosis than ratiocination. And because of this subjective approach to the problems at hand, metaphor is better suited than directness to their respective dispositions.

"I don't like the word 'bomb' in a song," Joan said one evening, watching a fire in her sister's small Carmel cabin. The flames were the kind that hissed and crackled, causing small coals to pop and sometimes explode with surprising violence. They seemed to reinforce her feeling that simple, explicit reference to heat and radiation was too easy to slough off, that it never evoked anything more than superficial interest and sympathy. Speaking or singing with regard to megatons, fallout, strontium 90, nuclear deterrents, overkill ratios, genetic mutation, all in so many facile phrases, might have been necessary for raising the initial indignation of the populace, but it was certainly not sufficient. "People don't listen to words like those," she said. "They hear them, sure, but they don't listen."

Certainly, popular American reaction to these bald concepts had been little short of apathetic. A more meaningful vocabulary was needed to loosen fundamental feelings. Students across the country were helplessly aware of this fact whenever their civil or political protests were met by blatantly bureaucratic responses from public officials, elders, and even fellow students. Posters scrawled with "Ban the Bomb" or "No More Jim Crow" were invariably treated with a disdain that belied any awareness of the gravity of the causal situation. The students, seeking a more profound language and finding such language in folk music, looked to folk musicians as their spokesmen; and the musicians said and sang what they could. Last year, however, the vivid and topical imagery of a self-styled Midwestern folk-poet finally lent their arguments more vigorous meaning. And even from the point of view of the bureaucrats, this meaning was difficult to evade.

"It ain't nothin' just to walk around and sing,"Dylan said: "You have to step out a little, right?" We were strolling in the predawn London fog a year and a half ago, six months before he made the now historic appearance at the Newport Folk Festival. "Take Joanie, man, she's still singin' about Mary Hamilton. I mean where's that at? She's walked around on picket lines, she's got all kinds of feeling, so why ain't she steppin' out?"

Joan quite possibly had asked herself the same question. As much as any of the young people who looked to her for guidance, she was, at the time, bewildered and confused by the lack of official response to the protesting college voices. She had very little material to help her. At one point she was concerned enough about the content of her repertoire to consider abandoning public appearances until she had something more substantial to offer. Traditional ballads, ethnic music from one culture or another were not satisfactory for someone whose conception of folk singing extended so far beyond an adequate rendering. Her most emphatic song was "What Have They Done to the Rain?" and she was, one felt, more personally moved by the image of a small boy standing alone in a tainted shower than by the implication of the remaining lyrical content.

By May 1963, however, she'd had a first-hand opportunity to hear Dylan perform at the Monterey Folk Festival in California. His strong-willed, untempered, but nonetheless poetic approach to the problem filled the gap and left her awed and impressed. Moreover, by the time she had finished going over the songs he left behind, it seemed his lyrics would finally provide the substance for her continuing, campaigning role. . . . By living the life many university students would like to live, were it not for the daily concerns of textbooks and money from home, and by spending most of her public time in and around the nation's campuses, she has had no trouble keeping a half-conscious finger on an eager college pulse. Young people are very much aware that she drives an XKE and that it has been in the repair pits an inordinate number of times. . . . To most students it comes as no surprise that she is refusing to pay 60 percent of her income tax, a figure that corresponds to the government's allocation for defense. Occasionally one gets the feeling that people try too hard to relegate her to a premature immortality and the subsequent rumors are in kind: she has come down with a mysterious paralysis and will never sing again; she has been arrested at the Mexican border with a Jaguar full of narcotics; she is living with Marlon Brando on a Choctaw Indian reservation. In what many would call the alarming calm of her California surroundings, the exoticism of these stories seems absurd.

It was to her home in Carmel that Dylan came last spring just after the Berkeley concert. He was on his way to Los Angeles in the station wagon, traveling with Paul Clayton, once the most recorded professional in the folk revival; Bobby Neuwirth, one of the half-dozen surviving hipster nomads who shuttle back and forth between Berkeley and Harvard Square; and a lazy-ridded, black-booted friend called Victor, who seemed to be his road manager. They arrived bearing gifts of French-fried almonds. glazed walnuts, bleached cashews, dried figs, oranges, and prunes. Here again the legions of image-makers might well have been disappointed by the progress of the evening. How could so volatile a company get itself together without some sort of apocalyptic scene dominating the action? Instead, Joan's mother, visiting from Paris, cooked a beef stew. We talked about old friends, listened to the Evenly Brothers, and finally got Clayton to do a number of songs that few others can sing with such understated composure. The only overt references to Dylan's music came when Joan said she might want to record an entire album of his songs and he told her, "Sure thing."

The college students' reaction to Dylan has been somewhat more complex than their acceptance of Joan. It was clear from his initial entry on the folk scene that he was neither as musically gifted and delicate, nor as consistent in performance as she. Yet Robert Shelton, now the editor of *Hootenanny* magazine, predicted that these very qualities would contribute to his popularity. "He's a moving target," Shelton said in New York, "and he'll fascinate the people who try to shoot him down." In the beginning, when he was better known for his Huck Finn corduroy cap than his abilities as a composer, he jumped back and forth between Boston and New York, developing a style and manner that brought the manifestation of the pregnant pause to uncanny perfection. Some still found a discomforting similarity to Jack Elliott, or too much affectation in his droll delivery; but everyone agreed his smirk implied a certain something left unsaid and that, whatever it was, if he got around to letting you in on the secret, it would be worthwhile.

It developed that this something was his writing. In no time at all, Dylan virtually abandoned established material for songs of his own composition. The transition from one to the other was nearly imperceptible since he had the good sense to keep his overall cadence within the framework of familiar traditional music. He begged and borrowed from the established ballad styles of the past (in some cases quite freely), from the prolific works of Woody Guthrie, from the contemporary production of friends like Clayton. But the stories he told in his songs had nothing to do with unrequited Appalachian love affairs or idealized whorehouses in New Orleans. They told about the cane murder of Negro servant Hattie Carroll, the death of boxer Davey Moore, the unbroken chains of injustice waiting for the hammers of a crusading era. They went right to the heart of his decade's most recurring preoccupation: that in a time of irreversible technological progress, moral civilization has pathetically faltered; that no matter how much international attention is focused on macrocosmic affairs, the plight of the individual must be considered, or we are forever lost.

Such a theme has often been associated with the output of folk poets; in fact, since the time John Henry laid down his hammer and died from the competition of the industrial revolution, they have celebrated little else. But even including the dynamic figures of Guthrie and Leadbelly in this century. no creator of the idiom has ever received such a wide cross-section of public attention. It is quite possible that already, within the astonishing space of a single year, Dylan has outdistanced the notoriety of still another spiritual forebear, Robert Burns. And like Burns he has the romantic's eye for trading bouts of hard writing with hard living. He often runs the two together, courting all the available kinds and degrees of disaster, sleeping little, partying late, and taking full-time advantage of the musician's scene in New York's Greenwich Village where he keeps a small apartment. Using a blowtorch on the middle of the candle is less aesthetic than burning it at both ends, but more people see the flame. He can dip in and out of traditional forms at will, shift temperament from cynical humor to objective tragedy and never lose sight of what people his age want to hear.

This wanting is in no way a passive or camouflaged matter. It is part and parcel of a generation's active desire to confront the very sources of hypocrisy, which in early years deceived them into thinking that God was perforce on their side, that good guys were always United States Marines, that if they didn't watch the skies day and night the Russians, Vietnamese, North Koreans, tribal Africans, and Lord knows who else would swoop down in the darkness and force them all into salt mines. Dylan feels a very critical trust was betrayed in these exaggerations. He feels further, in what amounts to a militant attitude, that it is up to him to speak out for the millions around him who lack the fortitude to do so for themselves.

Because he speaks for them, undergraduates in many ways seek to identify with his public image, just as they have with Joan's. They search for the same breed of rough Wellingtons and scuff them up with charcoal before wearing. They spend weekends hitchhiking, not so much to get somewhere as to log hours on the road. I've even come across an otherwise excellent guitarist and harmonica player from Fort Ord who tried a crash diet with Army food in order to achieve the necessary gaunt look. The image, of course, has shifted with Dylan's increasing maturity. Some fans are reluctant to accept his early attempts at playing with his past. Last winter, an article in *Newsweek* went to great pains recalling his middle-class upbringing in Hibbing,, Minnesota, and alluding to a prior, less attractive surname which had been removed in the courts. After the Berkeley concert a nineteen-year-old girl in a shawl told me, "He has a knack for saying what younger people want to hear. It's only too bad he had to change his name and not be able to accept himself." I reminded her that she liked his music, but she went on: "People want an image. They carry it around to make their scene look more important. There're so many guys wanting to be something they're not, that Bobby makes a nice alternative. At least he has integrity."

The seeming paradox between name-changing and integrity is significant. His admirers enjoy possessing a certain amount of private information and using it against him as insidiously as they try to hasten Joan's premature immortality. But he has done something they will never do: stepped so cleanly away from his antecedents and into the exhilarating world of creative action as to make the precise nature of an early history look insignificant. Behind the college students of America today, no matter what their protest against segregation, injustice, and thermonuclear war, are the realities of their parents, the monthly check and their hometown. *The Freewheelin' Bob Dylan,* as the title of his second album sets him up, lives in a world that is the realm of their alter ego.

But in the meantime the word still has to be passed and both Joan and Dylan go to the campuses to make sure that it gets there. After the evening of the French-fried almonds and beef stew, both of them journeyed into Southern California—Dylan with his friends in the station wagon, Joan in the XKE. There was some anticipatory talk of getting together at one or more of the concerts, but circumstances were not propitious and they went their separate ways. Dylan stayed at the Thunderbird Motel in Hollywood, drifting out to parties and local folk nightclubs between engagements; Joan stayed with friends of the family in Redlands, lying in the sun, going to bed early. She sang at her old high school one afternoon and was moved to tears by the standing ovation. When she did an encore, her mention of Dylan's name brought cheers. That same night, he returned the compliment to a devoted audience in Riverside.

It was during these performances, as with each of their concerts before predominantly young crowds, that their specific relationship to their generation is most unhindered and best understood. They utter a statement of unmistakably mortal grievance against what they stand to inherit as a result of the blunders of their immediate forebears. In the one case this statement is from the source, in the other through interpretation, but in neither is there any distance between expression and experience. To the young men and women who listen, the message is as meaningful as if it were uttered in the intimacy of their own secluded thought.

What Was It You Wanted?

Izzy Young

From an interview conducted by Izzy Young at his Folklore Center in New York, October 20 & 23, 1961.

"I DIDN'T KNOW THE TERM 'folk music' until I came to New York. 'Folk music' is just a name. I sing a lot of old jazz songs, sentimental cowboy songs, top forty hit parade stuff. People have to name it something so they call it folk music. Now there are very few people singing that way. There's been no one around to cut records like the old Leadbelly, Houston, and Guthrie. There are young people singing like that, but they're being held back by commercial singers. People who run radio programs don't play the ones singing like that. Folk music is being taken over by people who don't sing that way. It's all right, but to call it folk music . . ."

Younger Than That Now

"I don't want to make a lot of money, I want to get along. The more people I reach, and have the chance to sing the kind of music I sing, . . . But people have to be ready. They have to see me once already. People often say the first time they hear me, this isn't folk music. My songs aren't easy to listen to.

"The concert isn't going to be a planned concert. I can offer songs that tell something of this America. No foreign songs. The songs of the land that aren't offered over TV or radio and very few records. Offering a chance to hear them."

"I won't join a group. Groups are easy to be in. I've always learned the hard way. I will, now, too. When you fail in a group you can blame each other. When you fail alone, you yourself fail."

"I play a lot of cards. Believe in 'dead man's hand'—the aces and eights. It's time to cash in when you get aces and eights, dead man's hand. Sounds illogical? The other things I believe in are logical. Like the length of my hair. The less hair on the head, the more hair inside. Wear a crewcut and you have all that hair cluttering around your brain. I let my hair grow long to be wise and free to think . . . Or religion. Got no religion. Tried a bunch of different religions. The churches are divided. Can't make up their minds, and neither can I. Never saw a god; can't say until I see one."

"I've been with Jack Elliot . . . Jack hasn't taught me any songs. Jack doesn't know that many songs. He's had a lot of chances."

THE NEW YORKER, OCTOBER 24, 1964

The Crackin', Shakin', Breakin', Sounds

Nat Hentoff

THE WORD "FOLK" IN THE term "folk music" used to connote a rural, homogeneous community that carried on a tradition of anonymously created music. No one person composed a piece; it evolved through generations of communal care. In recent years, however, folk music has increasingly become the quite personal—and copyrighted—product of specific creators. More and more of them, in fact, are neither rural nor representative of centuries-old family and regional traditions. They are often city-bred converts to the folk style; and, after an apprenticeship during which they try to imitate rural models from the older approach to folk music, they write and perform their own songs out of their own concerns and preoccupations. The restless young, who have been the primary support of the rise of this kind of folk music over the past five years, regard two performers as their preeminent spokesmen. One is the twenty-three-year-old Joan Baez. She does not write her own material and she includes a considerable proportion of traditional, communally created songs in her programs. But Miss Baez does speak out explicitly against racial prejudice and militarism, and she does sing some of the best of the new topical songs. Moreover, her pure, penetrating voice and her open, honest manner symbolize for her admirers a cool island of integrity in a society that the folk-song writer Malvina Reynolds has characterized in one of her songs as consisting of "little boxes" ("And the boys go into business/ And marry and raise a family/ In boxes made of ticky tacky/ And they all look the same."). The second—and more influential—demiurge of the folk-music microcosm is Bob Dylan, who is also twenty-three. Dylan's impact has been the greater because he *is* a writer of songs as well as a performer. Such compositions of his as "Blowin' in the Wind," "Masters of War," "Don't Think Twice, It's All Right,"and "Only a Pawn in Their Game" have become part of the repertoire of many other performers, including Miss Baez, who has explained, "Bobby is expressing what I—and many other young people—feel, what we want to say. Most of the 'protest' songs about the bomb and race prejudice and conformity are stupid. They have no beauty. But Bobby's songs are powerful as poetry and powerful as music. And, oh, my God, how that boy can sing!" Another reason for Dylan's impact is the singular force of his personality. Wiry, tense, and boyish, Dylan looks and acts like a fusion of Huck Finn and a young Woody Guthrie. Both onstage and off, he appears to be just barely able to contain his prodigious energy. Pete Seeger, who, at forty-five, is one of the elders of American folk music, recently observed, "Dylan may well become the country's most creative troubadour—if he doesn't explode."

Dylan is always dressed informally—the possibility that he will ever be seen in a tie is as remote as the possibility that Miss Baez will perform in an evening gown—and his possessions are few, the weightiest of them being a motorcycle. A wanderer, Dylan is often on the road in search of more experience. "You can find out a lot about a small town by hanging around its poolroom," he says. Like Miss Baez, he prefers to keep most of his time for himself. He works only occasionally, and during the rest of the year he travels or briefly stays in a house owned by his manager, Albert Grossman, in Bearsville, New York—a small town adjacent to Woodstock and about a hundred miles north of New

York City. There Dylan writes songs, works on poetry, plays, and novels, rides his motorcycle, and talks with his friends. From time to time, he comes to New York to record for Columbia Records.

A few weeks ago, Dylan invited me to a recording session that was to begin at seven in the evening in a Columbia studio on Seventh Avenue near Fifty-second Street. Before he arrived, a tall, lean, relaxed man in his early thirties came in and introduced himself to me as Tom Wilson, Dylan's recording producer. He was joined by two engineers, and we all went into the control room. Wilson took up a post at a long, broad table, between the engineers, from which he looked out into a spacious studio with a tall thicket of microphones to the left and, directly in front, an enclave containing a music stand, two microphones, and an upright piano, and set off by a large screen, which would partly shield Dylan as he sang, for the purpose of improving the quality of the sound. "I have no idea what he's going to record tonight," Wilson told me. "It's all to be stuff he's written in the last couple of months."

I asked if Dylan presented any particular problems to a recording director.

"My main difficulty has been pounding mike technique into him," Wilson said. "He used to get excited and move around a lot and then lean in too far, so that the mike popped. Aside from that, my basic problem with him has been to create the kind of setting in which he's relaxed. For instance, if that screen should bother him, I'd take it away, even if we have to lose a little quality in the sound." Wilson looked toward the door. "I'm somewhat concerned about tonight. We're going to do a whole album in one session. Usually, we're not in such a rush, but this album has to be ready for Columbia's fall sales convention. Except for special occasions like this, Bob has no set schedule of recording dates. We think he's important enough to record whenever he wants to come to the studio."

Five minutes after seven, Dylan walked into the studio, carrying a battered guitar case. He had on dark glasses, and his hair, dark-blond and curly, had obviously not been cut for some weeks; he was dressed in blue jeans, a black jersey, and desert boots. With him were half a dozen friends, among them Jack Elliott, a folk singer in the Woody Guthrie tradition, who was also dressed in blue jeans and desert boots, plus a brown cowboy shirt and a jaunty cowboy hat. Elliott had been carrying two bottles of Beaujolais, which he now handed to Dylan, who carefully put them on a table near the screen. Dylan opened the guitar case, took out a looped-wire harmonica holder, hung it around his neck, and then walked over to the piano and began to play in a rolling, honky-tonk style.

"He's got a wider range of talents than he shows, " Wilson told me. "He kind of hoards them. You go back to his three albums. Each time, there's a big leap from one to the next—in material, in performance, in everything."

Dylan came into the control room, smiling. Although he is fiercely accusatory toward society at large while he is performing, his most marked offstage characteristic is gentleness. He speaks swiftly but softly, and appears persistently anxious to make himself clear. "We're going to make a good one tonight," he said to Wilson. "I promise." He turned to me and continued, "There aren't any finger-pointing songs in here, either. Those records I've already made, I'll stand behind them; but some of that was jumping into the scene to be heard and a lot of it was because I didn't see anybody else doing that kind of thing. Now a lot of people are doing finger-pointing songs. You know—pointing to all the things that are wrong. Me, I don't want to write *for* people anymore. You know—be a spokesman. Like I once wrote about Emmett Till in the first person, pretending I was him. From now on, I want to write from inside me, and to do that I'm going to have to get back to writing like I used to when I was ten—having everything come out naturally. The way I like to write is for it to come out the way I walk or talk." Dylan frowned. "Not that I even walk or talk yet like I'd like to. I don't carry myself yet the way Woody, Big Joe Williams, and Lightnin' Hopkins have carried themselves. I hope to someday, but they're older. They got to where music was a tool for them, a way to live more, a way to make themselves feel better. Sometimes I can make myself feel better with music, but other times it's still hard to go to sleep at night."

A friend strolled in, and Dylan began to grumble about an interview that had been arranged for him later in the week. "I hate to say no, because, after all, these guys have a job to do," he said, shaking his head impatiently. "But it bugs me that the first question usually turns out to be 'Are you going down South to take part in any of the civil-rights projects?' They try to fit you into things. Now, I've been down there, but I'm not going down just to hold a picket sign so they can shoot a picture of me. I know a lot of the kids in SNCC— you know, the Student Nonviolent Coordinating Committee. That's the only organization I feel a part of spiritually. The NAACP is a bunch of old guys. I found that out by coming directly in contact with some of the people in it. They didn't understand me. They were looking to use me for something. Man, everybody's hung up. You sometimes don't know if somebody wants you to do something because he's hung up or because he really digs who you are. It's awful complicated, and the best thing you can do is admit it."

Returning to the studio, Dylan stood in front of the piano and pounded out an accompaniment as he sang from one of his own new songs:

> "Are you for real baby, or are you
>   just on the shelf?
> I'm looking deep into your eyes, but
>   all I can see is myself.
> If you're trying to throw me, I've
>   already been tossed,
> If you're trying to lose me, I've
>   already been lost...."

Another friend of Dylan's arrived, with three children, ranging in age from four to ten. The children raced around the studio until Wilson insisted that they be relatively confined to the control room. By ten minutes to eight, Wilson had checked out the sound balance to his satisfaction, Dylan's friends had found seats along the studio walls, and Dylan had expressed his readiness—in fact, eagerness—to begin.

Younger Than That Now

Wilson, in the control room, leaned forward, a stopwatch in his hand. Dylan took a deep breath, threw his head back, and plunged into a song in which he accompanied himself on guitar and harmonica. The first take was ragged; the second was both more relaxed and more vivid. At that point, Dylan, smiling clearly appeared to be confident of his ability to do an entire album in one night. As he moved into succeeding numbers, he relied principally on the guitar for support, except for exclamatory punctuations on the harmonica.

Having glanced through a copy of Dylan's new lyrics that he had handed to Wilson, I observed to Wilson that there were indeed hardly any songs of social protest in the collection.

"Those early albums gave people the wrong idea," Wilson said. "Basically, he's in the tradition of all lasting folk music. I mean, he's not a singer of protest so much as he is a singer of *concern* about people. He doesn't have to be talking about Medgar Evers all the time to be effective. He can just tell a simple little story of a guy who ran off from a woman."

After three takes of one number, one of the engineers said to Wilson, "If you want to try another, we can get a better take."

"No." Wilson shook his head. "With Dylan, you have to take what you can get."

Out in the studio, Dylan, his slight form bent forward, was standing just outside the screen and listening to a playback through earphones. He began to take the earphones off during an instrumental passage, but then his voice came on, and he grinned and replaced them.

The engineer muttered again that he might get a better take if Dylan ran through the number once more.

"Forget it," Wilson said. "You don't think in terms of orthodox recording techniques, when you're dealing with Dylan. You have to learn to be as free on this side of the glass as he is out there."

Dylan went on to record a song about a man leaving a girl because he was not prepared to be the kind of invincible hero and all-encompassing provider she wanted. "It ain't me you're looking for, babe," he sang, with finality.

During the playback, I joined Dylan in the studio. "The songs so far sound as if there were real people in them," I said.

Dylan seemed surprised that I had considered it necessary to make the comment. "There are. That's what makes them so scary. If I haven't been through what I write about, the songs aren't worth anything." He went on, via one of his songs, to offer a complicated account of a turbulent love affair in Spanish Harlem, and at the end asked a friend, "Did you understand it?" The friend nodded enthusiastically. "Well, I didn't," Dylan said, with a laugh, and then became somber. "It's hard being free in a song—getting it all in. Songs are so confining. Woody Guthrie told me once that songs don't have to rhyme—that they don't have to do anything like that. But it's not true. A song has to have some kind of form to fit into the music. You can bend the words and the meter, but it still has to fit somehow. I've been getting freer in the songs I write, but I still feel confined. That's why I write a lot of poetry—if that's the word. Poetry can make its own form."

As Wilson signaled for the start of the next number, Dylan put up his hand. "I just want to light a cigarette, so I can see it there while I'm singing," he said, and grinned. "I'm very neurotic. I need to be secure."

By ten-thirty, seven songs had been recorded.

"This is the fastest Dylan date yet," Wilson said. "He used to be all hung up with the microphones. Now he's a pro."

Several more friends of Dylan's had arrived during the recording of the seven songs, and at this point four of them were seated in the control room behind Wilson and the engineers. The others were scattered around the studio, using the table that held the bottles of Beaujolais as their base. They opened the bottles and every once in a while poured out a drink in a paper cup. The three children were still irrepressibly present, and once the smallest burst suddenly into the studio, ruining a take. Dylan turned to the youngster in mock anger. "I'm gonna rub you out," he said. "I'll track you down and turn you to dust." The boy giggled and ran back into the control room.

As the evening went on, Dylan's voice became more acrid. The dynamics of his singing grew more pronounced, soft, intimate passages being abruptly followed by fierce surges in volume. The relentless, driving beat of his guitar was more often supplemented by the whooping thrusts of the harmonica.

"Intensity, that's what he's got," Wilson said, apparently to himself.

"By now, this kid is outselling Thelonious Monk and Miles Davis," he went on, to me. "He's speaking to a whole new generation. And not only here. He's just been in England. He had standing room only in Royal Festival Hall."

Dylan had begun a song called "Chimes of Freedom." One of his four friends in the control room, a lean, bearded man proclaimed, "Bobby's talking for every hung-up person in the whole wide universe." His three companions nodded gravely.

The next composition, "Motor-psycho Nitemare," was a mordantly satirical version of the vintage tale of the farmer, his daughter, and the traveling salesman. There were several false starts, apparently because Dylan was having trouble reading the lyrics.

"Man, dim the lights," the bearded friend counseled Wilson. "He'll get more relaxed."

"Atmosphere is not what we need," Wilson answered, without turning around. "Legibility is what we need."

During the playback, Dylan listened intently, his lips moving, and a cigarette cocked in his right hand. A short break followed, during which Dylan shouted, "Hey, we're gonna need some more wine!" Two of his friends in the studio nodded and left.

After the recording session resumed, Dylan continued to work hard and conscientiously. When he was preparing for a take or listening to a playback, he seemed able to cut himself off completely from the eddies of conversation and humorous byplay stirred up by his friends in the studio. Occasionally, when a line particularly pleased him, he burst into laughter, but he swiftly got back to business.

Dylan started a talking blues—a wry narrative in a sardonic recitative style, which had been developed by Woody Guthrie. "Now I'm a liberal, but to a degree," Dylan was drawling halfway through the song. "I want everybody to be free. But if you think I'll let Barry Goldwater move in next door and marry my daughter, you must think I'm crazy. I wouldn't let him do it for all the farms in Cuba." He was smiling broadly, and Wilson and the engineers were laughing. It was a long song, and toward the end Dylan faltered. He tried it twice more and each time he stumbled before the close.

"Let me do another song," he said to Wilson. "I'll come back to this."

"No," Wilson said. "Finish up this one. You'll hang us up on the order, and if I'm not here to edit, the other cat will get mixed up. Just do an insert of the last part."

"Let him start from the beginning, man," said one of the four friends sitting behind Wilson.

Wilson turned around, looking annoyed. "Why, man?"

"You don't start telling a story with Chapter Eight, man," the friend said.

"Oh, man," said Wilson. "What kind of philosophy is that? We're recording, not writing a biography."

As an obbligato of protest continued behind Wilson, Dylan, accepting Wilson's advice, sang the insert. His bearded friend rose silently and drew a square in the air behind Wilson's head.

Other songs, mostly of love lost or misunderstood, followed. Dylan was now tired, but he retained his good humor. "This last one is called 'My Back Pages,'" he announced to Wilson. It appeared to express his current desire to get away from "finger-pointing" and write more acutely personal material. "Oh, but I was so much older then," he sang as a refrain, "I'm younger than that now."

By one-thirty, the session was over. Dylan had recorded fourteen new songs. He agreed to meet me again in a week or so and fill me in on his background. "My background's not all that important though," he said as we left the studio. "It's what I'm doing now that counts."

Dylan was born in Duluth, on May 24, 1941, and grew up in Hibbing, Minnesota, a mining town near the Canadian border. He does not discuss his parents, preferring to let his songs tell whatever he wants to say about his personal history. "You can stand at one end of Hibbing on the main drag an' see clear past the city limits on the other end," Dylan once noted in a poem, "My Life in a Stolen Moment," printed in the program of a 1963 Town Hall concert he gave. Like Dylan's parents, it appears, the town was neither rich nor poor, but it was, Dylan has said, "a dyin' town." He ran away from home seven times: at ten, at twelve, at thirteen, at fifteen, at fifteen and a half, at seventeen, and at eighteen. His travels included South Dakota, New Mexico, Kansas, and California. In between flights, he taught himself the guitar, which he had begun playing at the age of ten. At fifteen, he was also playing the harmonica and the auto-harp, and, in addition, had written his first song, a ballad dedicated to Brigitte Bardot. In the spring of 1960, Dylan entered the University of Minnesota, in Minneapolis, which he attended for something under six months. In "My Life in a Stolen Moment," Dylan has summarized his college career dourly: "I sat in science class an' flunked out for refusin' to watch a rabbit die. I got expelled from English class for using four-letter words in a paper describing the English teacher. I also failed out of com-munication class for callin' up every day and sayin' I couldn't come. . . . I was kept around for kicks at a fraternity house. They let me live there, an' I did until they wanted me to join." Paul Nelson and Jon Pankake, who edit the *Little Sandy Review*, a quarterly magazine, published in Min-neapolis, that is devoted to critical articles on folk music and performers, remember meeting Dylan at the University of Minnesota in the summer of 1960, while he was part of a group of singers who performed at The Scholar, a coffeehouse near the university. The editors, who were stu-dents at the university then, have since noted in their publication: "We recall Bob as a soft-spoken, rather unprepossessing youngster . . . well-groomed and neat in the standard campus costume of slacks, sweater, and white oxford sneakers, poplin raincoat, and dark glasses."

Before Dylan arrived at the university, his singing had been strongly influenced by such Negro folk interpreters as Leadbelly and Big Joe Williams. He had met Williams in Evanston, Illinois, during his break from home at the age of twelve. Dylan had also been attracted to sev-eral urban-style rhythm-and-blues performers, notably Bo Diddley and Chuck Berry. Other shaping forces were white country-music figures, particularly Hank Williams, Hank Snow, and Jimmie Rodgers. During his brief stay at the university, Dylan became especially absorbed in the recordings of Woody Guthrie, the Oklahoma-born traveler who had created the most distinctive body of American topical folk material to come to light in this century. Since 1954, Guthrie, ill with Huntington's chorea, a progressive disease of the nervous system, had not been able to perform, but he was allowed to receive visitors. In the autumn of 1960, Dylan quit the University of Minnesota and decided to visit

Guthrie at Greystone Hospital, in New Jersey. Dylan returned briefly to Minnesota the following May, to sing at a university hootenanny, and Nelson and Pankake saw him again on that occasion. "In a mere half year," they have recalled in the *Little Sandy Review*, "he had learned to churn up exciting, bluesy, hard-driving, harmonica-and-guitar music, and had absorbed during his visits with Guthrie not only the great Okie musician's unpredictable syntax but his very vocal color, diction, and inflection. Dylan's performance that spring evening of a selection of Guthrie . . . songs was hectic and shaky, but it contained all the elements of the now-perfected performing style that has made him the most original newcomer to folk music."

The winter Dylan visited Guthrie was otherwise bleak. He spent most of it in New York, where he found it difficult to get steady work singing. In "Talkin' New York," a caustic song describing his first months in the city, Dylan tells of having been turned away by a coffeehouse owner who told him scornfully, "You sound like a hillbilly. We want folksingers here." There were nights when he slept in the subway, but, eventually he found friends and a place to stay on the lower East Side, and after he had returned from the spring hootenanny, he began getting more frequent engagements in New York. John Hammond, Director of Talent Acquisition at Columbia Records, who has discovered a sizable number of important jazz and folk performers during the past thirty years, heard Dylan that summer while attending a rehearsal of another folksinger, whom Hammond was about to record for Columbia Records. Impressed by the young man's raw force and by the vivid lyrics of his songs, Hammond auditioned him and immediately signed him to a recording contract. Then, in September 1961, while Dylan was appearing at Gerde's Folk City, a casual refuge for "citybillies" (as the young city singers and musicians are now called in the trade), on West Fourth Street, in Greenwich Village, he was heard by Robert Shelton, the folk-music critic for the *Times*, who wrote of him enthusiastically.

Dylan began to prosper. He enlarged his following by appearing at the Newport and Monterey Folk Festivals and giving concerts throughout the country. There have been a few snags, as when he walked off the Ed Sullivan television show in the spring of 1963 because the Columbia Broadcasting System would not permit him to sing a tart appraisal of the John Birch Society, but on the whole he has experienced accelerating success. His first three Columbia albums—*Bob Dylan, The Freewheelin' Bob Dylan,* and *The Times They Are A-Changin'*—have by now reached a cumulative sales figure of nearly four hundred thousand. In addition, he has received large royalties as a composer of songs that have become hits through recordings by Peter, Paul, and Mary, the Kingston Trio, and other performers. At present, Dylan's fees for a concert appearance range from two thousand to three thousand dollars a night. He has sometimes agreed to sing at a nominal fee for new, nonprofit folk societies, however, and he has often performed without charge at civil-rights rallies.

Musically, Dylan has transcended most of his early influences and developed an incisively personal style. His vocal sound is most often characterized by flaying harshness. Mitch Jayne, a member of the Dillards, a folk group from Missouri, has described Dylan's sound as "very much like a dog with his leg caught in barbed wire." Yet Dylan's admirers come to accept and even delight in the harshness, because of the vitality and wit at its core. And they point out that in intimate ballads he is capable of a fragile lyricism that does not slip into bathos. It is Dylan's work as a composer, however, that has won him a wider audience than his singing alone might have. Whether concerned with cosmic specters or personal conundrums, Dylan's lyrics are pungently idiomatic. He has a superb ear for speech rhythms, a generally astute sense of selective detail, and a natural storyteller's command of narrative pacing. His songs sound as if they were being created out of oral street history rather than carefully written in tranquility. On a stage, Dylan performs his songs as if he had an urgent story to tell. In his work there is little of the polished grace of such carefully trained contemporary minstrels as Richard Dyer-Bennet. Nor, on the other hand, do Dylan's performances reflect the calculated showmanship of Harry Belafonte or of Peter, Paul, and Mary. Dylan off the stage is very much the same as Dylan the performer—restless, insatiably hungry for experience, idealistic, but skeptical of neatly defined causes.

In the past year, as his renown has increased, Dylan has become more elusive. He felt so strongly threatened by his initial fame that he welcomed the chance to use the Bearsville home of his manager as a refuge between concerts, and he still spends most of his time there when he's not traveling. A week after the recording session, he telphoned me from Bearsville, and we agreed to meet the next evening at the Keneret, a restaurant on lower Seventh Avenue in the Village. It specializes in Middle Eastern food, which is one of Dylan's preferences, but it does not have a liquor license. Upon keeping our rendezvous, therefore, we went next door for a few bottles of Beaujolais and then returned to the Keneret. Dylan was as restless as usual, and as he talked, his hands moved constantly and his voice sounded as if he were never quite able to catch his breath.

I asked him what he had meant, exactly, when he spoke at the recording session of abandoning "finger-pointing" songs, and he took a sip of wine, leaned forward, and said, "I looked around and saw all these people pointing fingers at the bomb. But the bomb is getting boring, because what's wrong goes much deeper than the bomb. What's wrong is how few people are free. Most people walking around are tied down to something that doesn't let them really *speak,* so they just add their confusion to the mess. I mean, they have some kind of vested interest in the way things are now. Me, I'm cool." He smiled. "You know, Joanie—Joanie Baez—worries about me. She worries about whether people will get control over me and exploit me. But I'm cool. I'm in control, because I don't care about money, and all that. And I'm cool in myself, because I've gone through enough changes so that I know what's real to me and what isn't. Like this fame. It's done something to me. It's O.K. in the Village here. People don't pay attention to me. But in other towns it's funny knowing that people you don't know figure they know *you.* I mean, they think they know everything about you. One thing is groovy, though. I got birthday cards this year from people I'd never heard of. It's weird, isn't it? There are people I've really touched whom I'll never know." He lit a cigarette. "But in other ways being noticed can be a weight. So I disappear a lot. I go to places where I'm not going to be noticed. And I *can.*" He laughed. "I have no work to do. I have no job. I'm not committed to anything except making a few records and playing a few concerts. I'm weird that way. Most people, when they get up in the morning, have to do what they *have* to do. I could pretend there were all kinds of things I *had* to do every day. But why? So I do whatever I feel like. I might make movies of my friends around Woodstock one day. I write a lot. I get involved in scenes with people. A lot of scenes are going on with me all the time— here in the Village, in Paris during my trips to Europe, in lots of places."

I asked Dylan how far ahead he planned.

"I don't look past right now," he said. "Now there's this fame business. I know it's going to go away. It has to. This so-called mass fame comes from people who get caught up in a thing for a while and buy the records. Then they stop. And when they stop, I won't be famous anymore."

We became aware that a young waitress was standing by diffidently. Dylan turned to her, and she asked him for his autograph. He signed his name with gusto, and signed again when she asked if he would give her an autograph for a friend. "I'm sorry to have interrupted your dinner," she said, smiling. "But I'm really not."

"I get letters from people—young people—all the time," Dylan continued when she had left us. "I wonder if they write letters like those to other people they don't know. They just want to tell me things, and sometimes they go into their personal hang-ups. Some send poetry. I like getting them—read them all and answer some. But I don't mean I give any of the people who write to me any *answers* to their problems." He leaned forward and talked more rapidly. "It's like, when somebody wants to tell me what the 'moral' thing is to do, I want them to *show* me. If they have anything to say about morals, I want to know what it is they *do*. Same with me. All I can do is show the people who ask me questions how I live. All I can do is be me. I can't tell them how to change things, because there's only one way to change things, and that's to cut yourself off from all the chains. That's hard for most people to do."

I had Dylan's *The Times They Are A-Changin'* album with me, and I pointed out to him a section of his notes on the cover in which he

spoke of how he had always been running when he was a boy—
running away from Hibbing and from his parents.

Dylan took a sip of wine. "I kept running because I wasn't free," he
said. "I was constantly on guard. Somehow, way back then, I already
knew that parents do what they do because they're uptight. They're
concerned with their kids in relation to *themselves*. I mean, they want
their kids to please them, not to embarrass them—so they can be
proud of them. They want you to be what *they* want you to be. So I
started running when I was ten. But always I'd get picked up and sent
home. When I was thirteen, I was traveling with a carnival through
upper Minnesota and North and South Dakota, and I got picked up
again. I tried again and again, and when I was eighteen, I cut out for
good. I was still running when I came to New York. Just because you're
free to move doesn't mean you're free. Finally, I got so far out I was cut
off from everybody and everything. It was then I decided there was no
sense in running so far and so fast when there was no longer anybody
there. It was fake. It was running for the sake of running. So I stopped.
I've got no place to run from. I don't have to be anyplace I don't want
to be. But I am by no means an example for any kid wanting to strike
out. I mean, I wouldn't want a young kid to leave home because I did
it, and then have to go through a lot of the things I went through.
Everybody has to find his *own* way to be free. There isn't anybody who
can help you in that sense. Nobody was able to help me. Like seeing
Woody Guthrie was one of the main reasons I came East. He was an
idol to me. A couple of years ago, after I'd gotten to know him, I was
going through some very bad changes, and I went to see Woody, like
I'd go to somebody to confess to. But I couldn't confess to him. It was
silly. I did go and talk with him—as much as he could talk—and the
talking helped. But basically he wasn't able to help me at all. I finally
realized that. So Woody was my last idol."

There was a pause.

"I've learned a lot in these past few years," Dylan said softly. "Like
about beauty."

I reminded him of what he had said about his changing criteria of
beauty in some notes he did for a Joan Baez album. There he had

27

written that when he first heard her voice, before he knew her, his reaction had been:

> *"I hate that kind a sound," said I*
> *"The only beauty's ugly, man*
> *The crackin', shakin', breakin' sounds're*
> *The only beauty I understand."*

Dylan laughed. "Yeah," he said. "I was wrong. My hang-up was that I used to try to *define* beauty. Now I take it as it is, however it is. That's why I like Hemingway. I don't read much. Usually I read what people put in my hands. But I do read Hemingway. He didn't have to use adjectives. He didn't really have to define what he was saying. He just said it. I can't do that yet, but that's what I want to be able to do."

A young actor from Julian Beck's and Judith Malina's Living Theatre troupe stopped by the table, and Dylan shook hands with him enthusiastically. "We're leaving for Europe soon," the actor said. "But when we come back, we're going out on the street. We're going to put on plays right on the street, for anyone who wants to watch."

"Hey!" said Dylan, bouncing in his seat. "Tell Julian and Judith that I want to be in on that."

The actor said he would, and took Dylan's telephone number. Then he said, "Bob, are you doing only your own songs now—none of the old folk songs at all?"

"Have to," Dylan answered. "When I'm uptight and it's raining outside and nobody's around and somebody I want is a long way from me—and with someone else besides—I can't sing 'Ain't Got No Use for Your Red Apple Juice.' I don't care how great an old song it is or what its tradition is. I have to make a new song out of what *I* know and out of what *I'm* feeling."

The conversation turned to civil rights, and the actor used the term "the Movement" to signify the work of the civil-rights activists. Dylan looked at him quizzically. "I agree with everything that's happening," he said, "but I'm not part of no Movement. If I was, I wouldn't be able to do anything else but be in 'the Movement.' I just can't have people sit around and make rules for me. I do a lot of things no Movement would allow." He took a long drink of the Beaujolais. "It's like politics," he went on. "I just can't make it with any organization. I fell into a trap once—last December—when I agreed to accept the Tom Paine Award from the Emergency Civil Liberties Committee. At the Americana Hotel! In the Grand Ballroom! As soon as I got there, I felt uptight. First of all, the people with me couldn't get in. They looked even funkier than I did, I guess. They weren't dressed right, or something. Inside the ballroom, I really got uptight. I began to drink. I looked down from the platform and saw a bunch f people who had nothing to do with my kind of politics. I looked down and I got scared. They were supposed to be on my side, but I didn't feel any connection with them. Here were these people who'd been all involved with the left in the thirties, and now they were supporting civil-rights drives. That's groovy, but they also had minks and jewels, and it was like they were giving the money out of guilt. I got up to leave, and they followed me and caught me. They told me I had to accept the award. When I got up to make my speech, I couldn't say anything by that time but what was passing through my mind. They'd been talking about Kennedy being killed, and Bill Moore and Medgar Evers and the Buddhist monks in Vietnam being killed. I had to say something about Lee Oswald. I told them I'd read a lot of his feelings in the papers, and I knew he was uptight. Said I'd been uptight, too, so I'd got a lot of his feelings. I saw a lot of myself in Oswald, I said, and I saw in him a lot of the times we're all living in. And, you know, they started booing. They looked at me like I was an animal. They actually thought I was saying it was a good thing Kennedy had been killed. That's how far out they are. I was talking about Oswald. And then I started talking about friends of mine in Harlem—some of them junkies, all of them poor. And I said they need freedom as much as anybody else, and what's anybody doing for *them?* The chairman was kicking my leg under the table, and I told him, 'Get out of here.' Now, what I was supposed to be was a nice cat. I was supposed to say, 'I appreciate your award and I'm a great singer and I'm a great believer in liberals, and you buy my records and I'll support your cause.' But I didn't, and so I wasn't accepted that night. That's the cause of a lot of those chains I was talking about—

people wanting to be accepted, people not wanting to be alone. But, after all, what is it to be alone? I've been alone sometimes in front of three thousand people. I was alone that night."

The actor nodded sympathetically.

Dylan snapped his fingers. "I almost forgot," he said. "You know, they were talking about Freedom Fighters that night. I've been in Mississippi, man. I know those people on another level besides civil-rights campaigns. I know them as friends. Like Jim Forman, one of the heads of SNCC I'll stand on his side any time. But those people that night were actually getting me to look at colored people as colored people. I tell you, I'm never going to have anything to do with any political organization again in my life. Oh, I might help a friend if he was campaigning for office. But I'm not going to be part of any organization. Those people at that dinner were the same as everybody else. They're doing their time. They're chained to what they're doing. The only thing is, they're trying to put morals and great deeds on their chains, but basically they don't want to jeopardize their positions. They got their jobs to keep. There's nothing there for me, and there's nothing there for the kind of people I hang around with. The only thing I'm sorry about is that I guess I hurt the collection at the dinner. I didn't know they were going to try to collect money after my speech. I guess I lost them a lot of money. Well, I offered to pay them whatever it was they figured they'd lost because of the way I talked. I told them I didn't care how much it was. I hate debts, especially moral debts. They're worse than money debts."

Exhausted by his monologue, Dylan sank back and poured more Beaujolais. "People talk about trying to change society," he said. "All I know is that so long as people stay so concerned about protecting their status and protecting what they have, ain't nothing going to be done. Oh, there may be some change of levels inside the circle, but nobody's going to learn anything."

The actor left, and it was time for Dylan to head back upstate. "Come up and visit next week," he said to me, "and I'll give you a ride on my motorcycle." He hunched his shoulders and walked off quickly.

VILLAGE VOICE, MARCH 3, 1965

Dylan Meets the Press

J.R. Godard

THE PRESS: Bobby, We know you changed your name. Come on now, what's your real name?

DYLAN: Philip Ochs. I'm gonna change it back when I see it pays.

THE PRESS: Was Woody Guthrie your greatest influence?

DYLAN: I don't know that I'd say that, but for a spell, the idea of him affected me quite much.

THE PRESS: How about Brecht? Read much of him?

DYLAN: No. But I've read him.

THE PRESS: Rimbaud?

DYLAN: I've read his tiny little book *Evil Flowers* too.

THE PRESS: How about Hank Williams? Do you consider him an influence?

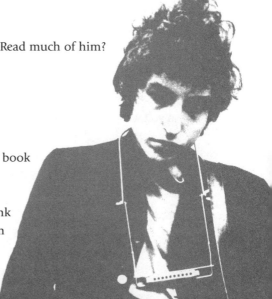

Younger Than That Now

DYLAN: Hey look, I consider Hank Williams, Captain Marvel, Marlon Brando, The Tennessee Stud, Clark Kent, Walter Cronkite, and J. Carrol Neish all influences. Now what is it—please—what is it exactly you people want to know?

THE PRESS: Tell us about your movie.

DYLAN: It's gonna be in black and white.

THE PRESS: Will it be in the Andy Warhol style?

DYLAN: Who's Andy Warhol? Listen, my movie will be—I can say definitely—it will be in the style of the early Puerto Rican films.

THE PRESS: Who's writing it?

DYLAN: Allen Ginsberg. I'm going to rewrite it.

THE PRESS: Who will you play in the film?

DYLAN: The hero.

THE PRESS: Who is it that you're going to be?

DYLAN: My mother.

THE PRESS: What about your friends The Beatles? Did you see them when you were there?

DYLAN: John Lennon and I came down to the Village early one morning. They wouldn't let us in The Figaro or The Hip Bagel or The Feenjon. This time I'm going to England. This April. I'll see 'em if they're there.

THE PRESS: Bob, what about the situation of American poets?

Kenneth Roxroth has estimated that since 1900 about thirty American poets have committed suicide.

DYLAN: Thirty poets! What about American housewives, mailmen, street cleaners, miners? Jesus Christ, what's so special about thirty people that are called poets? I've known some very good people that have committed suicide. One didn't do nothing but work in a gas station all his life. Nobody referred to him as poet, but if you're gonna call people like Robert Frost a poet, then I got to say this gas station boy was a poet too.

THE PRESS: Bob, to sum up—don't you have any important philosophy for the world?

DYLAN: Are you kidding? The world don't need me. Christ, I'm only five feet ten. The world could get along fine without me. Don'cha know, everybody dies. It don't matter how important you think you are. Look at Shakespeare, Napoleon, Edgar Allan Poe, for that matter. They are all
dead, right?

THE PRESS: Well, Bob, in your opinion, then, is there one man who can save the world?

DYLAN: Al Aronowitz.

The Paul J. Robbins Interview

Paul J. Robbins

ROBBINS: I don't know whether to do a serious interview or carry on in that absurdist way we talked last night.

DYLAN: It'll be the same thing anyway, man.

ROBBINS: Yeah, Okay . . . If you are a poet and write words arranged in some sort of rhythm, why do you switch at some point and write lyrics in a song so that you're singing the words as part of a Gestalt presence?

DYLAN: Well, I can't define that word poetry, I wouldn't even attempt it. At one time I thought that Robert Frost was poetry, other times I thought that Allen Ginsberg was poetry, sometimes I thought Francois Villon was poetry—but poetry isn't really confined to the printed page. Hey, then again, I don't believe in saying "Look at that girl walking! Isn't that poetry?" I'm not going to get insane about it. The lyrics to the songs . . . just so happens that it might be a

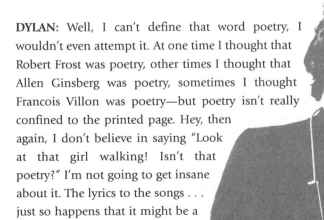

little stranger than in most songs. I find it easy to write songs. I been writing songs for a long time and the words to the songs aren't written out just for the paper; they're written as you can read it, you dig. If you take whatever there is to the song away—the beat, the melody—I could still recite it. I see nothing wrong with songs you can't do that with either—songs that, if you took the beat and the melody away, they wouldn't stand up. Because they're not supposed to do that, you know. Songs are songs . . . I don't believe in expecting too much out of any one thing.

ROBBINS: Whatever happened to Blind Boy Grunt?

DYLAN: I was doing that four years ago. Now there's a lot of people writing songs on protest subjects. But it's taken some kind of a weird step. Hey, I'd rather listen to Jimmy Reed or Howlin' Wolf, man, or the Beatles, or Francois Hardy, than I would listen to any protest song singers—although I haven't heard all the protest song singers there are. But the ones I've heard—there's this very emptiness which is like a song written "Let's hold hands and everything will be grand." I see no more to it than that. Just because someone mentions the word "bomb," I'm not going to go "Aalee!" and start clapping.

ROBBINS: Is it that they just don't work anymore?

DYLAN: It's not that it don't work, it's that there are a lot of people afraid of the bomb, right. But there are a lot of other people who're afraid to be seen carrying a *Modern Screen* magazine down the street, you know. Lot of people afraid to admit that they like Marlon Brando movies . . . Hey, it's not that they don't work anymore but have you ever thought of a place where they DO work? What exactly DOES work?

ROBBINS: They give a groovy feeling to the people who sing them, I guess that's about it. But what does work is the attitude, not the song. And there's just another attitude called for.

DYLAN: Yeah, but you have to be very hip to the fact about that attitude—you have to be hip to communication. Sure, you can make all sorts of protest songs and put them on a Folkways record. But who hears them? The people that do hear them are going to be agreeing with you anyway. You aren't going to get somebody to hear it who doesn't dig it. People don't listen to things they don't dig. If you can find a cat that can actually say "Okay, I'm a changed man because I heard this one thing—or I just saw this one thing. . . ." Hey it don't necessarily happen that way all the time. It happens with a collage of experience which somebody can actually know by instinct what's right and wrong for him to do. Where he doesn't actually have to feel guilty about anything. A lot of people can act out of guilt. They act because they think somebody's looking at *them*. No matter what it is. There's people who do anything because of guilt . . .

ROBBINS: And you don't want to be guilty?

DYLAN: It's not that I'm NOT guilty. I'm not any more guilty than you are. Like, I don't consider any elder generation guilty. I mean, they're having these trials at Nuremberg, right? Look at that and you can place it out. Cats say "I had to kill all those people or else they'd kill me." Now, who's to try them for that? Who are these judges that have got the right to try a cat? How do you know they wouldn't do the same thing?

ROBBINS: This may be a side trip, but this thing about the Statute of Limitations running out and everybody wants to extend it? You remember, in *Animal Farm*, what they wrote on the wall? "All animals are equal." But later they added "... but some are more equal than others." It's the same thing in reverse. That some are less equal than others. Like Nazis are *really* criminals, so let's *really* get them; change any law just to nail them all.

DYLAN: Yeah, all that shit runs in the same category. Nobody digs revenge, right? But you have these cats from Israel who, after *twenty* years, are still trying to catch these cats, who're *old* cats, man, who have escaped. God knows they aren't going to go anywhere, they're not going to do anything. And you have these cats from Israel running around catching them. Spending twenty years out of their lives. You take that job away from them and they're no more or less than a baker. He's got his whole life tied up in one thing. It's a one-thought thing, without anything between: "That's what it is, and I'm going to get it." Anything between gets wiped all away. I can't make that, but I can't really put it down. Hey: I can't put *anything* down, because I don't have to be around any of it. I don't have to put people down which I don't like, because I don't have to be around any of those people. Of course there is the giant great contradiction of What Do You Do. Hey, I don't know what you do, but all I can do is cast aside all the things *not* to do. I don't know where it's at once in a while, all I know is where it's *not* at. And as long as I know that, I don't really have to know, myself, where's it at. Everybody knows where it's at once in a while, but nobody can walk around all the time in a complete Utopia. Dig poetry. You were asking about poetry? Man, poetry is just bullshit, you know? I don't know about other countries, but in this one it's a total massacre. It's not poetry at all. People don't read poetry in this country—if they do, it offends them; they don't dig it. You go to school, man, and what kind of poetry do you read? You read Robert Frost's "The Two Roads," you read T. S. Eliot—you read all that bullshit and that's just bad, man, It's not good. It's not anything hard, it's just soft-boiled egg shit. And then, on top of it, they throw Shakespeare at some kid who can't read Shakespeare in high school, right? Who digs reading, *Hamlet*, man? All they give you is *Ivanhoe, Silas Mariner, Tale of Two Cities*—and they keep you away from things which you should do. You shouldn't even be there in school. You should find out from people. Dig! That's where it all starts. In the beginning—like from 13 to 19—that's where all the corruption is. These people all just overlook it, right? There's more V.D. in people 13 to 19 than there is in any other group, but they ain't ever going to say so. They're never going to go into the schools and give shots. But that's where it's at. It's all a hype, man.

ROBBINS: Relating all this: if you put it in lyrics instead of poetry, you have a higher chance of hitting the people who have to be hit?

DYLAN: I do, but I don't expect anything from it, you dig? All I can do is be me—whoever that is—for those people that I do play to, and not come on with them, tell them I'm something I'm not. I'm not going to tell them I'm the Great Cause Fighter or the Great Lover or the Great Boy Genius or whatever. Because I'm not, man. Why mislead them? That's all just Madison Avenue selling me, but it's not really selling ME, 'cause I was hip to it before I got there.

ROBBINS: Which brings up another thing. All the folk magazines and many folk people are down on you. Do they put you down because you changed or . . .

DYLAN: It's that I'm successful and they want to be successful, man. It's jealousy. Hey, anybody, with any kind of knowledge at all would know by instinct what's happening here. Somebody who doesn't know that, is still hung up with success and failure and good and bad . . . maybe he doesn't have a chick all the time . . . stuff like that. But I can't use comments, man. I don't take nothing like that seriously. If somebody praises me and say "How groovy you are!," it doesn't mean nothing to me, because I can usually sense where that person's at. And it's no compliment if someone who's a total freak comes up and says "How groovy you are!" And it's the same if they don't dig me. Other kinds of people don't *have* to say anything because, when you come down to it, it's all what's happening in the moment which counts. Who *cares* about tomorrow and yesterday? People don't live there, they live now.

ROBBINS: I have a theory, which I've been picking up and shaking out every so often. When I spoke with the Byrds, they were saying the same thing as I am saying—a lot of people are saying—you're talking it. It's why we have new so-called rock & roll sound emerging, it's a synthesis of all things a . . .

Younger Than That Now

DYLAN: It's further than that, man. People know nowadays more than before. They've had so much to look at by now and know the bullshit of everything. People now don't even care about going to jail. So what? You're still with yourself as much as if you're out on the streets. There's still those who don't care about anything, but I got to think that anybody who doesn't hurt anybody, you can't put that person down, you dig, if that person's happy doing that.

ROBBINS: But what if they freeze themselves into apathy? What if they don't care about anything at all anymore?

DYLAN: Whose problem is that? Your problem or theirs? No, it's not that, it's that nobody can learn by somebody else showing them or teaching them. People got to learn by themselves, going through something which relates. Sure, you say how do you make somebody know something . . . people know it by themselves; they can go through some kind of scene with other people and themselves which somehow will come out somewhere and it's grind into them and be them. And all that just comes out of them somehow when they're faced up to the next thing.

ROBBINS: It's like taking in until the times comes to put out, right. But people who don't care don't put anything out. It's a whole frozen thing where nothing's happening anywhere; it's just like the maintenance of status quo, of existing circumstances, whatever they are . . .

DYLAN: People who don't care? Are you talking about gas station attendants or a Zen doctor, man? Hey, there's a lot of people who don't care; a lot don't care for different reasons. A lot care about some things and not about others, and some who don't care about anything—it's just up to me not to let them bring me down and not to bring them down. It's like the whole world has a little thing: it's being taught that when you get up in the morning, you have to go out and bring somebody down. You walk down the street and, unless you've brought somebody down, don't come home today, right? It's a circus world.

ROBBINS: So who is it that you write and sing for?

DYLAN: Not writing and singing for anybody, to tell you the truth. Hey, really, I don't care what people say. I don't care what they make me seem to be or what they tell other people I am. If I did care about that, I'd tell you; I really have no concern with it. I don't even come in contact with these people. Hey, I dig people, though. But if somebody's going to come up to me and ask me some questions which have been on his mind for such a long time, all I can think of is "Wow, man, what else can be in that person's head besides me? Am I that important, man, to be in a person's head for such a long time he's got to know this answer?" I mean, can that really straighten him out—if I tell him something? Hey, come on . . .

ROBBINS: A local disc jockey, Les Claypool, went through a whole thing on you one night, just couldn't get out of it. For maybe 45 minutes, he'd play a side of yours and then an ethnic side in which it was demonstrated that both melodies were the same. After each pair he'd say, "Well, you see what's happening . . . This kid is taking other people's melodies; he's not all that original. Not only that," he'd say, "but his songs are totally depressing and have no hope."

DYLAN: Who's Les Claypool?

ROBBINS: A folk jockey out here who has a long talk show on Saturday nights and an hour one each night, during which he plays highly ethnic sides.

DYLAN: He played *those* songs? He didn't play something hopeful?

ROBBINS: No, he was loading it to make his point. Anyway, it brings up an expected question: Why do you use melodies that are already written?

DYLAN: I used to do that when I was more or less in folk. I knew the melodies; they were already there. I did it because I liked the melodies.

I did it when I really wasn't that popular and the songs weren't reaching that many people, and everybody around dug it. Man. I never introduced a song, "Here's the song I've stole the melody from, someplace." For me it wasn't that important; still isn't that important. I don't care about the melodies, man, the melodies are all traditional anyway. And if anybody wants to pick that out and say "That's Bob Dylan," that's their thing, not mine. I mean if they want to think that. Anybody with any sense at all, man, he says that I haven't any hope . . . Hey, I got *faith*. I know that there are people who're going to know that's total bullshit. I know the cat is just uptight. He hasn't really gotten into a good day and he has to pick on something. Groovy. He has to pick on me? Hey, if he can't pick on me, he picks on someone else, it don't matter. He doesn't step on me, 'cause I don't care. He's not coming up to me on the street and stepping on my head, man. Hey, I've only done that with very few of my songs, anyway. And then when I don't do it, everybody says they're rock & roll melodies. You can't satisfy the people—you just can't. You got to know, man; they just don't care about it.

ROBBINS: Why is rock & roll coming in and folk music going out?

DYLAN: Folk music destroyed itself. Nobody destroyed it. Folk music is still here, if you want to dig it. It's not that it's going in or out. It's all the soft mellow shit, man, that's just being replaced by something that people know there is now. Hey, you must've heard rock & roll long before the Beatles, you must've discarded rock & roll around 1960. I did that in 1957. I couldn't make it as a rock & roll singer then. There were too many groups. I used to play piano. I made some records, too.

ROBBINS: Okay, you got a lot of bread now. And your way of life isn't like it was four or five years ago. It's much grander. Does that kind of thing tend to throw you off?

DYLAN: Well, the transition never came from working at it. I left where I'm from because there's nothing there. I come from Minnesota, there was nothing there. I'm not going to fake it and say I went out to see the world. Hey, when I left there, man, I knew one thing: I had to get out of there and not come back. Just from my senses I knew there was something more than Walt Disney movies. I was never turned on or off by money. I never considered the fact of money as really that important. I could always play the guitar, you dig, and make friends—or fake friends. A lot of other people do other things and get to eat and sleep that way. Lot of people do a lot of things just to get around. You can find cats who get very scared, right? Who get married and settle down. But, after somebody's got something and sees it all around him, so he doesn't have to sleep out in the cold at night, that's all. The only thing is he don't die. But is he happy? There's nowhere to go. Okay, so I get the money, right? First of all, I had to move out of New York. Because everybody was coming down to see me—people which I didn't really dig. People coming in from weird-ass places. And I would think, for some reason, that I had to give them someplace to stay and all that. I found myself not really being by myself but just staying out of things I wanted to go to because people I knew would go there.

ROBBINS: Do you find friends—real friends—are they recognizable anymore?

DYLAN: Oh, sure, man, I can tell somebody I dig right away. I don't have to go through anything with anybody. I'm just lucky that way.

ROBBINS: Back to protest songs. The IWW's work is over now and the unions are pretty well established. What about the civil rights movement?

DYLAN: Well, it's okay. It's proper. It's not "Commie" anymore. *Harper's Bazaar* can feature it, you can find it on the cover of *Life*. But when you get beneath it, like anything, you find there's bullshit tied up in it. The Negro Civil Rights Movement is proper now, but there's more to it than what's in *Harper's Bazaar*. There's more to it than picketing in Selma, right? There's people living in utter poverty in New York. And then again, you have this big Right to Vote. Which is groovy. You want all these Negroes to vote? Okay, I can't go over the boat and shout "Hallelujah" only because they want to vote. Who're they going to vote for? Just politicians; same as the white people put in their politicians. Anybody that gets into politics is a little greaky anyway. Hey, they're just going to vote, that's all they're going to do. I hate to say it like that, make it sound hard, but it's going to boil down to that.

ROBBINS: What about the drive for education?

DYLAN: Education? They're going to school and learn about all the things the white private schools teach. The catechism, the whole thing. What're they going to learn? What's this education? Hey, the cat's much better off never going to school. The only thing against him is he can't be a doctor or a judge. Or he can't get a good job with the salesman's company. But that's the only thing wrong. If you want to say it's good that he gets an education and goes out and gets a job like that, groovy. I'm not going to do it.

ROBBINS: In other words, the formal intake of factual knowledge . . .

DYLAN: Hey, I have no respect for factual knowledge, man. I don't care what anybody knows, I don't care if somebody's a walking encyclopedia. Does that make him nice to talk to? Who cares if Washington was even the first president of the United States? You think anybody has actually ever been helped with this kind of knowledge?

ROBBINS: Maybe through a test. Well, what's the answer?

DYLAN: There aren't any answers, man. Or any questions. You must read my book . . . there's a little part in there about that. It evolves into a thing where it mentions words like "Answer." I couldn't possibly rattle off the words for these, because you'd have to read the whole book to see these specific words or Question and Answer. We'll have another interview after you read the book.

ROBBINS: Yeah, you have a book coming out. What about it? The title?

DYLAN: Tentatively, *Bob Dylan Off the Record*. But they tell me there's already books out with that "off the record" title. The book can't really be titled, that's the kind of book it is. I'm also going to write the reviews for it.

ROBBINS: Why write a book instead of lyrics?

DYLAN: I've written some songs which are kind of far out, a long continuation of verses, stuff like that—but I haven't really gotten into writing a completely free song. Hey, you dig something like cut-ups? I mean, like William Burroughs?

ROBBINS: Yeah, there's a cat in Paris who published a book with no pagination. The book comes in a box and you throw it in the air and, however it lands, you read it like that.

DYLAN: Yeah, that's where it's at. Because that's what it means, anyway. Okay, I wrote the book because there's a lot of stuff in there I can't possibly sing . . . all the collages. I can't sing it because it gets too long or it goes too far out. I can only do it around a few people who would know. Because the majority of the audience—I don't care where they're from, how hip they are—I think it would just get totally lost. Something that had no rhyme, all cut up, no nothing, except something happening, which is words.

ROBBINS: You wrote the book to say something?

DYLAN: Yeah, but certainly not any kind of profound statement. The book don't begin or end.

ROBBINS: But you had something to say. And you wanted to say it to somebody.

Younger Than That Now

DYLAN: Yeah, I said it to myself. Only, I'm lucky, because I could put it into a book. Now somebody else is going to be allowed to see what I said to myself.

ROBBINS: You have four albums out now, with a fifth any day. Are these albums sequential in the way that you composed and sung them?

DYLAN: Yeah, I've got about two or three albums that I've never recorded, which are lost songs. They're old songs; I'll never record them. Some very groovy songs. Some old songs which I've written and sung maybe once in a concert and nobody else ever heard them. There are a lot of songs which would fill in between the records. It was growing from the first record to the second, then a head change on the third. And the fourth. The fifth I can't even tell you about.

ROBBINS: So if I started with Album One, Side One, Band One, I could truthfully watch Bob Dylan grow?

DYLAN: No, you could watch Bob Dylan laughing to himself. Or you could see Bob Dylan going through changes. That's really the most.

ROBBINS: What do you think of the Byrds? Do you think they're doing something different?

DYLAN: Yeah, they could. They're doing something really new now. It's like a danceable Bach sound. Like "Bells of Rhymney." They're cutting across all kinds of barriers which most people who sing aren't even hip to. They know it all. If they don't close their minds, they'll come up with something pretty fantastic.

"Bob Dylan"

Jenny De Yong and Peter Roche

"I try to harmonize with songs the lonesome sparrow sings," sang Bob Dylan, alone on the stage at a packed City Hall last Friday: Dylan is himself sparrow-like—a thin, faded, ruffled sparrow—but one that sings to the tune of L2,000 per concert.

His dark-circled eyes seemed to peer above the conglomeration surrounding him (two microphones, a table with two glasses of much-needed water and a harmonica cradle round his polo-sweatered neck), while his penetrating songs convinced even the most cynical that Bob Dylan is worthy of the mound of superlatives which has been heaped upon him and under which his earlier followers feared he might suffocate.

An essential part of the popular image is the loneliness of Bob Dylan. He sings about it, in haunting symbols. He sings too about bitterness, of "The felsh-colored Christs that glow in the dark." Make no mistakes though—Dylan can write in glowing images about war and violence but he can write with equal insight, and strictly for laughs, about the things that are reality to a greater part of his audience, like the boy trying to persuade his girl to stay for the night.

Younger Than That Now

Dylan has been set up as everything from a blue-denim god to a guitar-playing Socrates, corrupting youth by opening the door on hooliganism, warning the universal parent: "Your sons and your daughters are beyond your command." It was for this reason that we approached him with some trepidation (and considerable difficulty, owing to positive festoons of red tape). We anticipated meeting the "sullen, bored Mr. Dylan" about whom so much has been written in the press lately—and found instead an individual who was very tired but very willing to talk. He answered our questions in his room at the Grand Hotel, perched on the edge of a couch, a cup of black coffee in one hand, a cigarette (Player's, untipped) in the other. Around him his entourage: a tough, voluble manager with flowing grey hair; a hip-talking young man with glasses and [a lovely?] jacket; a tall negro with an engaging chin; a dark, chatty girl hitching a plastic iris.

Dylan talks rapidly—his voice very soft—even when discussing topics about which he obviously feels strongly (the press, for example) his tone remains quiet, matter-of-fact. His thin, pale face has a fragile, almost transparent quality—although this was probably due in part to lack of sleep ("He's had no proper sleep for three days," Joan Baez had told us earlier). Miss Baez, who plans to tour Britain herself some time in the Autumn, sat quietly in a corner of the room, watching Dylan intently as he talked.

———

Q: To start with the obvious question: What do you think of Donovan and "Catch the Wind"?

A: Well, I quite like that song, and he sings it quite well. He's very young though, and people might like to try to make him into something that he isn't; that's something he'll have to watch. But the song is O.K.

Q: Isn't the tune a lot like your "Chimes of Freedom"?

A: Oh, I don't care what he takes from me; I don't care what other singers do to my songs either, they can't hurt me any. Like with the Animals and "Baby Let Me Follow You Down," I didn't worry none about that. I met the Animals over in New York, and we all went out and got scoused. Is that what you say? (Someone behind him suggests "sloshed.") Oh yeah, that's it, sloshed. Anyway, the Animals are O.K., I liked their last one, "Don't Let Me be Misunderstood," that was a good one.

Q: Coming on to your latest single, "Subterranean Homesick Blues," [many] people seem worried about the electric guitars and drums.

A: Yeah, well we had a lot of swinging cats on that track, real hip musicians, not just some cats I picked up off the street, and we all got together and we just had a ball. Anyway, that's just one track off the album.

Q: So why release it as a single?

A: That's not me, that's the Company. The Company says to me "It's time to do your next album," so I go along and record [???h] tracks for the album. [What we] do with the songs then, we [leave it] up to them. But I record [???] I wouldn't record a single.

Q: Aren't you afraid though that they'll turn you into a pop star?

A: They can't turn me into anything; I just write my songs and that's it. They can't change me any, and they can't change my songs. "Subterranean" sounds a bit different because of the backing, but I've had backing on my songs before, I had some backing on "Corrain."

Q: What are your own favorite songs?

A: You mean the ones I've written? Well, it depends on how I'm feeling; I think to be really good a song has to hit you at the right moment. But I like most of the ones on my new album, and on my last album I guess the one I liked best was "I Don't Believe You."

Younger Than That Now

Q: Your songs have changed a lot over the last couple of years. Are you consciously trying to change your style, or would you say that this was a natural development?

A: Oh, it's a natural one, I think. The big difference is that the songs I was writing last year, songs like "Ballad in Plain D," they were what I call one-dimensional songs, but my new songs I'm trying to make more three-dimensional, you know, there's more symbolism, they're written on more than one level.

Q: How long does it take you to write a song? Say a song like "Hard Rain"?

A: Well, I wrote "Hard Rain" while I was still on the streets, I guess that was the first three-dimension song I wrote. It took me about—oh, about two days.

Q: Is that normal?

A: No, that was kind of long; usually I write them a lot quicker, sometimes in a couple of hours.

Q: Would you say that your songs contain sufficient poetry to be able to stand by themselves, without music?

A: If they can't do that, then they're not what I want them to be. Basically, I guess I'm more interested in writing than in performing.

Q: Does that explain all those poems on the backs of your albums?

A: Oh, those (laughing)—well they were kind of written out of terror, I used to get scared that I wouldn't be around much longer, so I'd write my poems down on anything I could find—the backs of my albums, the backs of Joan's albums, you know, anywhere I could find.

Q: Why do you suppose that the national press tries to make you out to be angry and bored and all the rest?

A: That's because they ask the wrong questions, like, "What did you have for breakfast," "What's your favorite color," stuff like that. Newspaper reporters, man, they're just hung-up writers, frustrated novelists, they don't hurt me none by putting fancy labels on me. They got all these preconceived ideas about me, so I just play up to them.

Q: How do you feel about being labeled as the voice of your generation?

A: Well, I don't know. I mean, I'm 24, how can I speak for people of 17 or 18, I can't be anyone else's voice. If they can associate with me that's O.K., but I can't give a voice to people who have no voice. Would you say that I was your voice?

Q: Well you manage to say a lot of things that I'd like to say, only I don't have the words.

A: Yeah, but that's not the same as being your voice.

Q: No, but it's something.

Someone mentions food and at once Dylan and followers remember that they haven't eaten for hours. Not much is said but it becomes increasingly obvious that food has the edge on aesthetics . . . We took that as our cue to leave.

DISC WEEKLY, MAY 12, 1965

Mr. Send Up

Laurie Henshaw

HENSHAW: Can you tell me when and where you were born?

DYLAN: No, you can go and find out. There's many biographies and you can look to that. You don't ask me where I was born, where I lived. Don't ask me those questions. You find out from other papers.

HENSHAW: I'd rather hear it from you.

DYLAN: I'm not going to tell you.

HENSHAW: Can you tell me exactly when you entered the profession? When you first started writing songs?

DYLAN: When I was 12.

HENSHAW: And you were writing poetry at the time? And you are writing a book now?

DYLAN: I've got a book done.

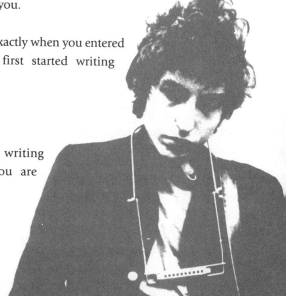

Younger Than That Now

HENSHAW: Is it already published?

DYLAN: It's going to be published in the fall.

HENSHAW: What's it called?

DYLAN: I'm not going to tell you.

HENSHAW: Can you give me an idea what it is about?

DYLAN: No.

HENSHAW: Can you tell me your favorite song among the ones you've written?

DYLAN: I don't have any. I've no personal songs that I wouldn't consider apart from any other.

HENSHAW: You must obviously make a lot of money nowadays?

DYLAN: I spend it all. I have six Cadillacs. I have four houses. I have a plantation in Georgia. Oh, I'm also working on a rocket. A little rocket. Not a big rocket. Not the kind of rocket they have in Cape Canaveral. I don't know about those kind of rockets.

HENSHAW: Do you have personal things—cameras, watches, and that sort of thing?

DYLAN: No, I don't. I buy cars. I have lot of cars, the Cadillacs. I also have a few Oldsmobiles, about three.

HENSHAW: Do you have fears about anything political.

DYLAN: No.

HENSHAW: Of course your songs have a very strong content . . .

DYLAN: Have you heard my songs?

HENSHAW: I have. "Masters Of War." "Blowin' In The Wind."

DYLAN: What about "Spanish Lover"? [sic] Have you heard that? Why don't you listen to that? Listen, I couldn't care less what your paper writes about me. Your paper can write anything, don't you realize? The people that listen to me don't read your paper, you know, to listen to me. I'm not going to be known from your paper.

HENSHAW: You're already known. Why be so hostile?

DYLAN: Because you're hostile to me. You're using me. I'm an object to you. I went through this before in the United States, you know. There's nothing personal. I've nothing against you at all. I just don't want to be bothered with your paper, that's all. I just don't want to be a part of it. Why should I have to go along with something just so that somebody else can eat? Why don't you just say that my name is Kissenovitch. You know, and I, er, come from Acapulco, Mexico. That my father was an escaped thief from South Africa. OK. You can say anything you want to say.

HENSHAW: Let's talk about you. Your clothes for instance. Are your taste in clothes changing at all?

DYLAN: I like clothes. I don't have any particular interests at all. I like to wear drapes, umbrellas, hats.

HENSHAW: You're not going to tell me you carry an umbrella.

DYLAN: I most certainly do carry an umbrella. Where I come from everybody carries an umbrella. Have you ever been to South Dakota? Well, I come from South Dakota, and in South Dakota people carry umbrellas.

Younger Than That Now

HENSHAW: What would you say has been the greatest influence in your life?

DYLAN: You! Your paper happens to influence me a lot. I'm going to go out and write a song after I've seen you—your know—what I'm used for. I feel what I'm doing and I feel what your paper does. And you have the nerve and gall to ask me what influences me and why do I think I'm so accepted. I don't want to be interviewed by your paper. I don't need it. You don't need it either. You can build up your own star. Why don't you just get a lot of money and bring some kid out here from the north of England and say "We're gonna make you a star! You just comply with everything, everything we do. Everytime you want an interview you can just sign a paper that means we can have an interview and write what we want to write. And you'll be a star and make money!" Why don't you just do that? I'm not going to do it for you.

HENSHAW: Why should we bother to interview you if we didn't think you were worth interviewing?

DYLAN: Because I'm news. That's why I don't blame you, you have a job to do. I know that. There's nothing personal here. But don't try to pick up too much you know.

HENSHAW: When did you start making records?

DYLAN: I started making records in 1947, that was my first recording. A race record. I made it down south. Actually the first record I made was in 1935. John Hammond came and recorded me. Discovered me in 1935, sitting on a farm. The man who discovered Benny Goodman saw me down the street. He had me in to do a session. It happened just like that. Otherwise I wouldn't be here.

HENSHAW: Do you have a favorite guitar?

DYLAN: Favorite guitar? I have 33 guitars! How can you have one favorite? I'm going to quit playing the guitar anyway. I'm playing the banjo.

HENSHAW: Have you heard Manfred Mann doing "With God On Our Side"?

DYLAN: No, I haven't heard it. I've only heard about it.

HENSHAW: It was sung on "Ready Steady Goes Live" and it made quite an impact.

DYLAN: I would like to have seen it.

HENSHAW: How do you feel about other groups doing your songs?

DYLAN: Well, how would you feel about other groups doing your songs?

HENSHAW: I'd be complimented.

DYLAN: I'd feel the same as you.

HENSHAW: What sort of people do you like? What type do you cultivate?

DYLAN: I would cultivate the kind of person that sticks to his job. Sticks to his job and gets his job done. And is not too nervous. But nervous enough not to come back!

HENSHAW: What kind of people do you take an instant dislike to?

DYLAN: I take an instant dislike to people that shake a lot. An instant dislike—wham! Most of the time I throw them against a wall. I have a bodyguard, Toppo. (Dylan here puts his hands to his mouth and calls to the next room) Toppo! Is Toppo in there? I have a bodyguard to get rid of people like that. He comes out and wipes them out. He wiped out three people last week.

HENSHAW: Do you paint?

DYLAN: Yeah, sure.

HENSHAW: What sort of painting.

DYLAN: I painted my house.

(at this point Dylan abruptly ended the interview)

Bob Dylan Interview

Nora Ephron & Susan Edmiston

This interview took place in late summer of 1965 in the office of Dylan's manager, Albert Grossman. Dylan had just been booed in the historic Forest Hills concert where he abandoned folk purity to the use of electric accompaniment. he was wearing a red-and-navy op-art shirt, a navy blazer, and pointy high-heeled boots. His face, so sharp and harsh when translated through media, was then infinitely soft and delicate. His hair was not bushy or electric or Afro; it was fine-spun soft froth like the foam of a wave. He looked like an underfed angel with a nose from the land of the Chosen People.

Q: Some American folk singers—Carolyn Hester, for example—say that what you're now doing, the new sound, "folk rock," is liberating them.

A: Did Carolyn say that? You tell her she can come around and see me any time now that she's liberated.

Younger Than That Now

Q: Does labeling, using the term, "folk rock," tend to obscure what's happening?

A: Yes.

Q: It's like "pop gospel." What does the term mean to you?

A: Yeah, classical gospel could be the next trend. There's country rock, rockabilly. What does it mean to me? Folk rock. I've never even said that word. It has a hard gutter sound. Circussy atmosphere. It's nose-thumbing. Sound like you're looking down on what is . . . fantastic, great music.

Q: The definition most often given of folk rock is the combination of the electronic sound of rock and roll with the meaningful lyrics of folk music? Does that sum up what you're doing?

A: Yes. It's very complicated to play with electricity. You play with other people. You're dealing with other people. Most people don't like to work with other people, it's more difficult. It takes a lot. Most people who don't like rock and roll can't relate to other people.

Q: You mention the Apollo Theatre in Harlem on one of your album covers. Do you go there often?

A: Oh, I couldn't go up there. I used to go up there a lot about four years ago. I even wanted to play in one of the amateur nights, but I got scared. Bad things can happen to you. I saw what the audience did to a couple of guys they didn't like. And I would have had a couple of things against me right away when I stepped out on the stage.

Q: Who is Mr. Jones in "Ballad of a Thin Man"?

A: He's a real person. You know him, but not by that name.

Q: Like Mr. Charlie?

A: No. He's more than Mr. Charlie. He's actually a person. Like I saw him come into the room one night and he looked like a camel. He proceeded to put his eyes in his pocket. I asked this guy who he was and he said, "That's Mr. Jones." Then I asked this cat, "Doesn't he do anything but put his eyes in his pocket?" And he told me, "He puts his nose on the ground." It's all there, it's a true story.

Q: Where did you get that shirt?

A: California. Do you like it? You should see my others. You can't get clothes like that here. There are a lot of things out there we haven't got here.

Q: Isn't California on the way here?

A: It's uptight here compared to there. Hollywood I mean. It's not really breathable here. It's like there's air out there. The Sunset Strip can't be compared to anything here, like 42nd Street. The people there look different, they look more like . . . you want to kiss them out there.

Q: Do you spend a lot of time out there?

A: I don't have much time to spend anywhere: The same thing in England. In England everybody looks very hip East Side. They wear things . . . they don't wear things that bore you. They've got other hang-ups in other directions.

Q: Do you consider yourself primarily a poet?

A: No. We have our ideas about poets. The word doesn't mean any more than the word "house." There are people who write _po_ems and people who write po_ems_. Other people write _poems_. Everybody who writes poems do you call them a poet? There's a certain kind of rhythm in some kind of way that's visible. You don't necessarily have to write to be a poet. Some people work in gas stations and they're poets. I don't call myself a poet because I don't like the word. I'm a trapeze artist.

Q: What I meant was, do you think your words stand without the music?

A: They would stand but I don't read them. I'd rather sing them. I write things that aren't songs—I have a book coming out.

Q: What is it?

A: It's a book of words.

Q: Is it like the back of your albums? It seemed to me that the album copy you write is a lot like the writing of William Burroughs. Some of the accidental sentences—

A: Cut-ups.

Q: Yes, and some of the imagery and anecdotes. I wondered if you had read anything by him.

A: I haven't read *Naked Lunch* but I read some of his shorter things in little magazines, foreign magazines. I read one in Rome. I know him. I don't really know him—I just met him once. I think he's a great man.

Q: Burroughs keeps an album, a collection of photographs that illustrate his writing. Do you have anything similar to that?

A: I do that too. I have photographs of "Gates of Eden" and "It's All Over Now, Baby Blues." I saw them after I wrote the songs. People send me a lot of things and a lot of the things are pictures, so other people must have that idea too. I gotta admit, maybe I wouldn't have chosen them, but I can see what it is about the pictures.

Q: I heard you used to play the piano for Buddy Holly.

A: No. I used to play the rock and roll piano, but I don't want to say who it was for because the cat will try to get hold of me. I don't want to see the cat. He'll try to reclaim the friendship. I did it a long time ago, when I was seventeen years old. I used to play a country piano too.

Q: This was before you became interested in folk music?

A: Yes. I became interested in folk music because I had to make it somehow. Obviously I'm not a hard-working cat. I played the guitar, that was all I did. I thought it was great music. Certainly I haven't turned my back on it or anything like that. There is—and I'm sure nobody realizes this, all the authorities who write about what it is and what it should be, when they say keep things simple, they should be easily understood—folk music is the only music where it isn't simple. It's never been simple. It's weird, man, full of legend, myth, Bible, and ghosts. I've never written anything hard to understand, not in my head anyway, and nothing as far out as some of the old songs. They were out of sight.

Q: Like what songs?

A: "Little Brown Dog." "I bought a little brown dog, its face is all gray. Now I'm going to Turkey flying on my bottle." And "Nottemun Town," that's like a herd of ghosts passing through on the way to Tangiers. "Lord Edward," "Barbara Allen," they're full of myth.

Q: And contradictions?

A: Yeah, contradictions.

Q: And chaos?
A: Chaos, watermelon, clocks, everything.

Younger Than That Now

Q: You wrote on the back of one album, "I accept chaos but does chaos accept me."

A: Chaos is a friend of mine. It's like I accept him, does he accept me.

Q: Do you see the world as chaos?

A: Truth is chaos. Maybe beauty is chaos.

Q: Poets like Eliot and Yeats—

A: I haven't read Yeats.

Q: They saw the world as chaos, accepted it as chaos and attempted to bring order from it. Are you trying to do that?

A: No. It exists and that's all there is to it. It's been here longer than I have. What can I do about it? I don't know what the songs I write are. That's all I do is write songs, right? Write. I collect things too.

Q: Monkey wrenches?

A: Where did you read about that? Has that been in print? I told this guy out on the coast that I collected monkey wrenches, all sizes and shapes of monkey wrenches, and he didn't believe me. I don't think you believe me either. And I collect the pictures too. Have you talked to Sonny and Cher?

Q: No.

A: They're a drag. A cat got kicked out of a restaurant and he went home and wrote a song about it.

Q: They say your fan mail has radically increased since you switched sounds.

A: Yeah. I don't have time to read all of it, but I want you to put that I answer half of it. I don't really. A girl does that for me.

Q: Does she save any for you—any particularly interesting letters?

A: She knows my head. Not the ones that just ask for pictures, there's a file for them. Not the ones that say, I want to make it with you, they go in another file. She saves two kinds. The violently put-down—

Q: The ones that call you a sellout?

A: Yeah. Sellout, fink, Fascist, Red, everything in the book. I really dig those. And ones from old friends.

Q: Like, "You don't remember me but I was in the fourth grade with you"?

A: No, I never had any friends then. These are letters from people who knew me in New York five, six years ago. My first fans. Not the people who call themselves my first fans. They came in three years ago, two years ago. They aren't really my first fans.

Q: How do you feel about being booed at your concert at Forest Hills?

A: I thought it was great, I really did. If I said anything else I'd be a liar.

Q: And at Newport Folk Festival?

A: That was different. They twisted the sound. They didn't like what I was going to play and they twisted the sound on me before I began.

Q: I hear you are wearing a sellout jacket.

A: What kind of jacket is a sellout jacket?

Younger Than That Now

Q: Black leather.

A: I've had black leather jackets since I was five years old. I've been wearing black leather all my life.

Q: I wonder if we could talk about electronic music and what made you decide to use it.

A: I was doing fine, you know, singing and playing my guitar. It was a sure thing, don't you understand, it was a sure thing. I was getting very bored with that. I couldn't go out and play like that. I was thinking of quitting. Out front it was a sure thing. I knew what the audience was gonna do, how they would react. It was very automatic. Your mind just drifts unless you can find some way to get in there and remain totally there. It's so much of a fight remaining totally there all by yourself. It takes too much. I'm not ready to cut that much out of my life. You can't have nobody around. You can't be bothered with anybody else's world. And I like people. What I'm doing now—it's a whole other thing. We're not playing rock music. It's not a hard sound. These people call it folk rock—if they want to call it that, something that simple, it's good for selling records. As far as it being what it is, I don't know what it is. I can't call it folk rock. It's a whole way of doing things. It has been picked up on, I've heard songs on the radio that have picked it up. I'm not talking about words. It's a certain feeling, and it's been on every single record I've ever made. That has not changed. I know it hasn't changed. As far as what I was totally, before, maybe I was pushing it a little then. I'm not pushing things now. I know it. I know very well how to do it. The problem of how I want to play something—I know it in front. I know what I am going to say, what I'm going to do. I don't have to work it out. The band I work with—they wouldn't be playing with me if they didn't play like I want them to. I have this song, "Queen Jane Approximately"—

Q: Who is Queen Jane?

A: Queen Jane is a man.

Q: Was there something that made you decide to change sounds? Your trip to England?

A: I like the sound. I like what I'm doing now. I would have done it before. It wasn't practical to do it before. I spend most of my time writing. I wouldn't have had the time. I had to get where I was going all alone. I don't know what I'm going to do next. I probably will record with strings some time, but it doesn't necessarily change. It's just a different color. And I know it's real. No matter what anybody says. They can boo till the end of time. I know that the music is real, more real than the boos.

Q: How do you work?

A: Most of the time I work at night. I don't really like to think of it as work. I don't know how important it is. It's not important to the average cat who works eight hours a day. What does he care? The world can get along very well without it. I'm hip to that.

Q: Sure, but the world can get along without any number of things.

A: I'll give you a comparison. Rudy Vallee. Now that was a lie, that was a downright lie. Rudy Vallee being popular. What kind of people could have dug him? You know, your grandmothers and mothers. But what kind of people were they? He was so sexless. If you want to find out about those times and you listen to his music you're not going to find out anything about the times. His music was a pipedream. All escapes. There are no more escapes. If you want to find out anything that's happening now, you have to listen to the music. I don't mean the words, although "Eve of Destruction" will tell you something about it. The words are not really gonna tell it, not really. You gotta listen to the Stapes (Staple?) Singers, Smokey and the Miracles, Martha and the Vandellas. That's scary to a lot of people. It's sex that's involved. It's not hidden. It's real. You can overdo it. It's not only sex, it's a whole beautiful feeling.

Q: But Negro rhythm and blues has been around underground for at least twelve years. What brought it out now?

A: The English did that. They brought it out. They hipped everybody. You read an interview asking who the Beatles' favorite singer was and they say Chuck Berry. You never used to hear Chuck Berry records on the radio, hard blues. The English did that. England is great and beautiful, though in other ways kinda messy. Though not outside London.

Q: In what way messy?

A: There's a snobbishness. What you see people doing to other people. It's not only class. It's not that simple. It's a kind of Queen kind of thing. Some people are royalty and some are not. Here, man, somebody don't like you he tells you. There it's very tight, tight kinds of expressions, their whole tone of speaking changes. It's an everyday kind of thing. But the kids are a whole other thing. Great. They're just more free. I hope you don't think I take this too seriously—I just have a headache.

A: I think you started out to say that music was more in tune with what's happening than other art forms.

A: Great paintings shouldn't be in museums. Have you ever been in a museum? Museums are cemeteries. Paintings should be on the walls of restaurants, in dime stores, in gas stations, in men's rooms. Great paintings should be where people hang out. The only thing where it's happening is on radio and records, that's where people hang out. You can't see great paintings. You pay half a million and hang one in your house and one guest sees it. That's not art. That's a shame, a crime. Music is the only thing that's in tune with what's happening. It's not in book form, it's not on the stage. All this art they've been talking about is non-existent. It just remains on the shelf. It doesn't make anyone happier. Just think how many people would really feel great if they could see a Picasso in their daily diner. It's not the bomb that has to go, man, it's the museums.

One Foot on the Highway . . .

Robert Shelton

"I have a death thing—I have a suicidal thing, I know. . . . If the songs
are dreamed, it's like my voice is coming out of their dream."
—DYLAN, 1966

"Judas!"
—HECKLER AT ALBERT HALL, 1966

"Bob Dylan, go home."
—PARIS JOUR, 1966

IN THE DARK, LINCOLN MUNICIPAL Airport
blended into the surrounding farmland. It was just
past the break of midnight on a Saturday in mid-
March 1966. As Dylan, The Band, two
roadies, and I arrived, runway lights
flashed on, tower controllers stirred,
and mechanics busied themselves
around Dylan's private plane, the
two-engine Lockheed Lodestar jet.

Younger Than That Now

Denver was next, then back to New York, then up to the Pacific Northwest, Hawaii, Australia, Scandinavia, Ireland, England, France, then back home. This was the beginning of the end of one of Dylan's many careers. As he walked into the lunch-canteen room, a mechanic in white overalls peered into the night. "It must get lonely out here," Bob said. Both looked at the field. "It does," the mechanic replied, "but it's a job. I just take the hours they give me." "I know how that feels, I really do," Dylan said, as they stared across prairie land.

He had just evaded fifty fans at his hotel, but a half dozen clustered around the plane. He scribbled his autograph a few times. A shy youth, about seventeen, approached. "Mr. Dylan," he said, nervously, "I'm interested in poetry too." "Yeah, is that so?" Dylan replied. "Yes, sir," the boy answered. "I was wondering if you could spare a few minutes, sometime, to read some poems I've written." "Sure," Bob responded. The young man handed Dylan a large envelope that bulged like a football. "Are all these poems?" Dylan asked. "Yes . . . I've been writing more since I began to study your songs." "Well," Dylan said, "thank you. I'll try to read some tonight. Is your address on the envelope? I'll let you know what I think of them." The boy glowed: "That's wonderful. I hope you like them."

Inside the plane, The Band members were dozing off, a pile of slumping bodies. Road managers Bill Avis and Victor Maimudes checked everyone's seat belt. Dylan and I sat face-to-face. On one knee rested a packet of proofs of his book, *Tarantula*. On his other knee was the fan's envelope. I fussed with my tape recorder, cursing the engine noise. His eyes were nearly slits, but he told me he wouldn't have slept even if I hadn't been there. He just had too much to do.

"It takes a lot of medicine to keep up this pace," Dylan said. "It's very hard, man. A concert tour like this has almost killed me. It's been like this since October. . . . It really drove me out of my mind. . . . I'm really going to cut down. Next year, the concert tour is only going to last a month or two. I'm only doing it like this because I want everyone to know what we're doing." Dylan sent a cloud of cigarette smoke over his head, tugged his shirt collar, and continued: "It's just absurd for people to sit around being offended by their own meaninglessness, so that they have to force everything else to come into the hole with them, and die trying. That's the hang-up here. But I'm not involved with that anymore. I've told you that many times. I don't know if you think I'm kidding, or if you think it's a front. I really just don't *care*—honestly just don't *care*—what people say about me. I don't care what people think about me. I don't care what people know about me.

"Playing on the stage is a kick for me, now. It wasn't before, because I knew what I was doing then was just too empty . . . It was just dead ambassadors who would come and see me and clap and say: 'Oh, groovy, I would like to meet him and have a cocktail. Perhaps I'll bring my son, Joseph, with me.' And the first thing you know you've got about five or six little boys and girls hanging around with Coke bottles and ginger-ale bottles . . . and you're confronted by some ambassador who's got his hand in your pocket trying to shake your spine and give you compliments. I won't let *anybody* backstage anymore. Even to give me a compliment. I just don't care. . . ."

His eyes cleared: "You can't ask me about how I sleep. You can't ask me about how I make it, and you cannot ask me what I think I am doing here. Other than that, we'll just get along fine. You just ask me anything and I will shoot right back . . . Now, we have one thing straight about the book. I'm going to tell Albert we have come to an understanding about the book. I'll give you as much time as I can. I'll come very quickly to the point in all the things that I want done, but you can easily go back on me . . . But I won't forgive you for doing that, man. It's not going to be a biography, because I'm not dead yet. It's going to be a timeless thing, right?

"Nobody knows about me. What do people really know? That my father's name is Zimmerman and my mother's family is middle class? I'm not about to go around telling people that this is false . . . I'm not covering up anything I did before. I'm not going back on anything, any statement or anything I've ever done. . . . I've given up trying to tell any-body that they are wrong in their thinking about anything, about the world, or me, or whatever. . . . Now, you are not going to say 'author-ized by Bob Dylan.' I'll write that on the cover. I'll write four sentences on the cover and sign my name, to something like: 'Bob Shelton wrote me up in the *New York Times* five years ago. And he's a nice guy and I like him. And he wrote this book and for that, it is not'—just to make sure it sells in Nebraska and Wyoming—'it's not chintzy.' " Dylan laughed.

"There is nothing anybody can expose about me. Everybody thinks that there is such an exposé, on millions of little tiny things, like name change. It doesn't really matter to me. Obviously, there are people who like to read that shit. And people might say 'Oh, I don't believe it,' or 'That doesn't matter to me.' But it tickled them, you know." Twisting restlessly, Dylan was getting angry at the hungers of his audience. He seemed to want to *explain* himself. He tried a new beginning: "I think of all that I do as my *writing*. It cheapens it to call it anything else but writing. But there is not a person on the earth who takes it less seriously than I do. I know that it's not going to help me into heaven one little bit. It's not going to keep me out of the fiery furnace. It's not going to extend my life any and it's not going to make me happy."

What did he think would make him happy? I asked. "I'm happy, you know," he said. "I'm happy to just be able to come across things. I don't need to be happy. Happiness is a kind of cheap word. Let's face it, I'm not the kind of cat that's going to cut off an ear if I can't do something. I would commit suicide. I would shoot myself in the brain if things got bad. I would jump from a window . . . You know, I can think about death openly. It's nothing to fear. It's nothing sacred. I've seen so many people die." I asked: Is life sacred? "Life's not sacred either," Dylan replied. "Look at all the spirits that actually control the atmosphere, which are not living and yet which attract you, as ideas, or like games with the solar system. Or look at the farce of politics, economy, and war."

Another variation on an old theme: inner despair battling outer hope. "It's become so easy for me to do everything, you have no idea, man, everything at my command. I can make money now doing absolutely anything. But I don't want that kind of money. I'm not a millionaire now, in terms of everything I have. But it is really close . . . This next year, I'm going to be a millionaire, but that means nothing. To be a millionaire means that next year you can lose it all. You must realize that I have not copped out on one thing. I mean, I love what I do. I also make money off it—Hey, I sing honest stuff, man, and it's consistent. It's *all* I do. I don't give a damn what anybody says. Nobody can criticize what I do that's going to have any effect on me. I never really read what people say about me. I'm just not interested.

"When I first really knew that I had money that I couldn't see, I looked around to see what a few of my agents were doing with it. First of all, I like chauffeurs. When I came back from England last time, I didn't buy a chauffeur, but I sure rented one. I make no bones about it . . . I *need* the money to *employ* people. It all works hand in hand. If I had no money, I could walk *invisible*. But it costs me money now to be able to walk invisible. That's the *only* reason I need the money. I don't need the money to buy clothes or nothing. . . ." Again his anger mounted. "I'm sick of giving creeps money off my soul. When I lose my teeth tomorrow, they are not going to buy me a new pair of teeth. I don't like little short people who smoke Tiparillo cigarettes and have their pockets turned inside out all the time and wear glasses and who once wanted to be Groucho Marx making all the money off me. And there are a lot of them. . . . All in the music business.

"Oh, if it's not the promoter cheating you, it's the box office cheating you. Somebody is always giving you a hard time. . . . Even the record company figures won't be right. Nobody's going to be straight with you because nobody wants the information out. Do you know that up to a certain point I made more money on a song I wrote if it were on an album by Carolyn Hester, or anybody, than if I did it myself. That's the contract they gave me. Horrible! Horrible! . . .

"I'm not going to be accepted, but I would like to be accepted . . . by the *Hogtown Dispatch* literary crowd, who wear violets in their crotch and make sure that they get on all the movie and TV reviews and also write about the ladies' auxiliary meetings and the PTA gatherings, you know, all in the same column. I would like to be accepted by them people. But I don't think I'm ever going to be. Whereas the Beatles have been." Did he want the Beatles' sort of acceptance? "No, no, no . . . I'm not saying that. I'm just saying the Beatles have arrived, right? In all music forms, whether Stravinsky or Leopold Jake the Second, who plays in the Five Spot, the Black Muslim Twins, or whatever. The Beatles are accepted, and you've got to accept them for what they do. They play songs like 'Michelle' and 'Yesterday.' A lot of smoothness there."

When I told him Joan Baez planned to record "Yesterday" on her next album, Bob responded: "Yeah, it's the thing to do, to tell all the teeny-boppers, 'I dig the Beatles,' and you sing a song like 'Yesterday' or 'Michelle.' Hey, God knows, it's such a cop-out, man, both of those songs. If you go into the Library of Congress, you can find a lot better than that. There are millions of songs like 'Michelle' and 'Yesterday' written in Tin Pan Alley." There aren't millions of songs like *his* being written by anyone, I suggested. "I don't know if I fully appreciate that because it's going to get to the point where nobody else is going to be able to sing my songs but me. Like, I'm going to drive myself right out of business. I'll have to put out ten thousand records a year, for God's sake, because nobody will record the songs I write." Did he influence young people because he broke the rules? "It's not a question of breaking the rules, don't you understand? I don't break the rules, because I don't see any rules to break. As far as I'm concerned, there aren't any rules. . . ."

Like Lenny Bruce, he was riffing, in and out of communication, like a jazzman going in and out of a melody line. It was word music, chin music, symbol music. "My thing is with colors. It's not black and white. It's always been with colors, whether with clothes or anything. Color. Now, with something like that driving you, sometimes it gets very fiery red, you understand? And at times it gets very jet black.

"You just have to make it. When I say 'make it,' I don't mean being a popular folk-rock star. Making it means finding your line. Everybody's line is there, someplace. People think they just have to go through living hell on earth, but I don't really believe that attitude. The only people who believe . . . that life is a tragedy, are the people who are simple, closed-minded, who have to make excuses for themselves. Despite everybody who has been born and has died, the world has just gone on. I mean, look at Napoleon— but we went right on. Look at Harpo Marx—the world went around, it didn't stop for a second. It's sad but true. John Kennedy, right?"

Isn't the difference in what people did when they were here on earth? "Don't you see they did *nothing*? Has anybody done anything? Name anybody you think has done something." Shaw, I said. "George Bernard Shaw," Dylan slowly repeated. "Who has he helped?" "He helped a lot of people to use their heads," I replied, adding: "You've helped a lot of people to use their heads and their ears." "Well," Dylan rejoined, "I don't think I have, that's all. It's funny people think I have. I'm certainly not the one to go around saying that that is what I do. . . . At one time I did read a lot of the stuff that was written about me, maybe three or four years ago. Now, I don't even read anything anymore. So I have no idea what people say about me. I really don't. I do know that a lot of people really like me. I know that. . . ."

Eight miles high, over the Great Plains, he joggled *Tarantula* on one knee and the Nebraska boy's poems on the other, an unconscious seesaw. Did he think *Tarantula* was going to be accepted by the literary establishment, by serious poets? ". . . I think a poet is anybody who wouldn't call himself a poet. Anybody who could possibly call himself a poet just cannot be a poet . . . When people start calling me a poet, I say: 'Oh, groovy, how groovy to be called a poet!' But it didn't do me any good, I'll tell you that. It didn't make me any happier.

"Hey, I would love to say that I am a poet. I would really like to think of myself as a poet, but I just can't because of all the slobs who are called poets." Who was a poet, then? Allen Ginsberg? "He's a poet," Dylan fired back. "To be a poet does not necessarily mean that you have to write words on paper. One of those truck drivers at the motel is a poet. He talks like a poet. I mean what else does a poet have to do? Poets—" his voice trailed off inchoately, ideas running too fast for his tongue. "People like Robert Frost poetry about trees and branches, but that isn't what I mean. . . . Allen Ginsberg is the only writer I know. The rest of the writers I don't have that much respect for. If they really want to do it, they're going to have to *sing* it. . . . I wouldn't call myself a poet for any more reason than I would call myself a protest singer. All that would do would put me in a category with a whole lot of people who would just bother me. To tell anybody I'm a poet would just be fooling people. That would put me in a class, man, with people like Carl Sandburg, T. S. Eliot,

Younger Than That Now

Stephen Spender, and Rupert Brooke. Hey, name them—Edna St. Vincent Millay and Robert Louis Stevenson and Edgar Allan Poe and Robert Lowell.

"I know two saintly people," Bob continued. "I know just two holy people. Allen Ginsberg is one. The other, for lack of a better term I just want to call 'this person named Sara.' What I mean by 'holy' is crossing all the boundaries of time and usefulness. . . . William Burroughs is a poet, I like all his old books and Jean Genet's old books. Genet's scholastical lectures are just a waste of time, they are just boring. But if we are talking now in terms of writers I think can be called poets, then Allen must be the best. I mean Allen's 'Kaddish,' not 'Howl.' Allen doesn't have to sing 'Kaddish,' man. You understand what I mean? He just has to lay it down. He's the only poet that I know of. He's the only person I respect who writes, that just totally writes. He don't have to do nothing, man. Allen Ginsberg, he's just holy." How is Sara holy? "I don't want to put her in this book. I want to keep her out of this. I don't want to call her 'a girl.' I know it's very corny, but the only thing I can think of is, more or less, 'madonna-like.' "

I was beginning to think he'd forgotten my tape recorder, when he asked: "Are you getting it all? How much tape do you have left? Is it still running?" He plunged on: "Love and sex are things that really hang everybody up. When things aren't going right and you're really nobody, if you don't get laid in one way or another, you get mean, you know. You get cruel. Now, why in the world sex should force this is beyond me. I truthfully can tell you that male and female are not here to have sex, you know, that's not the purpose. I don't believe that that's God's will, that females have been created so that they can be a counterpart of man's urge. There are too many other things that people just won't let themselves be involved in. Sex and love have nothing to do with female and male. It is just whatever two souls happen to be. It could be male and female, and it might not be male and female. It might be female and female or it might be male and male. You can try to pretend that it doesn't happen, and you can make fun of it and be snide, but that's not really the rightful thing. I know, I know."

His verbal floodstream seemed driven by pressure built up during years of talking guardedly for publication. Inevitably, music displaced all other topics, even though he had remarked to me before we got on the plane that "music is only twenty percent of what I am." "I want you to have explanations of my songs in your book," Dylan said. "Things nobody else will ever have." "Such as," I broke in, "who Mr. Jones is to you?" "Well," Bob parried, "I'm not going to tell you that way. I'm going to tell you about the stuff that *I* want to tell you about. . . . I could tell you who Mr. Jones is in my life, but, like, everybody has got their Mr. Jones, so I can't really say that he is the same for everyone." Nothing struck me so strongly as this passage in his two-in-the-morning monologue: "Mr. Jones's loneliness can easily be covered up to the point where he can't recognize that he is alone . . . suddenly locked in a room . . . it's not so incredibly absurd, and it's not so imaginative, to have Mr. Jones in a room with three walls with a midget and a geech and a naked man. Plus a voice, a voice coming in his dream. I'm just a voice speaking. Anytime I'm singing about people, and if the songs are dreamed, it's like my voice is coming out of their dream. . . ."

He was speeding along, now attacking some false myths: "I hung around college, but it's a cop-out from life, from experience. A lot of people started out to be lawyers, but I venture to say that one hundred percent of the really groovy lawyers haven't gotten through school the way they ought to. They've always been freaks in their school, and have always had a hard time making it . . . so many lawyers just take people for what they're worth. They all made deals and all are very criminal . . . but doctors, lawyers, all these kinds of people—they're just in it for money . . . and for resentment. They put in their time and they're going to get it back. I agree with them that way. But I'm sure it could be done in other ways, and it's not. . . . I've known people who've been really loaded down with burdens and who have been in the right to collect, and who have been so innocent, that when they got lawyers to get them what they deserve . . . Do you follow me? The parties they are suing make deals with their lawyers. Like, it happens all the time, man. How anybody could have respect for lawyers baffles me! I have lawyers working for me I never see. I don't see my lawyers. Anytime they see the chance, they jump on it. . . ."

Did he want to talk about Joan Baez? Would he shed any light on his attitudes *then* toward one of the most intriguing show-business liaisons of the times, or would he bite my head off? "Me and Joan?" Bob asked. "I'll tell you. I hope you do explain it, if you can do this book straight. She brought me up. . . . I rode on her, but I don't think I owe her anything. . . . I want you to print that, because I am not joking. I feel sorry for her, knowing that I don't have to feel sorry for her, or anybody to feel sorry for her. . . . I feel bad for her because she has nobody to turn to that's going to be straight with her. . . . She hasn't got that much in common with the street vagabonds who play insane instruments. She's not that kind of person. Her family is a very gentle kind of family. She's very fragile and very sick and I lived with her and I loved the place. . . . Can you write this in your book? If you can't, man, it's a waste of time. I mean, is your book going to be a mature book, or is this all just a waste of time?" I reassured him.

Dylan's strangely defiant mood seemed to stress his most unappealing, antiheroic side, daring me, it seemed, to take at face value all his negative thinking or self-destructive patterns. I think that he wanted it understood that behind all the applause, there was a lot of pain. He talked of when we had knocked around the Village together. "After Suze moved out of the house . . . I got very, very strung out for a while. I mean, really, very strung out." But, he told me, he'd survived. "I can do anything, knowing in front that it's not going to catch me and pull me . . . 'cause I've been through it once already. I've been through people. A lot of times you get strung out with people. They are just like junk. . . . The same thing, no more, no less. They kill you the same way. . . . They rot you the same way. . . ." I suggested it reminded me of the line in Sartre's *No Exit*: "Hell is other people." Dylan joked: "Whatever it is, man. I don't know Sartre. He's cross-eyed, that's all I know about him. Anybody cross-eyed can't be all bad. . . ." Then he seemed to hit bottom: "I have a death thing, I know. I have a suicidal thing, I know. . . ."

Later, I asked if he wanted to leave all this despair on the record. He said: "I haven't explained those things I said against myself. . . . A lot of people *think* that I shoot heroin. But that's *baby talk*. . . . I do a lot of things. Hey, I'm not going to sit here and lie to you . . . and make you wonder about all the things I do. I do a lot of things, man, which help me. . . . And I'm smart enough to know that I don't depend on them for my existence, you know, and that's all. Man, that's where it lays, like that. . . ."

I'd been thinking then of how one night at the Gaslight Dylan had advised me "to just write about something that is really important to you." At that time, I couldn't envision that it would be about the man who'd given me the advice. Dylan continued: "I can't be hurt, man, if the book is honest. No kidding, I can't be hurt. Hey, I'm trusting you. . . ." We were bitter then because the folk world was so hostile toward his electric merging of folk and rock. "Nobody told me to go electric," Bob said emphatically. "No, I didn't even ask anybody. I asked not a soul, believe me. . . . Hey, I went electric on my second record. Why don't you bring that out in the book?" Dylan reminded me that the *Freewheelin'* album, released in May 1963, had been meant to include "four electric songs. The only reason they cut out the electric ones was because I didn't write them. . . . Columbia still has them. I don't know if they would play them for you, because I know they are trying to retouch them."

Before The Beatles were known in America and before the folk-rock craze of 1965, Dylan had tried to show he was not a performer to pigeonhole. "I hate all the labels people have put on me . . . because they are labels. It's just that they are ugly, and I know, in my heart, that it's not me. . . . I have not *arrived* at where I am at now, I have just *returned* to where I am now, knowing it's the only way. What I am doing now is what I must do before I move on."

Dylan dug his heels in about the music world and his early attraction toward folk music: "I hate to say this, because I don't want it to be taken the wrong way, but I latched on, when I got to New York City, because I saw a huge audience was there. People I *knew* I was not taking advantage of. I knew I wasn't going to stay there. I knew it wasn't my thing. Many times I spoiled it. Many times I went against it. Anytime they tried to think I was like them, I knew I wasn't like them. I just told them whatever happened to be in my mind at the time. I didn't have any respect for any of the organizations. In New York City, they are all organizations. I had respect for the people.

"Woody [Guthrie] turned me on romantically. . . . Woody used his own time, in a way nobody else did. He was just a little bit better . . . just a little smarter, because he was from the country. . . . I met Woody and I talked with him. I dug him. I would dig him, I imagine, if he were around today. . . ." He cited some reservations about Guthrie's style, and I asked if Woody's work seemed too simple for him. "No, not simple at all! The fundamental objection is that I can see *why* he wrote what he wrote. I can see him sitting down and writing what he wrote, in a very calm kind of a way. I am *not* putting him down. I'm not copping out on my attraction to him and his influence on me. His influence on me was never in inflection or in voice. What drew me to him was that hearing his voice I could tell he was very lonesome, very alone, and very lost out in his time. That's why I dug him."

Dylan stressed that at the height of his involvement in the folk world, he still loved rock 'n' roll. "Suze Rotolo could tell you, because Suze knows more than anybody else that I played, back in 1961 and 1962, when nobody was around, all those Elvis Presley records. She'll tell you how many nights I stayed up and wrote songs and showed them to her and asked her: 'Is this right?' Because I knew her father and mother were associated with unions and she was into this equality-freedom thing long before I was. I checked the songs out with her. . . . Suze is a very talented girl, man, but she is very frightened. . . ."

We talked about *Sing Out!*, the folk-song magazine. In defense of Dylan's changes, I had wrangled with them. He cautioned me against my wasting time with polemics. Dylan: "Don't you understand? If you're smart, you just gotta keep going, you're just not going to stand still. Everyone else is going to die. I don't mean *die*. I mean, they are going to decay and go crazy. If I could help them, I would love to see them straightened out. But I know in my heart that it is impossible to straighten all these people out, because they are all so nine-to-five, and so involved with that life that it is impossible. I don't want nothing to do with it. *Sing Out!* has a big organization . . . they know they control a lot. They have a very big hand in a lot of money. They have an Establishment. The only person in that organization I respect . . . is Moe Asch, who is old and hip. He's the only one who knows that he's not a clown, that the whole world is not a circus. He knows. The rest of the people there don't know it. They have power . . . fake, phony power. . . . They're dumb, man. . . . They're clods. I never signed their petitions. If you're out of it, groovy! But I'm telling you, man, get out of it. It's not that you have to put them down to leave it."

He eyed the boy's poems, knowing he wouldn't read them that night. I told him how touching it was when he told that airport mechanic how lonely it got out there. "Well, I loved him, man," Dylan replied. "He's a poor cat. What's he doing out there in Nebraska? I just wanted to know. Hey, it's lonesome everyplace. The people that can't live with it, that can't accept it . . . They are just going to blow up the world . . . and make things bad for everybody, only because they feel so out of place. . . . Everybody has that in common—they are all going to die.

"I quit after England, and it was just done. I could quit again." Already, he told me, he'd withdrawn for a while from Woodstock. Dylan: "I moved out a long time ago. Before the summer [of 1965] ended, I moved into New York City. I couldn't make it up there anymore because it wasn't private anymore. It will *never, ever* happen again. I'm *never* going to tell anybody where I live again. . . . People want to tear me apart, man. Hey, I don't take people up to the country now, because the country is a very alone place. And if you don't dig being alone, if you haven't got something to do, you're just going to take the bus back. I can be alone . . . as long as I have to be alone. I don't have anything to say to anybody. But it's hard for other people like that."

Dylan's search for the place to be "alone" has kept a lot of real-estate agents and moving men busy. He asked me: "Do you know what I did when I got back from England, man? I bought me a thirty-one-room house . . . can you imagine that? . . . It turned into a nightmare, because, first of all, I wrote *Highway 61 Revisited* there and I don't believe in writing some total other thing in the same place twice. It's just a hang-up, a voodoo kind of thing. I just can't do it. When I need someplace to make something new, I can't go back there because . . . Have you ever smelled birth? Well, I just can't stand the smell of birth. It just lingers, so I just lived there and tried to go on, but couldn't. And so the house is up for sale now, and I've moved back into Albert's."

We talked a bit about the Beatles, whom he had first met at New York's Delmonico Hotel during their 1964 tour. He told me, however, that he felt, at that point, much closer to Marlon Brando than he did to any of the Beatles. "I wish you could meet Brando," Bob said. "There's nobody like Brando. . . . Nobody has treated him right, in the press. . . ."

I'd seen a lot of cracks developing in Dylan's relationship with his manager. Dylan: "There are some things Albert and I naturally agree on, and some things that I have to tell him to agree on. He's only come across once on his side. The rest of the time, I don't want him telling me shit. . . ." I suggested that people should realize a manager is a star's employee, not his employer, but Dylan flared. Like the man who grumbles about his wife but won't let anyone else criticize her, Dylan leaped to Grossman's defense: ". . . It's not that Albert works for me. . . . People who put Albert down ought to be . . . I mean, critic people. . . . First of all, did you know? Sara told me this, and it's true—that in hell there is a special place for critics? Did you ever know that? That was before Dante's time. Before the *Inferno* and before the Black Plague. And when you think about it, it is very weird. Obviously, now, you see the ragman walking around a couple of thousand years B.C. did not like to be confronted with a bunch of mouths. That's still where it's at. . . ."

I'd grown accustomed to Dylan's wide swings in mood. After one encounter this trip, in which he expressed deep and pervasive pessimism, I tried to counter his depression. A few days later, he scorned me: "I am *not* pessimistic," he told me. "If I am pessimistic, I am not even going to talk, I'm just going to go in the corner. One thing I have never done and will never do is force my moods on other people. Why should I sit around and talk to somebody for hours and then . . . have them think that I am pessimistic? That's an insult! I'll tell you what the drag is, what hangs everybody up is that I'm not *stopping*. They call me dead. It is very silly for them to call me dead, and they know it. There was a time, last year, when it just went overboard. Everybody recorded my songs and it would have been very easy for me, at that time, to have written up another huge batch. Everyone would have done them. They would have just lapped them up," he said.

Dylan's ambivalence has confounded everyone who has ever been close to him. It sometimes confuses him. As late as 1976, he would say his Gemini personality "forces me to extremes. I'm never really balanced in the middle. I go from one side to the other without staying in either place very long. I'm happy, sad, up, down, in, out, up in the sky, and down in the depths of the earth. . . . " Ten years earlier, as we rode on this plane, he was swinging widely. When I said I'd like to interview Phil Spector, Dylan said, "Sure, sure, go see him." Then he told me how Spector had annoyed him, but "tell him that when I think about him, I really love him. . . . " More ambivalence about the press, critics, tastemakers, and opinion-molders: "Hey, magazines, critics, *Newsweek, Time, Look, Life* . . . all of it is very meaningless. It doesn't seem to me to change anybody's mind. When people *like* something, other people go around trying to figure out why people like these things. I mean, when they really like something, they like it. They just get involved in something, that's all. It happens to them. *Like* and *dislike* are just unreal words."

Sic transit the Fourth Estate, in the estimation of one who has used the press with much artfulness. I tried to move to his enthusiasm for black musicians. "Ask Aretha Franklin about me, man," Dylan said. "Or talk to The Staple Singers. Why don't you talk to Mavis Staples? I'd be interested in what she says. And to Purvis and Roebuck Staples too. Remember that night when Mahalia Jackson came out from the dugout with her goddamn maids, who lifted up her dresses and opened up her doors? She sure has class!

"A lot of people think that the modern spade musicians are getting a raw deal. A lot of them are, because there are real genius people playing in dives. But an awful lot of the records you hear are all copies. They too are imitating who they think they should imitate. . . . That don't mean you have to give them a million dollars and a house in the suburbs and a golf course. That's what we're talking about here. We're not talking about equality . . . or enough food to eat. . . ."

Why had he become so hopeless about the civil rights movement? "I'm not pessimistic about it," Bob replied. "No, no, I don't want to be misunderstood about Negro rights. But I don't know what a Negro is. What's a Negro? A black person? How black? What's a Negro? A person living in a two-room shack with twelve kids? A lot of white people live in a two-room shack with twelve kids. Does this make them Negro? What's a Negro? Someone with African blood? A lot of white people have African blood. What's a Negro? An Ethiopian kind of thing? That's not a Negro, that's an ancient, religious, pajama-riding freak! I've got nothing against Negro rights. I never did."

Dylan reminisced about some black friends from his early days in New York: about Mel and Lillian Bailey, who had treated him like a son and a brother, about Jim Forman, former leader of the Student Non-Violent Coordinating Committee. He spoke nostalgically about some other young blacks from Albany, Georgia, like Bernice Johnson and Cordell Reagon. "I love Cordell. He's a madman. He's the only faithful madman, the only madman—let me put it this way—that can wipe you out with pure strength who I could trust to go anywhere with. I never get to see so many people. That's why I would like you to say things about a lot of people that I loved. Say that I said good things about them. Hey, I've turned down everybody, Bob. I'm giving you all this. I'm trusting you to go along with me. Hey, I've never been wrong. I'll tell you something about this book. If I tell you something, I'm not trying to horn in. I don't want any of your bread."

Knowing how mercurial Dylan was, I began to explore how he changes his mind about people, his own music, his past work. I said: "You have always been wildly enthusiastic about the recording you have just finished, and then you turn around a few months later and say it was nothing. At least, you always did that in the past." "No, no," Dylan flashed. "I like the last record. Hey, I made *Bringing It All Back Home* and I love that record. I made *Highway 61 Revisited* and I love that record. I love the *Blonde on Blonde* album. What I was trying to do on my fourth album—on *Another Side of Bob Dylan*—well, I was just too out of it, man, to come across with what I was trying to do. It was all done too fast. All done in one session. I liked the idea of it. No, I don't like the first album. You know, though, I've done some stuff on that first record that still stands up. Like my harmonica playing. Like in 'Man of Constant Sorrow,' the arrangement of that I like. 'In My Time of Dying' still stands up. But as a whole, it's not consistent."

Wasn't he really his own worst critic? "Of course I am my own worst critic! Those aren't my words, those are your words. A lot of the stuff I've done, man, the last three things I've done on records, is beyond criticism. I'm not saying that because I think I'm any kind of god. I'm just saying that because I just know. I've been at it too long. . . . I wanted to call that album *Highway 61 Revisited*. Nobody understood it. I had to go up the fucking ladder until finally the word came down and said: 'Let him call it what he wants to call it.' I have to fight for songs on the albums. I put them on there because I know it is right. And sure enough, it turns out to be right."

Dylan had been repeatedly irked by problems of sound amplification, especially in sports arenas, despite the setup that audio engineer Richard Alderson had assembled. "It turns out that we have wasted a lot of time . . . no matter how groovy and good it is, if it can't be heard, then it doesn't do anybody any good." Dylan asked me my reactions to the amplification at the various concerts I'd heard. He said he wanted, at the end of this tour, to bring the show into Carnegie Hall. I jokingly suggested that for optimum acoustics he try the Metropolitan Opera House. Dylan laughed, then asked, seriously: "How many people does it hold?"

I asked him about "My Life in a Stolen Moment." Dylan wove a web of ambivalence: "I don't disavow it. It is just not *me*. Somebody else wrote that. But I am not the person of five years ago. It's almost as if I were him," he said, pointing at one of the sleeping Band members. I asked him: "Can I say that when I quote things you wrote or said in the past, then?" Dylan replied: "Sure. All right, but put it in context. It was done out of . . . It was bled from my hand and from my arm. . . ." "By who?" I asked. "By my brain," Dylan replied. "I remember all of it. I remember the drafts. I remember the words. I used to write them, thinking, they might some day be novels. I remember why I did them. I remember all the shucks and all the cons. All the cute, funny things. Like, man, I am so lucky now. . . . I wouldn't be lucky if I couldn't produce. That's what I thought the last six months. Oh, I was really down. I mean, in ten recording sessions, man, we didn't get one song," he said, referring to *Blonde on Blonde*. What slowed things down? "It was the band. But you see, I didn't know that. I didn't want to think that. If I go back to Nashville, man . . . and everybody down there can't make it, I'm going to take a plane until something else happens. I don't have the right to blame anybody else. It's not that I blame myself, man, it is just that I was down. I was down. . . ."

I chanced a Hollywood-star interview question—just what does he do with his money? "Tell them," Dylan said, making his first and last full financial disclosure, "tell them to check their pockets." We laughed. What did he see in his future? "I can't talk of the future," Dylan said slowly. "I can only talk a little more about it than I used to be able to talk about it, but, still, I can't talk about it all that much. I know there's a movie. I'm going to make a movie, and it's going to be groovy, you know. Then, there's this book for Macmillan," Dylan said, tapping one of the envelopes. "It's already been fucking publicized and written about, and everybody's expected it and that kind of stuff," he went on, eyeing the *Tarantula* envelope warily. "Every time I look in the paper there is something about this book. And I gave away the title, which I shouldn't have done. So, I'm thinking of changing it now. You know, I just don't like the obvious. Obvious things are a step backward. Nobody should step backward because nobody knows what's behind them. The only direction you can see is in front of you, not in back of you. . . ."

The plane's vibrations had been diminishing, even though it hadn't been descending sharply. We'd forgotten that at Denver the ground comes up to meet a plane arriving from the East. The Band stirred. They were surprised he was still wide awake, still talking. Bob gave directions to Victor and Bill about deplaning. He asked Robbie Robertson if he was up to a few hours' work when they got to the motel, and Robbie nodded. As the plane touched down, Dylan kept talking. He looked at the package of poems and said he'd have to read them some other time. His eyes went back and forth between the two envelopes on his lap as he said: "I know how that boy feels. I know what it's like being a boy in a small town, somewhere, trying to become a writer."

We arrived in Denver at nearly three A.M. I thought that Dylan was finished for the night. "Give us about ten minutes, Bob," Dylan said, "and then come down to the room." Robbie and Dylan were again sprawled out on twin beds, each holding acoustic guitars, starting an hour's jamming. I drank some coffee and tried to bring myself to life to tape them at work. It was all new material; I couldn't put a title on anything. When Dylan came to "Sad-Eyed Lady," he said: "This is the best song I've ever written. Wait till you hear the whole thing." Robbie's face was gray with fatigue. I assumed that tomorrow would be a long sleep-in. Dylan said: "Let's go out to Central City tomorrow morning. You'll like it. Meet me here at about eleven."

Next morning Bob called Grossman in New York. "I've got five new songs to tape," Dylan told the telephone. "Uh-huh, uh-huh . . . Sinatra wants it? What about Otis Redding? I'd rather he do it. . . ." After the Central City outing, we returned to the Denver motel for more inter- view taping. I asked him how he could get any work done on such a rough tour. "It's very hard, man. It's killed me, ever since September. I never really had it like that before. I don't know how long until some- body will just clamp down, you know what I mean?"

We talked about people who had been important to him along the way. "Suze, I will be kind to her the rest of my life. Suze, anytime she wants anything, she could always come to me." But he had no patience with some others: "Just con people—they shouldn't be associated with me, because they are just going to get hung up by idiots that know they have known me."

In Denver, Dylan gave another concert for three thousand people. The amplification at the Denver Municipal Auditorium was a jangled echo. After the concert, I returned to Dylan's crowded motel room, where he started to describe Lennon and McCartney beating a retreat from his Albert Hall concert a year earlier. Dylan mimicked the Beatles running downstairs, halting for breath at landings, looking to see if they were pursued, then running down another flight. It was good pantomime. The Hawks roared. Some fans began calling up and friends dropped in. Bob was expansive, but couldn't conceal his fatigue. He saw me to the door.

"Now, Bob, I'm trusting you to be honest with your story," Dylan said. There was the old graciousness coming out, through all the fatigue and stoned haze. "See if you can't make it to El Paso, or to England. It'll be different there. It'll be better there. Say hello to Ralph." Ralph? Oh, yes! I had told him several days ago that I was going to see Ralph Gleason in San Francisco. I couldn't believe that with all he had on his mind he could remember something that I said *I* was going to do. He returned to the room and started telling everyone that it was getting late and he had some things to do. The party was over, for that night.

Tour's Roaring Ovations
Leave Dylan Quietly Pleased

John Rockwell

PHILADELPHIA, JAN. 7—BOB DYLAN, dressed in jeans, a zippered sweatshirt and a fur hat sat barefooted and cross-legged on the living room couch of a suite in the Sheraton Hotel this afternoon, wiping sleep from his eyes and gradually overcoming a certain frog-throatedness usually associated with the early morning hours.

Then, in one of his rare press interviews, he discussed the enthusiastic response to his current national tour, his first in eight years.

"Now that it's happened, it pleases me," he said. "But if it hadn't happened, it wouldn't have disappointed me either. Being on tour is like being in limbo. It's like going from nowhere to nowhere."

AUDIENCES ARE GOOD

"But at least the audiences are different. The audiences on this tour have been very warm," he said. "Chicago's always good. But on our last tour Stockholm and London and New York and Austin—we are not making it to Austin on this trip—they were good, too. After we finish this we'll sit down and decide what we're going to do next. Maybe we'll go to Europe."

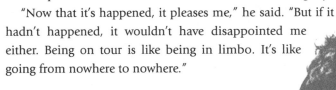

Younger Than That Now

The mood among those associated with the nationwide Dylan tour that began last Thursday in Chicago might best be described as prudently euphoric. David Geffen of Elektra/Asylum Records, who brought Mr. Dylan and the Band back together for the occasion, calls the reception at the first four concerts "fantastic." Robbie Robertson, lead guitarist and spokesman for the Band, says it's been "incredible." And even Mr. Dylan, who appears to be moving cautiously but surely out of the reclusive shell he had built up around himself, is obviously pleased.

AVOIDED PRESS

Mr. Dylan has avoided interviews in recent years. "I used to feel used by the press, but that was because no one was in control of it for me."

As he answered questions in Mr. Geffen's suite in the hotel today, however, he was friendly and straightforward, if still ultimately guarded in his responses.

Mr. Robertson, talking later in his own room, wasn't so calm. "The ticket orders and the audience response have been just great," he says. "We've all been waiting a long time, especially Bob. And when we finally get there, to have it be a disappointment would have been really heartbreaking. But it's been wonderful."

"The last tour we did, in 1965-66, was like a hurricane," Mr. Dylan recalled. "This one is more like a hard rain. The last tour, we were going all the time, even when we weren't going. We were always doing something else, which is just as draining as performing. We were looking for Loch Ness monsters, staying up for four days running—and making all those 8 o'clock curtains, besides. There won't be any of that on this tour—for me, anyway."

Mr. Dylan is obviously not personally sympathetic to the glitter-rock phenomenon that has become popular in rock of late. Although he says he has "no feelings" about the glitter rockers, he does offer on reflection that he likes David Bowie—"He probably got started listening to us, back in '65 or '66—and even Alice Cooper—"good, basic rock 'n roll."

Mr. Robertson is more explicit in his distaste. "It's heartening—the audiences' response so far. We don't take our clothes off, or hang ourselves onstage, or paint our hair. We don't have anything to offer but the music. We are not a bunch of cutie-pies; we're grown-up people."

The current tour repertory has been drawn from a group of about 50 Dylan songs that Mr. Dylan and the Band ran through loosely together last November and December in Malibu, Calif. "We've tried to do as much as possible," Mr. Dylan offers.

"We want to keep things fresh," Mr. Robertson adds. "There aren't any arrangements as such of any of the Dylan songs we are doing. There's no set beginning, or end, or key. We just play along together, and hope it comes out right."

Mr. Dylan has been experimenting with additions to the program and with the format at every concert, and plans to continue with that experimentation. He says he was surprised at the roaring ovations that have greeted the beginning and end of his solo acoustic sets, but says he doesn't plan to expand that portion beyond the present five or six numbers. Mr. Robertson says the Band will eventually begin introducing some new original songs, definitely by the New York dates late this month.

Mr. Dylan admits to being pleased about the way his new Asylum album, *Planet Waves,* has turned out, and Mr. Geffen—understandably but apparently genuinely—waxes downright lyrical about it.

"I particularly like the song 'Something There Is About You,' " Mr. Dylan said. "It completes a circle for me, about certain things running through my pattern. But I think they are all good," he added quickly. "I don't play favorites.

"I still write songs the same way I always did: I get a first line, the words and the tune together, and then I work out the rest wherever I happen to be, whenever I have time. If it's really important, I'll just make the time and try to finish it. I do write less songs now than I used to, though. Seems like I do a lot less of everything now. Although yes, family life [Mr. Dylan and his wife, Sara, have five children]—that takes its part, too."

The thought of his performances in the New York area—Jan. 28 and 29 at the Nassau Coliseum on Long Island and three shows Jan. 30 and 31 at Madison Square Garden—brings a smile. "Oh, I love New York," he says. "I'm not really livin' in Los Angeles—we're just passin' through. I'm gonna have places all over."

Although he says his neck is still sometimes affected by the weather since his near-fatal motorcycle accident in 1966, Mr. Dylan is clearly sanguine about his life these days, and appears genuinely glad that his days as a cult hero seem to be over.

"It had to be somebody, and it happened to be me. I just picked this suit of cards—or it was handed to me. Now I want to do a lot of different things. I'd like eventually to make my own kind of movie, but first I'll have to do two or three more to get into 'em. Eventually, my turn will come.

"And I'd like to put out a book of my drawings, and later on maybe retire to a ranch some day. What part of the country? Why, I don't even know what country. Whatever happens will just happen by itself."

PEOPLE MAGAZINE, NOVEMBER 10, 1975

Bob Dylan: A Myth Materializes with a New Protest Record and a New Tour

Jim Jerome

BOB DYLAN AT 34: "We each have our own vision and a voice inside that talks only to us. We have to be able to hear it."

It was a windowless recording studio, six floors above a deserted Manhattan side street. The artists were sealed off, as if under a siege that would not end until the tape was finally right. Meal breaks were out—instead, carrots, crunchy cauliflower, curry sauce, Camembert, French bread, beer, wine, and tequila were brought in. The mood otherwise, though, was of a warm, conspiratorial intimacy. The harsh overhead lights were replaced by soothing red and green spots. A homey floor lamp illuminated the music stand of the lead singer. The producer was supportive: "Just hold that tempo, Bobby," he encouraged from the control room. "That last take was startin' to smoke." The star leaned into his mike and responded: "We're gonna get it, man, I know we are. Let's get this thing in the can and out on the streets." Bobby was Dylan and, after his latest 18-month retreat, he was returning to the streets again.

The recording is "Hurricane," a protest song with the gritty urgency and outrage that had once enflamed a whole American generation. It pleads against the controversial eight-year incarceration for murder of ex-boxer Rubin ("Hurricane") Carter. Simultaneously, Dylan was readying his first road show since his tumultous comeback tour of '74. The itinerary would detour the megabuck impresarios, the multiseat superdomes, the computerized ticket networks and re-create the modest small-club minitours that characterized the years when he first left Hibbing, Minn. But his entourage includes friends like his ex-lady Joan Baez, plus Ronee Blakley, the discovery of the movie *Nashville*. Undeniably, Dylan creates in a genre in which minimal art is almost impossible, and so his latest comeback may live up to its ironic title—the Rolling Thunder Revue.

Dylan is himself, after all, the most influential figure in American pop music (and thus pop culture) since 1960. His garbage was analyzed years before Henry Kissinger's. Every syllable or solecism of his life is subject to fearful scrutiny. Dylan, now 34, and as scruffy, wiry, and taut as ever, looks back and sees it all as only a colossal accident. "It was never my intention to become a big star. It happened, and there was nothing I could do about it. I tried to get rid of that burden for a long time. I eat and sleep and, you know, have the same problems anybody else does, and yet people look at me funny."

If Dylan had his way, he would not be looked at—at all. He has granted very few major interviews in eight years, and this was his first in some 18 months. "I was playing music in the '50s," he begins, "and man, it was all I did. It saved my life. I'm not a hermit. Exclusive, maybe, but not reclusive."

"I didn't consciously pursue the Bob Dylan myth," he continues. "It was given to me—by God. Inspiration is what we're looking for. You just have to be receptive to it." While reports of Dylan's ardent Zionism are almost certainly exaggerated, he has unquestionably returned to his Jewish roots, or at least to a generalized spiritualism.

"I was locked into a certain generation," he says. "I still am. A certain area, a certain place in the universe at a certain time." The middle '60s, a period of drug-boosted frenzy, were reflected in Dylan's electric, clamorous rock'n'roll and in his manic jet-stream imagery—and they culminated on the edge of death on a shattered motorcycle in the summer of

1966. Then followed a two-year withdrawal which only intensified the myth. "I just wanted to be alone," he now says. He surfaced in 1968-69 with the subdued self-examination of *John Wesley Harding* and, later his watershed country LP, *Nashville Skyline*. Asked if he had it to do all over again, Dylan summons his samurai-quick sardonicism: "Maybe I would have chosen not to have been born at all—bypass the whole thing."

Dylan regards himself as an artist rather than a musician ("Put my guitar playing next to Segovia's and I'm sure you could tell who was the musician"), whose role is to create, not preach. "I can move, and fake. I know some of the tricks and it all applies artistically, not politically or philosophically."

He has a way of leaving reviewers as well as disciples in the dust. "I don't care what people expect of me," Dylan says defiantly. "Doesn't concern me. I'm doin' God's work. That's all I know." His classics like "Blowin' in the Wind" and "The Times, They Are a Changin'" became anthems of the opposition, and the terrorist Weathermen took their name from his lyrics. But pressed about his influence, Dylan says only, "You'll have to ask them, those people who are involved in that state of panic where my works seen to take them. It's not for me. I wouldn't have time for that. I'm not an activist. I am not politically inclined. I'm for people, people who are suffering. I don't have any pull in the government."

The accusation that he copped out from the antiwar and other protest movements which his music catalyzed leaves him livid—especially criticism of his refusal to participate in Woodstock. "I didn't want to be part of that thing," he says. "I liked the town. I felt they exploited the shit out of that, goin' up there and gettin' 15 million people all in the same spot. That don't excite me. The flower generation—is that what it was? I wasn't into that at all. I just thought it was a lot of kids out and around wearing flowers in their hair takin' a lot of acid. I mean what _can_ you think about that?"

"Today the youth are living in a certain amount of fantasy," he adds. "But in a lot of ways they become more disillusioned with life a lot earlier. It's a result of the overload, the mass overload which we are all gonna have to face. Don't forget when I started singin', marijuana was known only in certain circles—actors, musicians, dancers, poets, architects, people who were aware of what it could do for you. You never went down to make a phone call at a phone booth and had some cop hand you a joint. But now it's almost legal. The consciousness of the whole country has changed in a very short time."

He is impatient with fans who expected his own expression to stay the same. "Those people were stupid," he snaps. "They want to see you in the same suit. Upheaval distorts their lives. They refuse to be loose and make themselves flexible to situations. They forget they might have a different girlfriend every night, that their lives change too." Certainly there were formative changes in Dylan's life: marriage in 1965 to fashion model Sarah Lowndes; the accident; the growth of his own family to five (including one child from Sarah's previous marriage).

Yet, professionally, Dylan points out, "A songwriter tries to grasp a certain moment, write it down, sing it for that moment and then keep that experience within himself, so he can be able to sing the song years later. He'll change, and he won't want to do that song. He'll go on." But Dylan is not speaking of himself. Of his own massive anthology of poems, he says, "I can communicate *all* of my songs. I might not remember all the lyrics," he laughs, "but there aren't any in there I can't identify with on some level."

"I write fast," he continues. "The inspiration doesn't last. Writing a song, it can drive you crazy. My head is so crammed full of things I tend to lose a lot of what I think are my best songs, and I don't carry around a tape recorder."

"Music," Dylan says, "is an outgrowth of family—and my family comes first." He moved them to the beach at Malibu from Woodstock several years ago, and has been intermittently rumored to be splitting from Sarah. He concedes, "I haven't been able to spend as much time with my wife as I would like to," but pinning Dylan down on personal matters is like collecting quicksilver. A sample colloquy:

Q: Are you living with your wife?

A: When I have to, when I need to. I'm living with my wife in the same world.

Q: Do you . . .

A: Do I know where she is most of the time? She doesn't have to answer to me.

Q: So you don't live . . .

A: She has to answer to herself.

Q: Do you live under one roof?

A: Right now things are changing in all our lives. We will always be together.

Q: Where are you living now?

A: I live in more than one place.

Q: Can you be more specific?

A: I don't want to give out my address.

Q: Region?

A: I live where I have to live, where my priorities are.

Q: Right now, is that in New York City?

A: Right now it is, and off and on since last spring.

"Traveling is in my blood," said Dylan, as he rehearsed for his latest tour. "There is a lot of gypsy in me. What I'm trying to do is set my standards, get that organized now. There is a voice inside us all that talks only to us. We have to be able to hear that voice. I'm through listening to other people tell me how to live my life." Did Bob Dylan, of all

Younger Than That Now

Americans, feel himself mortgaged to others? "I'm just doing now what I feel is right for me," he concludes. "For my own self."

The TV Guide Interview

Neil Hickey

"MY BEING A GEMINI EXPLAINS a lot, I think," Bob Dylan is saying. "It forces me to extremes. I'm never really balanced in the middle. I go from one side to the other without staying in either place very long. I'm happy, sad, up, down, in, out, up in the sky and down in the depths of the earth. I can't tell you how Bob Dylan has lived his life. And it's far from over." Outside the auto's air-conditioned shell, the Malibu coastline of California, baking in 95-degree heat, is slipping past. Dylan observes the bathers idly. "I'm not really very articulate. I save what I have to say for what I do." What Bob Dylan does is write songs and perform them. Over the last 15 years, since he was 20, he has created a body of work unique among American artists: songs of such power and pertinence that they stand as a definition of the country and the man in those years: songs of rage over inhumanity; songs of inexpressible love, bitter vindictiveness and ribald joy; songs of spiritual longing, confusion and affirmation; songs in such extraordinary numbers that it often seemed miraculous that a largely self-educated youth—son of a

Younger Than That Now

Jewish furniture dealer from the Mesabi iron range of northern Minnesota—could have created them all: "Blowin' in the Wind" (an anthem of the 1960s civil-rights movement), "Like a Rollin' Stone" (one of the greatest rock songs ever written), "Masters of War," "With God on Our Side," "A Hard Rain's A-Gonna Fall," "Don't Think Twice, It's All Right." He has been, in sum, the single biggest cultural influence on millions in his own generation. He has taken American music by the hand into uncharted regions. Dylan turns from consideration of the bathers, smothers a grin, and says: "Somebody called me the Ed Sullivan of rock and roll." He laughs loudly at the thought. "I don't know what that means," he says, "but it sounds right." Indeed, Dylan is both master and star of his own troupe, the so-called Rolling Thunder Revue, a company of strolling players who recently completed a 50-concert tour—one performance of which was taped at Colorado State University and will be visible on NBC Tuesday night (Sept. 14): Bob Dylan's first TV special, "Hard Rain." Rarely interviewed (the last full-fledged one was seven years ago) and rarely seen publicly or privately over long periods, Dylan has chosen to be one of the least accessible figures in the entertainment world.

Born in Duluth, Minn., he grew up in nearby Hibbing and migrated early to New York's Greenwich Village, where he acquired a recording contract and became a major concert star. After a motorcycle accident in Woodstock, N.Y., in July 1966, in which he almost died (indeed, rumors of his death were persistent), he remained in virtual seclusion for several years. In late 1969 he appeared at the Isle of Wight Festival of Music—his first paid concert in four years—and 200,000 people from Great Britain, the European continent, Canada, and the U.S. showed up to hear him. Since then, he has toured the U.S. several times and issued a series of highly successful albums. "I don't really talk about what I do," Bob Dylan is saying. "I just try to be poetically and musically straight. I think of myself as more than a musician, more than a poet. The real self is something other than that. Writing and performing is what I do in this life and in this country. But I could be happy being a blacksmith. I would still write and sing. I can't imagine not doing that. You do what you're geared for."

This year, along the presidential campaign trail, Jimmy Carter has been quoting Dylan in many of his stump speeches, and even in his acceptance speech at the Democratic convention. "I don't know what to think about that. People have told me there was a man running for president and quoting me. I don't know if that's good or bad." He laughs broadly. "But he's just another guy running for president. I sometimes dream of running the country and putting all my friends in office." He grins at the thought. "That's the way it works now, anyway. I'd like to see Thomas Jefferson, Benjamin Franklin, and a few of those other guys come back. If they did, I'd go out and vote. They knew what was happening."

Sports cars bearing upturned surfboards stream along Pacific Coast Highway in the noon sun. "Over there," says Dylan, pointing to a roadside cafe rimmed with tables and benches. "There's a place to stop." Striding toward the cafe in a bent-kneed lope, Dylan—wearing jeans, sandals, a thin, frayed, black leather jacket and white burnoose swathing longish brown curls—resembles a hip shepherd from some Biblical Brigadoon. Settled with a beer, he fixes pale blue eyes on his companion and reflects on the press and its treatment of him. "The press has always misrepresented me. They refuse to accept what I am and what I do. "They always sensationalize and blow things up. I let them write whatever they want as long as I don't have to talk to them. They can see me any time—doing what I do. It's best to keep your mouth shut and do your work. It makes me feel better to write one song than talk to a thousand journalists." He rarely watches television, he says, including news. "I'm not influenced by it. I don't feel that to live in this country you have to watch TV news." How does he absorb the world's information before processing it into the topical songs that are so substantial a part of his work? "You learn from talking to other people. You have to know how people feel, and you don't get that from television news." (In 1963, when Dylan was a sky-rocketing young folk balladeer, Ed Sullivan invited him to appear on his show and Dylan accepted. He'd sing a new composition of his own called "Talkin' John Birch Society Blues," Dylan told Sullivan—a satire on the right-wing political group. Sullivan liked the song and scheduled it, but CBS censors refused to let Dylan perform it. Dylan refused to alter his choice of material and angrily chose not to appear on the show. Since then, he has consistently declined offers of network television, except for two brief appearances: one on ABC's old *Johnny Cash Show*—out of friendship for Cash; another on a recent PBS tribute to Columbia Records executive John Hammond, who gave him his first recording contract.)

What does he read? He laughs. "You don't want to know that. It would sound stupid." Still, the on-screen credits for this week's TV special carry "thanks" to (among others) Arthur Rimbaud, the French symbolist, mystical poet; and to American novelist Herman Melville. "Yes. Rimbaud has been a big influence on me. When I'm on the road and want to read something that makes sense to me, I go to a bookstore and read his words. Melville is somebody I can identify with because of how he looked at life. I also like Joseph Conrad a lot, and I've loved what I've read of James Joyce. Allen Ginsberg is always a great inspiration." Dylan visited Israel in 1971, an event that triggered talk among Dylan experts that Judaic tradition was about to become an overt aspect of his art. "There was no great significance to that visit," he insists. But, he says: "I'm interested in the fact that Jews are Semites, like Babylonians, Hittites, Arabs, Syrians, Ethiopians. But a Jew is different because a lot of people hate Jews. There's something going on here that's hard to explain." Many of Dylan's songs abound in religious mystical images: the album *John Wesley Harding* for example ("the first biblical rock album," he calls it, and the first to be released after his motorcycle accident), contains songs based almost entirely on stories and symbols from the Bible.

"There's a mystic in all of us," he says. "It's part of our nature. Some of us are shown more than others. Or maybe we're all shown the same things, but some make more use of it." How does Bob Dylan imagine God? He laughs abruptly, and then says, "How come nobody ever asks Kris Kristofferson questions like that?" After a pause, he says, "I can see God in a daisy. I can see God at night in the wind and rain. I see creation just about everywhere. The highest form of song is prayer. King David's, Solomon's, the wailing of a coyote, the rumble of the earth. It must be wonderful to be God. There's so much going on out there that you can't get to it all. It would take longer than forever. "You're talking to somebody who doesn't comprehend the values most people operate under. Greed and lust I can understand, but I can't understand the values of definition and confinement. Definition destroys. Besides, there's nothing definite in this world." He sips at his beer and asks solicitously, "Want to go and sit on the beach for a while?" We return to the car and, Dylan driving, roll slowly northward. Dylan reminisces about Greenwich Village in the early 1960s and its role as the spawning ground for the great "folk boom" that swept the nation in those years. One reason he had traveled there was to track down Woody Guthrie, the folk poet and balladeer who was Dylan's idol. The village's cafes and coffeehouses were home to scores of guitar-playing folkniks whose music was filtering out to the marketplace. The enormously popular Newport Folk Festivals, ABC's overslick TV series *Hootenanny* and hundreds of record albums by folk-style performers all fed the public's new appetite for simple, homemade music. (The folk boom ended, effectively, when the Beatles took the U.S. by storm in 1964, and when Dylan himself turned to the use of electrified instruments at about the same time.) "There was a lot of space to be born in then," Dylan is saying. "The media were onto other things. You could develop whatever creative interests you had without having to deal with categories and definitions. It lasted about three years. There's just as much going on now, but it's not centrally located like it was then." A few skeptics have suggested that Dylan wrote his so-called protest songs in the 1960s because his finely attuned commercial antennae told him there was a market for them. He denies it. "I wrote them because that's what I was in the middle of. It swept me up. I felt "Blowin' in the Wind." When Joan [Baez] and I sing it [as they do on the TV special], it's like an old folk song to me. It never occurs to me that I'm the person who wrote that. "The bunch of us who came through that time probably have a better sense about today's music. A lot of people in the '70s don't know how all this music got here. They think Elton John appeared overnight. But the '50s and '60s were a high-energy period." And how did the Beatles fit into all this? Dylan wags his head earnestly. "America should put up statues to the Beatles. They helped give this country's pride back to it. They used all the music we'd been listening to— everything from Little Richard to the Everly Brothers. A lot of barriers broke down, but we didn't see it at the time because it happened too fast." Dylan draws up at the curb, exits the car and walks to a 20-foot-high bluff over a near-vertical incline leading down to the beach. He scrambles down agilely and turns to catch cans of beer thrown after him. Settled in the sun, burnoose in place, peering out at the ocean, he resumes: "I consider myself in the same spirit with the Beatles and the Rolling Stones. That music has meaning for me. And Joan Baez means more to me than 100 of these singers around today. She's more powerful. That's what we're looking for. That's what we respond to. She always had it and always will—power for the species, not just for a select group." What records does he play for his own amusement? "Personally, I like sound-effects records," he says, laughing. "Sometimes late at night, I get a mint julep and just sit there and listen to sound effects. I'm surprised more of them aren't on the charts." He is still laughing. "If I had my own label, that's what I'd record." A teenage girl approaches Dylan, Frisbee in hand, and asks if it belongs to him. "No," says Bob Dylan politely, and the girl nods and ambles off down the beach, obviously unaware tht she has addressed (in the view of many) the generation's greatest rock-and-roll singer-writer. "I pass on crowded streets without being recognized. I don't want to be one of those big stars who can't go nowhere. Change that to anywhere. My mother might read this."

How is it, he is asked, that the Bob Dylan one encounters today, recumbent on this Malibu beach, seems so much more serene than the turbulent, often self-destructive, angry young man one recalls from the 1960s. (He's now the father of five, married to the former Sara Lowndes, living in the languor of southern California rather than New York's bustle.) He squints toward the horizon. "Anger is often directed at oneself. It all depends on where you are in place and time. A person's body chemistry changes every seven years. No one on earth is the same now as he was seven years ago, or will be seven years from today. It doesn't take a whole lot of brains to know that if you don't grow you die. You have to burst out; you have to find the sunlight."

Where is he, musically, these days? "I play rag rock. It's a special brand of music that I play. I'll be writing some new songs soon, and then, look out! The music will be up to a whole new level." Does he write every day, and does it come easily? "Are you kidding? Almost anything else is easy except writing songs. The hardest part is when the inspiration dies along the way. Then you spend all your time trying to recapture it. I don't write every day. I'd like to but I can't. You're talking to a total misfit. Gershwin, Bacharach—those people—they've got songwriting down. I don't really care if I write." Pause. "I can say that now, but as soon as the light changes, it'll be the thing I care about most. When I'm through performing, I'll still be writing, probably for other people." Any regrets? "The past doesn't exist. For me there's the next song, the next poem, the next performance." Any messages to the world? "I've been thinking about that. I'd like to extend my gratitude to my mother. I'd like to say hello to her if she's reading this." Ever see her? Pause. "Not as much as when I was a kid." He plucks his beer can from the sand. "I hope there's not a snake in my beer," he says, apropos of not very much. Then he reclines languorously and watches the sun descend slowly to the Pacific horizon.

PLAYBOY, MARCH 1978

The Playboy Interview

Ron Rosenbaum

It was in March 1966 that *Playboy* published the first full-length interview with Bob Dylan. In the intervening years, he has talked to journalists only rarely, and, shortly before completing his first feature film, he agreed to talk with us. We asked writer Ron Rosenbaum, who grew up listening to Dylan songs, to check in with the elusive artist. His report:

Call it a simple twist of fate, to use a Dylan line, but perhaps psychic twist of fate is more accurate. Because there was something of a turning point in our ten-day series of conversations when we exchanged confidences about psychics. Until that point, things had not been proceeding easily. Dylan has seldom been forthcoming with any answers, particularly in inter-view situations and has long been notorious for ques-tioning the questions rather than answering them, replying with put-ons and tall tales and surrounding his real feelings with mystery and circumlocu-tion. We would go round in circles, some-times fascinating metaphysical circles, and I'd got a sense of his intellect but little of his heart. He hadn't given anyone a major interview for many years, but after my initial excitement at being chosen to do this one, I began to wonder whether Dylan really wanted to do it. It's probably unnecessary to explain why getting answers from Bob Dylan has come to mean so much to many people. One has only to recall how Dylan, born Robert Zimmerman in 1941 in Duluth, Minnesota, burst upon the early sixties folk-music scene with an abrasive voice and an explosive intensity, how he created songs such as "Blowin' in the Wind" and "The Times They Are A-Changin'" that became anthems of the civil rights and antiwar movements. How he and his music raced through the sixties at breakneck speed, leaving his folk followers behind and the politicos mystified with his electrifying, elliptical explorations of uncharted states of mind. How, in songs such as "Mr. Tambourine Man," "Desolation Row," "Like a Rolling Stone," and "Just like a Woman," he created emotional road maps for an entire generation. How, in the midst of increasingly frenzied rock-'n'-roll touring, Dylan continued to surround the details of his personal life with mystery and wise-guy obfuscation, mystery that deepened ominously after his near-fatal motorcycle accident in 1966. And how, after a long period of bucolic retreat devoted to fatherhood, family, and country music, he suddenly returned to the stage with big nationwide tours in 1974 and, most recently, in 1976 with the all-star rock 'n' roll ensemble known as The Rolling Thunder Revue. How his latest songs, particularly on the Blood on the Tracks *and* Desire *albums, take us into new and often painful investigations of love and lust, and pain and loss, that suggest the emotional predicaments of the seventies in a way few others can approach. The anthologies that chronicle all of that are littered with the bodies of interviewers he's put on, put down, or put off. I was wondering if I were on my way to becoming another statistic when we hit upon the psychic connection. Late one afternoon, Dylan began telling me about Tamara Rand, an L.A. psychic reader he'd been seeing, because when the world falls on your head, he said, "you need someone who can tell you how to crawl out, which way to take." I presumed he was referring obliquely to the collapse of his twelve-year marriage to Sara Dylan. (Since the child-custody battle was in progress as we talked, Dylan's lawyer refused to permit him to address that subject directly.) Dylan seemed concerned that I understand that Tamara was no con artist, that she had genuine psychic abilities. I assured him I could believe it because my sister, in addition to being a talented writer, has some remarkable psychic* abilities and is in great demand in New York for her prescient readings. Dylan asked her name (it's Ruth) and when I told him, he looked impressed. "I've heard of her," he said. I think that made the difference, because after that exchange, Dylan became far more forthcoming with me. Some of the early difficulties of the interview might also be explained by the fact that Dylan was physically and mentally drained from an intense three-month sprint to finish editing and dubbing Renaldo & Clara, the movie he'd been writing, directing, and coediting for a full two years. He looked pale, smoked a lot of cigarettes and seemed fidgety. The final step in the moviemaking process—the sound mix—was moving slowly, largely because of his own nervous perfectionism. Most of our talks took place in a little shack of a dressing room outside dubbing stage five at the Burbank Studios. Frequently, we'd be interrupted as Dylan would have to run onto the dubbing stage and watch the hundredth run-through of one of the film's two dozen reels to see if his detailed instructions had been carried out. I particularly remember one occasion when I accompanied him onto the dubbing stage. Onscreen, Renaldo, played by Bob Dylan, and Clara, played by Sara Dylan (the movie was shot before the divorce—though not long before), are interrupted in the midst of connubial foolery by a knock at the door. In walks Joan Baez, dressed in white from head to toe, carrying a red rose. She says she's come for Renaldo. When Dylan, as Renaldo, sees who it is, his jaw drops. At the dubbing console, one of the sound men stopped the film at the jaw-drop frame and asked, "You want me to get rid of that footstep noise in the background, Bob?" "What footstep noise?" Dylan asked. "When Joan comes in and we go to Renaldo, there's some kind of footstep noise in the background, maybe from outside the door." "Those aren't footsteps," said Dylan. "That's the beating of Renaldo's heart." "What makes you so sure?" the sound man asked teasingly. "I know him pretty well," Dylan said, "I know him by heart." "You want it kept there, then?" "I want it louder," Dylan said. He turned to me. "You ever read that thing by Poe, 'The Tell-Tale Heart'?" I was surprised at how willing Dylan was to explain the details of his film; he'd never done that with his songs. But he's put two years and more than a piece of his heart into this five-hour epic and it seems clear that he wants to be taken seriously as a film-maker with serious artistic ambitions. In the "Proverbs of Hell," William Blake (one of Dylan's favorite poets) wrote: "The road of excess leads to the *palace of wisdom." Eleven years ago, Dylan's motorcycle skidded off that road and almost killed him. But unlike most Dionysian sixties figures, Dylan survived. He may not have reached the palace of wisdom (and, indeed, the strange palace of marble and stone he has been building at Malibu seems, according to some reports, to be sliding into the sea). But despite his various sorrows, he does seem to be bursting with exhilaration and confidence that he can still create explosive art without having to die in the explosion.*

———————•◦•———————

PLAYBOY: Exactly 12 years ago, we published a long interview with you in this magazine, and there's a lot to catch up on. But we'd like at least to try to start at the beginning. Besides being a singer, a poet, and now a filmmaker, you've also been called a visionary. Do you recall any visionary experiences while you were growing up?

DYLAN: I had some amazing projections when I was a kid, but not since then. And those visions have been strong enough to keep me going through today.

PLAYBOY: What were those visions like?

DYLAN: They were a feeling of wonder. I projected myself toward what I might personally, humanly do in terms of creating any kinds of reality. I was born in, grew up in a place so foreign that you had to be there to picture it.

PLAYBOY: Are you talking about Hibbing, Minnesota?

DYLAN: It was all in upper Minnesota.

PLAYBOY: What was the quality of those visionary experiences?

DYLAN: Well, in the winter, everything was still, nothing moved. Eight months of that. You can put it together. You can have some amazing hallucinogenic experiences doing nothing but looking out your window. There is also the summer, when it gets hot and sticky and the air is very metallic. There is a lot of Indian spirit. The earth there is unusual, filled with ore. So there is something happening that is hard to define. There is a magnetic attraction there. Maybe thousands and thousands of years ago, some planet bumped into the land there. There is a great spiritual quality throughout the Midwest. Very subtle, very strong, and that is where I grew up. New York was a dream.

PLAYBOY: Why did you leave Minnesota?

DYLAN: Well, there comes a time for all things to pass.

PLAYBOY: More specifically, why the dream of New York?

DYLAN: It was a dream of the cosmopolitan riches of the mind.

PLAYBOY: Did you find them there?

DYLAN: It was a great place for me to learn and to meet others who were on similar journeys.

PLAYBOY: People like Allen Ginsberg, for instance?

DYLAN: Not necessarily him. He was pretty established by the time I got there. But it was Ginsberg and Jack Kerouac who inspired me at first—and where I came from, there wasn't the sophisticated transportation you have now. To get to New York, you'd have to go by thumb. Anyway, those were the old days when John Denver used to play sideman. Many people came out of that period of time. Actors, dancers, politicians, a lot of people were involved with that period of time.

PLAYBOY: What period are you talking about?

Younger Than That Now

DYLAN: Real early sixties.

PLAYBOY: What made that time so special?

DYLAN: I think it was the last go-round for people to gravitate to New York. People had gone to New York since the 1800s, I think. For me, it was pretty fantastic. I mean, it was like, there was a cafe—what was it called?—I forgot the name, but it was Aaron Burr's old livery stable. You know, just being in that area, that part of the world was enlightening.

PLAYBOY: Why do you say it was the last go-round?

DYLAN: I don't think it happened after that. I think it finished. New York died after that, late to middle sixties.

PLAYBOY: What killed it?

DYLAN: Mass communication killed it. It turned into one big carnival sideshow. That is what I sensed and I got out of there when it was just starting to happen. The atmosphere changed from one of creativity and isolation to one where the attention would be turned more to the show. People were reading about themselves and believing it. I don't know when it happened. Sometime around Peter, Paul, and Mary, when they got pretty big. It happened around the same time. For a long time, I was famous only in certain circles in New York, Philadelphia, and Boston, and that was fine enough for me. I am an eyewitness to that time. I am one of the survivors of that period. You know as well as I do that a lot of people didn't make it. They didn't live to tell about it, anyway.

PLAYBOY: Why do you think they didn't survive?

DYLAN: People were still dealing with illusion and delusion at that time. The times really change and they don't change. There were different characters back then and there were things that were undeveloped that are fully developed now. But back then, there was space, space—well, there wasn't any pressure. There was all the time in the world to get it done. There wasn't any pressure, because nobody knew about it. You know, I mean, music people were like a bunch of cotton pickers. They see you on the side of the road picking cotton, but nobody stops to give a shit. I mean, it wasn't that important. So Washington Square was a place where people you knew or met congregated every Sunday and it was like a world of music. You know the way New York is; I mean, there could be 20 different things happening in the same kitchen or in the same park; there could be 200 bands in one park in New York; there could be 15 jug bands, 5 bluegrass bands and an old crummy string band, 20 Irish confederate groups, a Southern mountain band, folk singers of all kinds and colors, singing John Henry work songs. There was bodies piled sky-high doing whatever they felt like doing. Bongo drums, conga drums, saxophone players, xylophone players, drummers of all nations and nationalities. Poets who would rant and rave from the statues. You know, those things don't happen anymore. But then that was what was happening. It was all street. Cafes would be open all night. It was a European thing that never really took off. It has never really been a part of this country. That is what New York was like when I got there.

PLAYBOY: And you think that mass communications, such as *Time* magazine's putting Joan Baez on the cover—

DYLAN: Mass communication killed it all. Oversimplification. I don't know whose idea it was to do that, but soon after, the people moved away.

PLAYBOY: Just to stay on the track, what first turned you on to folk singing? You actually started out in Minnesota playing the electric guitar with a rock group, didn't you?

DYLAN: Yeah. The first thing that turned me onto folk singing was Odetta. I heard a record of hers in a record store, back when you could listen to records right there in the store. That was in '58 or something like that. Right then and there, I went out and traded my electric guitar and amplifier for an acoustical guitar, a flat-top Gibson.

PLAYBOY: What was so special to you about that Odetta record?

DYLAN: Just something vital and personal. I learned all the songs on that record. It was her first and the songs were—"Mule Skinner," "Jack of Diamonds," "Water Boy," "'Buked and Scorned."

PLAYBOY: When did you learn to play the guitar?

DYLAN: I saved the money I had made working on my daddy's truck and bought a Silvertone guitar from Sears Roebuck. I was 12. I just bought a book of chords and began to play.

PLAYBOY: What was the first song you wrote?

DYLAN: The first song I wrote was a song to Brigitte Bardot.

PLAYBOY: Do you remember how it went?

DYLAN: I don't recall too much of it. It had only one chord. Well, it is all in the heart. Anyway, from Odetta, I went to Harry Belafonte, the Kingston Trio, little by little uncovering more as I went along. Finally, I was doing nothing but Carter Family and Jesse Fuller songs. Then later I got to Woody Guthrie, which opened up a whole new world at the time. I was still only 19 or 20. I was pretty fanatical about what I wanted to do, so after learning about 200 of Woody's songs, I went to see him and I waited for the right moment to visit him in a hospital in Morristown, New Jersey. I took a bus from New York, sat with him, and sang his songs. I kept visiting him a lot and got on friendly terms with him. From that point on, it gets a little foggy.

PLAYBOY: Folk singing was considered pretty weird in those days, wasn't it?

DYLAN: It definitely was. *Sing Out* was the only magazine you could read about those people. They were special people and you kept your distance from them.

PLAYBOY: What do you mean?

DYLAN: Well, they were the type of people you just observed and learned from, but you would never approach them. I never would, anyway. I remember being too shy. But it took me a long time to realize the New York crowd wasn't that different from the singers I'd seen in my own hometown. They were right there, on the backroad circuit, people like the Stanley Brothers, playing for a few nights. If I had known then what I do now, I probably would have taken off when I was 12 and followed Bill Monroe. 'Cause I could have gotten to the same place.

PLAYBOY: Would you have gotten there sooner?

DYLAN: Probably would have saved me a lot of time and hassles.

PLAYBOY: This comes under the category of setting the record straight: By the time you arrived in New York, you'd changed your name from Robert Zimmerman to Bob Dylan. Was it because of Dylan Thomas?

DYLAN: No. I haven't read that much of Dylan Thomas. It's a common thing to change your name. It isn't that incredible. Many people do it. People change their town, change their country. New appearance, new mannerisms. Some people have many names. I wouldn't pick a name unless I thought I was that person. Sometimes you are held back by your name. Sometimes there are advantages to having a certain name. Names are labels so we can refer to one another. But deep inside us we don't have a name. We have no name. I just chose that name and it stuck.

PLAYBOY: Do you know what Zimmerman means in German?

Younger Than That Now

DYLAN: My forebears were Russian. I don't know how they got a German name coming from Russia. Maybe they got their name coming off the boat or something. To make a big deal over somebody's name, you're liable to make a big deal about any little thing. But getting back to Dylan Thomas, it wasn't that I was inspired by reading some of his poetry and going "Aha!" and changing my name to Dylan. If I thought he was that great, I would have sung his poems, and could just as easily have changed my name to Thomas.

PLAYBOY: Bob Thomas? It would have been a mistake.

DYLAN: Well, that name changed me. I didn't sit around and think about it too much. That is who I felt I was.

PLAYBOY: Do you deny being the enfant terrible in those days—do you deny the craziness of it all that has been portrayed?

DYLAN: No, it's true. That's the way it was. But . . . can't stay in one place forever.

PLAYBOY: Did the motorcycle accident you had in 1966 have anything to do with cooling you off, getting you to relax?

DYLAN: Well, now you're jumping way ahead to another period of time. . . . What was I doing? I don't know. It came time. Was it when I had the motorcycle accident? Well, I was straining pretty hard and couldn't have gone on living that way much longer. The fact that I made it through what I did is pretty miraculous. But, you know, sometimes you get too close to something and you got to get away from it to be able to see it. And something like that happened to me at the time.

PLAYBOY: In a book you published during that period, *Tarantula*, you wrote an epitaph for yourself that begins: "Here lies Bob Dylan / murdered / from behind / by trembling flesh. . . ."

DYLAN: Those were in my wild, unnatural moments. I'm glad those feelings passed.

PLAYBOY: What were those days like?

DYLAN: [Pause] I don't remember. [Long pause]

PLAYBOY: There was a report in the press recently that you turned the Beatles on to grass for the first time. According to the story, you gave Ringo Starr a toke at J.F.K. Airport and it was the first time for any of them. True?

DYLAN: I'm surprised if Ringo said that. It don't sound like Ringo. I don't recall meeting him at J.F.K. Airport.

PLAYBOY: OK. Who turned you on?

DYLAN: Grass was everywhere in the clubs. It was always there in the jazz clubs and in the folk-music clubs. There was just grass and it was available to musicians in those days. And in coffeehouses way back in Minneapolis. That's where I first came into contact with it, I'm sure. I forget when or where, really.

PLAYBOY: Why did the musicians like grass so much?

DYLAN: Being a musician means—depending on how far you go—getting to the depths of where you are at. And most any musician would try anything to get to those depths, because playing music is an immediate thing—as opposed to putting paint on a canvas, which is a calculated thing. Your spirit flies when you are playing music. So, with music, you tend to look deeper and deeper inside yourself to find the music. That's why, I guess, grass was around those clubs. I know the whole scene has changed now; I mean, pot is almost a legal thing. But in the old days, it was just for a few people.

Younger Than That Now

PLAYBOY: Did psychedelics have a similar effect on you?

DYLAN: No. Psychedelics never influenced me. I don't know, I think Timothy Leary had a lot to do with driving the last nails into the coffin of that New York scene we were talking about. When psychedelics happened, everything became irrelevant. Because that had nothing to do with making music or writing poems or trying to really find yourself in that day and age.

PLAYBOY: But people thought they were doing just that—finding themselves.

DYLAN: People were deluded into thinking they were something that they weren't: birds, airplanes, fire hydrants, whatever. People were walking around thinking they were stars.

PLAYBOY: As far as your music was concerned, was there a moment when you made a conscious decision to work with an electric band?

DYLAN: Well, it had to get there. It had to go that way for me. Because that's where I started and eventually it just got back to that. I couldn't go on being the lone folkie out there, you know, strumming "Blowin' in the Wind" for three hours every night. I hear my songs as part of the music, the musical background.

PLAYBOY: When you hear your songs in your mind, it's not just you strumming alone, you mean?

DYLAN: Well, no, it is to begin with. But then I always hear other instruments, how they should sound. The closest I ever got to the sound I hear in my mind was on individual bands in the *Blonde on Blonde* album. It's that thin, that wild mercury sound. It's metallic and bright gold, with whatever that conjures up. That's my particular sound. I haven't been able to succeed in getting it all the time. Mostly, I've been driving at a combination of guitar, harmonica, and organ, but now I find myself going into territory that has more percussion in it and [pause] rhythms of the soul.

PLAYBOY: Was that wild mercury sound in "I Want You"?

DYLAN: Yeah, it was in "I Want You." It was in a lot of that stuff. It was in the album before that, too.

PLAYBOY: *Highway 61 Revisited?*

DYLAN: Yeah. Also in *Bringing It All Back Home.* That's the sound I've always heard. Later on, the songs got more defined, but it didn't necessarily bring more power to them. The sound was whatever happened to be available at the time. I have to get back to the sound, to the sound that will bring it all through me.

PLAYBOY: Can't you just reassemble the same musicians?

DYLAN: Not really. People change, you know, they scatter in all directions. People's lives get complicated. They tend to have more distractions, so they can't focus on that fine, singular purpose.

PLAYBOY: You're searching for people?

DYLAN: No, not searching, the people are there. But I just haven't paid as much attention to it as I should have. I haven't felt comfortable in a studio since I worked with Tom Wilson. The next move for me is to have a permanent band. You know, usually I just record whatever's available at the time. That's my thing, you know, and it's—it's legitimate. I mean, I do it because I have to do it that way. I don't want to keep doing it, because I would like to get my life more in order. But until now, my recording sessions have tended to be last-minute affairs. I don't really use all the technical studio stuff. My songs are done live in the studio; they always have been and they always will be done that way. That's why they're alive. No matter what else you say about them, they are alive.

Younger Than That Now

You know, what Paul Simon does or Rod Stewart does or Crosby, Stills, and Nash do—a record is not that monumental for me to make. It's just a record of songs.

PLAYBOY: Getting back to your transition from folk to rock, the period when you came out with *Highway 61* must have been exciting.

DYLAN: Those were exciting times. We were doing it before anybody knew we would—or could. We didn't know what it was going to turn out to be. Nobody thought of it as folk-rock at the time. There were some people involved in it like The Byrds, and I remember Sonny and Cher and the Turtles and the early Rascals. It began coming out on the radio. I mean, I had a couple of hits in a row. That was the most I ever had in a row—two. The top ten was filled with that kind of sound—the Beatles, too—and it was exciting, those days were exciting. It was the sound of the streets. It still is. I symbolically hear that sound wherever I am.

PLAYBOY: You hear the sound of the street?

DYLAN: That ethereal twilight light, you know. It's the sound of the street with the sunrays, the sun shining down at a particular time, on a particular type of building. A particular type of people walking on a particular type of street. It's an outdoor sound that drifts even into open windows that you can hear. The sound of bells and distant railroad trains and arguments in apartments and the clinking of silverware and knives and forks and beating with leather straps. It's all—it's all there. Just lack of a jackhammer, you know.

PLAYBOY: You mean if a jackhammer were—

DYLAN: Yeah, no jackhammer sounds, no airplane sounds. All pretty natural sounds. It's water, you know water trickling down a brook. It's light flowing through the . . .

PLAYBOY: Late-afternoon light?

DYLAN: No, usually it's the crack of dawn. Music filters out to me in the crack of dawn.

PLAYBOY: The "jingle jangle morning"?

DYLAN: Right.

PLAYBOY: After being up all night?

DYLAN: Sometimes. You get a little spacey when you've been up all night, so you don't really have the power to form it. But that's the sound I'm trying to get across. I'm not just up there re-creating old blues tunes or trying to invent some surrealistic rhapsody.

PLAYBOY: It's the sound that you want.

DYLAN: Yeah, it's the sound and the words. Words don't interfere with it. They—they—punctuate it. You know, they give it purpose. [Pause] And all the ideas for my songs, all the influences, all come out of that. All the influences, all the feelings, all the ideas come from that. I'm not doing it to see how good I can sound, or how perfect the melody can be, or how intricate the details can be woven or how perfectly written something can be. I don't care about those things.

PLAYBOY: The sound is that compelling to you?

DYLAN: Mmm-hnh.

PLAYBOY: When did you first hear it, or feel it?

DYLAN: I guess it started way back when I was growing up.

PLAYBOY: Not in New York?

Younger Than That Now

DYLAN: Well, I took it to New York. I wasn't born in New York. I was given some direction there, but I took it, too. I don't think I could ever have done it in New York. I would have been too beaten down.

PLAYBOY: It was formed by the sounds back in the ore country of Minnesota?

DYLAN: Or the lack of sound. In the city, there is nowhere you can go where you don't hear sound. You are never alone. I don't think I could have done it there. Just the struggle of growing up would be immense and would really distort things if you wanted to be an artist. Well . . . maybe not. A lot of really creative people come out of New York. But I don't know anyone like myself. I meet a lot of people from New York that I get along with fine, and share the same ideas, but I got something different in my soul. Like a spirit. It's like being from the Smoky Mountains or the backwoods of Mississippi. It is going to make you a certain type of person if you stay 20 years in a place.

PLAYBOY: With your love of the country, what made you leave Woodstock in 1969 and go back to the Village?

DYLAN: It became stale and disillusioning. It got too crowded, with the wrong people throwing orders. And the old people were afraid to come out on the street. The rainbow faded.

PLAYBOY: But the Village, New York City, wasn't the answer, either.

DYLAN: The stimulation had vanished. Everybody was in a pretty down mood. It was over.

PLAYBOY: Do you think that old scene you've talked about might be creeping back into New York?

DYLAN: Well, I was there last summer. I didn't sense any of it. There are a lot of rock-'n'-roll clubs and jazz clubs and Puerto Rican poetry clubs, but as far as learning something new, learning to teach. . . . New York is full of teachers, that is obvious, but it is pretty depressing now. To make it on the street, you just about have to beg.

PLAYBOY: So now you're in California. Is there any kind of scene that you can be part of?

DYLAN: I'm only working out here most, or all, of the time, so I don't know what this town is really like. I like San Francisco. I find it full of tragedy and comedy. But if I want to go to a city in this country, I will still go to New York. There are cities all over the world to go to. I don't know, maybe I am just an old dog, so maybe I feel like I've been around so long I am looking for something new to do and it ain't there. I was looking for some space to create what I want to do. I am only interested in that these days. I don't care so much about hanging out.

PLAYBOY: Do you feel older than when you sang, "I was so much older then, I'm younger than that now"?

DYLAN: No, I don't feel old. I don't feel old at all. But I feel like there are certain things that don't attract me anymore that I used to succumb to very easily.

PLAYBOY: Such as?

DYLAN: Just the everyday vices.

PLAYBOY: Do you think that you have managed to resist having to grow up or have you found a way of doing it that is different from conventional growing up?

DYLAN: I don't really think in terms of growing up or not growing up. I think in terms of being able to fulfill yourself. Don't forget, you see, I've been doing what I've been doing since I was very small, so I have never known anything else. I have never had to quit my job to do this. This is all that I have ever done in my life. So I don't think in terms of economics or status or what people think of me one way or the other.

PLAYBOY: Would you say you still have a rebellious, or punk, quality toward the rest of the world?

DYLAN: Punk quality?

PLAYBOY: Well, you're still wearing dark sunglasses, right?

DYLAN: Yeah.

PLAYBOY: Is that so people won't see your eyes?

DYLAN: Actually, it's just habit-forming after a while, I still do wear dark sunglasses. There is no profound reason for it, I guess. Some kind of insecurity, I don't know: I like dark sunglasses. Have I had these on through every interview session?

PLAYBOY: Yes. We haven't seen your eyes yet.

DYLAN: Well, Monday for sure. [The day that *Playboy* photos were to be taken for the opening page.]

PLAYBOY: Aside from the dark glasses, is it something in the punk quality of Elvis or James Dean that makes you dress a certain way or act a certain way?

DYLAN: No. It's from the early sixties. Elvis was there. He was there when there wasn't anybody there. He was Elvis and everybody knows about what Elvis did. He did it to me just like he did it to everybody else. Elvis was in that certain age group and I followed him right from Blue Moon in Kentucky. And there were others; I admired Buddy Holly a lot. But Elvis was never really a punk. And neither was James Dean a punk.

PLAYBOY: What quality did Dean represent?

DYLAN: He let his heart do the talking. That was his one badge. He was effective for people of that age, but as you grow older, you have different experiences and you tend to identify with artists who had different meanings for you.

PLAYBOY: Let's talk some more about your influences. What musicians do you listen to today.

DYLAN: I still listen to the same old black-and-blue blues. Tommy McClennan, Lightnin' Hopkins, the Carter Family, the early Carlyles. I listen to Big Maceo, Robert Johnson. Once in a while, I listen to Woody Guthrie again. Among the more recent people, Fred McDowell, Gary Stewart. I like Memphis Minnie a whole lot. Blind Willie McTell. I like bluegrass music. I listen to foreign music, too. I like Middle Eastern music a whole lot.

PLAYBOY: Such as?

DYLAN: Om Kalthoum.

PLAYBOY: Who is that?

DYLAN: She was a great Egyptian singer. I first heard of her when I was in Jerusalem.

PLAYBOY: She was an Egyptian singer who was popular in Jerusalem?

DYLAN: I think she's popular all over the Middle East. In Israel, too. She does mostly love and prayer-type songs, with violin and drum accompaniment. Her father chanted those prayers and I guess she was so good when she tried singing behind his back that he allowed her to sing professionally, and she's dead now but not forgotten. She's great. She really is. Really great.

Younger Than That Now

PLAYBOY: Any popular stuff?

DYLAN: Well, Nana Maskouri.

PLAYBOY: How about the Beatles?

DYLAN: I've always liked the way George Harrison plays guitar-restrained and good. As for Lennon, well, I was encouraged by his book *[In His Own Write]*. Or the publishers were encouraged, because they asked me to write a book and that's how Tarantula came about. John has taken poetics pretty far in popular music. A lot of his work is overlooked, but if you examine it, you'll find key expressions that have never been said before to push across his point of view. Things that are symbolic of some inner reality and probably will never be said again.

PLAYBOY: Do you listen to your own stuff?

DYLAN: Not so much.

PLAYBOY: What about your literary influences? You've mentioned Kerouac and Ginsberg. Whom do you read now?

DYLAN: Rilke. Chekhov. Chekhov is my favorite writer. I like Henry Miller. I think he's the greatest American writer.

PLAYBOY: Did you meet Miller?

DYLAN: Yeah, I met him. Years ago. Played ping-pong with him.

PLAYBOY: Did you read *Catcher in the Rye* as a kid?

DYLAN: I must have, you know. Yeah, I think so.

PLAYBOY: Did you identify with Holden Caulfield?

DYLAN: Uh, what was his story?

PLAYBOY: He was a lonely kid in prep school who ran away and decided that everyone else was phony and that he was sensitive.

DYLAN: I must have identified with him.

PLAYBOY: We've been talking about the arts, and as we've been speaking, you've been in the midst of editing your first film, *Renaldo & Clara*. What do you feel you can do in films that you can't do in songs?

DYLAN: I can take songs up to a higher power. The movie to me is more a painting than music. It is a painting. It's a painting coming alive off a wall. That's why we're making it. Painters can contain their artistic turmoil; in another age, moviemakers would most likely be painters.

PLAYBOY: Although *Renaldo & Clara* is the first movie you've produced, directed, and acted in, there was a documentary made in 1966 that marked your first appearance in a film—*Don't Look Back*. What did you think of it?

DYLAN: *Don't Look Back* was . . . somebody else's movie. It was a deal worked out with a film company, but I didn't really play any part in it. When I saw it in a moviehouse, I was shocked at what had been done. I didn't find out until later that the camera had been on me all the time. That movie was done by a man who took it all out of context. It was documented from his personal point of view. The movie was dishonest, it was a propaganda movie. I don't think it was accurate at all in terms of showing my formative years. It showed only one side. He made it seem like I wasn't doing anything but living in hotel rooms, playing the typewriter, and holding press conferences for journalists. All that is true, you know. Throwing some bottles, there's something about it in the movie. Joan Baez is in it. But it's one-sided. Let's not lean on it too hard. It just wasn't representative of what was happening in the sixties.

Younger Than That Now

PLAYBOY: Don't you feel it captured the frenzy of your tour, even though it focused on you in terms of stardom?

DYLAN: I wasn't really a star in those days, any more than I'm a star these days. I was very obviously confused then as to what my purpose was. It was pretty early, you know. "The Times They Are A-Changin'" was on the English charts then, so it had to be pretty early.

PLAYBOY: And you didn't really know what you were doing then?

DYLAN: Well, look what I did after that. Look what I did after that. I didn't really start to develop until after that. I mean, I did, but I didn't. *Don't Look Back* was a little too premature. I should have been left alone at that stage.

PLAYBOY: You were involved in another movie around that period—1966—that was never released, called *Eat the Document.* How did that happen?

DYLAN: That started as a television special. I wasn't the maker of that film, either. I was the—I was the victim. They had already shot the film, but at that time, of course, I did—I had a—if I hadn't gotten into that motorcycle accident, they would have broadcast it, and that would have been that. But I was sort of—I was taken out of it, you know, and—I think it was the fall of that year. I had a little more time to, you know, concentrate on what was happening to me and what had happened. Anyway, what had happened was that they had made another *Don't Look Back*, only this time it was for television. I had nothing better to do than to see the film. All of it, including unused footage. And it was obvious from looking at the film that it was garbage. It was miles and miles of garbage. That was my introduction to film. My film concept was all formed in those early days when I was looking at that footage.

PLAYBOY: From looking at those miles of garbage, you got your concept of film?

DYLAN: Yeah, it was mostly rejected footage, which I found beauty in. Which probably tells you more—that I see beauty where other people don't.

PLAYBOY: That reminds us of a poem you wrote for the jacket of an early Joan Baez album, in which you claimed that you always thought something had to be ugly before you found it beautiful. And at some point in the poem, you described listening to Joan sing and suddenly deciding that beauty didn't have to start out by being ugly.

DYLAN: I was very hung up on Joan at the time. [Pause] I think I was just trying to tell myself I wasn't hung up on her.

PLAYBOY: OK. Would you talk some more about the film concept you got from the rejected footage?

DYLAN: Well, up until that time, they had been concerned with the linear story line. It was on one plane and in one dimension only. And the more I looked at the film, the more I realized that you could get more onto film than just one train of thought. My mind works that way, anyway. We tend to work on different levels. So I was seeing a lot of those levels in the footage. But technically, I didn't know how to do what my mind was telling me could be done.

PLAYBOY: What did you feel could be done?

DYLAN: Well, well, now, film is a series of actions and reactions, you know. And it's trickery. You're playing with illusion. What seems to be a simple affair is actually quite contrived. And the stronger your point of view is, the stronger your film will be.

PLAYBOY: Would you elaborate?

DYLAN: You're trying to get a message through. So there are many ways to deliver that message. Let's say you have a message: "White is white."

Bergman would say, "White is white" in the space of an hour—or what seems to be an hour. Bunuel might say, "White is black, and black is white, but white is really white." And it's all really the same message.

PLAYBOY: And how would Dylan say it?

DYLAN: Dylan would probably not even say it. [Laughs] He would—he'd assume you'd know that. [Laughs]

PLAYBOY: You wriggled out of that one.

DYLAN: I'd say people will always believe in something if they feel it to be true. Just knowing it's true is not enough. If you feel in your gut that it's true, well, then, you can be pretty much assured that it's true.

PLAYBOY: So that a film made by someone who feels in his guts that white is white will give the feeling to the audience that white is white without having to say it.

DYLAN: Yes. Exactly.

PLAYBOY: Let's talk about the message of *Renaldo & Clara*. It appears to us to be a personal yet fictional film in which you, Joan Baez, and your former wife, Sara, play leading roles. You play Renaldo, Baez plays a "woman in white," and Sara plays Clara. There is also a character in the film called Bob Dylan played by someone else. It is composed of footage from your Rolling Thunder Revue tour and fictional scenes performed by all of you as actors. Would you tell us basically what the movie's about?

DYLAN: It's about the essence of man being alienated from himself and how, in order to free himself, to be reborn, he has to go outside himself. You can almost say that he dies in order to look at time and by strength of will can return to the same body.

PLAYBOY: He can return by strength of will to the same body . . . and to Clara?

DYLAN: Clara represents to Renaldo everything in the material world he's ever wanted. Renaldo's needs are few. He doesn't know it, though, at that particular time.

PLAYBOY: What are his needs?

DYLAN: A good guitar and a dark street.

PLAYBOY: The guitar because he loves music, but why the dark street?

DYLAN: Mostly because he needs to hide.

PLAYBOY: From whom?

DYLAN: From the demon within. [Pause] But what we all know is that you can't hide on a dark street from the demon within. And there's our movie.

PLAYBOY: Renaldo finds that out in the film?

DYLAN: He tries to escape from the demon within, but he discovers that the demon is, in fact, a mirrored reflection of Renaldo himself.

PLAYBOY: OK. Given the personalities involved, how do you define the relationship between you, your personal life, and the film?

DYLAN: No different from Hitchcock making a movie. I am the overseer.

PLAYBOY: Overseeing various versions of yourself?

DYLAN: Well, certain truths I know. Not necessarily myself but a certain accumulation of experience that has become real to me and a knowledge that I acquired on the road.

PLAYBOY: And what are those truths?

DYLAN: One is that if you try to be anyone but yourself, you will fail; if you are not true to your own heart, you will fail. Then again, there's no success like failure.

PLAYBOY: And failure's no success at all.

DYLAN: Oh, well, we're not looking to succeed. Just by our being and acting alive, we succeed. You fail only when you let death creep in and take over a part of your life that should be alive.

PLAYBOY: How does death creep in?

DYLAN: Death don't come knocking at the door. It's there in the morning when you wake up.

PLAYBOY: How is it there?

DYLAN: Did you ever clip your fingernails, cut your hair? Then you experience death.

PLAYBOY: Look, in the film, Joan Baez turns to you at one point and says, "You never give any straight answers." Do you?

DYLAN: She is confronting Renaldo.

PLAYBOY: Evasiveness isn't only in the mind; it can also come out—in an interview.

DYLAN: There are no simple answers to these questions. . . .

PLAYBOY: Aren't you teasing the audience when you have scenes played by Baez and Sara, real people in your life, and then expect the viewers to set aside their preconceptions as to their relationship to you?

DYLAN: No, no. They shouldn't even think they know anyone in this film. It's all in the context of Renaldo and Clara and there's no reason to get hung up on who's who in the movie.

PLAYBOY: What about scenes such as the one in which Baez asks you, "What if we had gotten married back then?"

DYLAN: Seems pretty real, don't it?

PLAYBOY: Yes.

DYLAN: Seems pretty real. Just like in a Bergman movie, those things seem real. There's a lot of spontaneity that goes on. Usually, the people in his films know each other, so they can interrelate. There's life and breath in every frame because everyone knew each other.

PLAYBOY: All right, another question: In the movie, Ronnie Hawkins, a 300-pound Canadian rock singer, goes by the name of Bob Dylan. So is there a real Bob Dylan?

DYLAN: In the movie?

PLAYBOY: Yes.

DYLAN: In the movie, no. He doesn't even appear in the movie. His voice is there, his songs are used, but Bob's not in the movie. It would be silly. Did you ever see a Picasso painting with Picasso in the picture? You only see his work. Now, I'm not interested in putting a picture of myself on the screen, because that's not going to do anybody any good, including me.

PLAYBOY: Then why use the name Bob Dylan at all in the movie?

DYLAN: In order to legitimize this film. We confronted it head on: The persona of Bob Dylan is in the movie so we could get rid of it. There should no longer be any mystery as to who or what he is—he's there, speaking in all kinds of tongues, and there's even someone else claiming to be him, so he's covered. This movie is obvious, you know. Nobody's hiding anything. It's all right there. The rabbits are falling out of the hat before the movie begins.

PLAYBOY: Do you really feel it's an accessible movie?

DYLAN: Oh, perfectly. Very open movie.

PLAYBOY: Even though Mr. Bob Dylan and Mrs. Bob Dylan are played by different people. . . .

DYLAN: Oh, yeah.

PLAYBOY: And you don't know for sure which one he is?

DYLAN: Sure. We could make a movie and you could be Bob Dylan. It wouldn't matter.

PLAYBOY: But if there are two Bob Dylans in the film and Renaldo is always changing. . . .

DYLAN: Well, it could be worse. It could be three or four. Basically, it's a simple movie.

PLAYBOY: How did you decide to make it?

DYLAN: As I said, I had the idea for doing my own film back in '66. And I buried it until '76. My lawyer used to tell me there was a future in movies. So I said, "What kind of future?" He said, "Well, if you can come up with a script, an outline, and get money from a big distributor." But I knew I couldn't work that way. I can't betray my vision on a little piece of paper in hopes of getting some money from somebody. In the final analysis, it turned out that I had to make the movie all by myself, with people who would work with me, who trusted me. I went on the road in '76 to make the money for this movie. My last two tours were to raise the money for it.

PLAYBOY: How much of your money are you risking?

DYLAN: I'd rather not say. It is quite a bit, but I didn't go into the bank. The budget was like $600,000, but it went over that.

PLAYBOY: Did you get pleasure out of the project?

DYLAN: I feel it's a story that means a great deal to me, and I got to do what I always wanted to do—make a movie. When something like that happens, it's like stopping time, and you can make people live into that moment. Not many things can do that in your daily life. You can be distracted by many things. But the main point is to make it meaningful to someone. Take *Shane*, for example. That moved me. *On the Water-front* moved me. So when I go to see a film, I expect to be moved. I don't want to go see a movie just to kill time, or to have it just show me something I'm not aware of. I want to be moved, because that's what art is supposed to do, according to all the great theologians. Art is supposed to take you out of your chair. It's supposed to move you from one space to another. *Renaldo & Clara* is not meant to put a strain on you. It's a movie to be enjoyed as a movie. I know nothing about film, I'm not a filmmaker. On the other hand, I do consider myself a filmmaker because I made this film: So I don't know. . . . If it doesn't move you, then it's a grand, and was made in the spirit of "All right, if all you people out there want to talk about Dylan breaking up with his wife, about his having an affair with Joan Baez, I'll just put those people into my film and rub people's noses in the gossip, because only I know the truth?"

DYLAN: It's not entirely true, because that's not what the movie is about. I'm not sure how much of Bob Dylan and Joan Baez concern anybody. To me, it isn't important. It's old news to me, so I don't think it's of much interest to anybody. If it is, fine. But I don't think it's a relevant issue. The movie doesn't deal with anything current. This is two years ago. I'm smart enough to know I shouldn't deal with any current subject on an emotional level, because usually it won't last. You need experience to write, or to sing or to act. You don't just wake up and say you're going to do it. This movie is taking experience and turning it into something else. It's not a gossipy movie.

PLAYBOY: We began this discussion of your movie by comparing filmmakers to painters. Were you as interested in painting as in, say, rock music when you were growing up?

DYLAN: Yeah, I've always painted. I've always held on to that one way or another.

PLAYBOY: Do you feel you use colors in the same way you use notes or chords?

DYLAN: Oh, yeah. There's much information you could get on the meaning of colors. Every color has a certain mood and feeling. For instance, red is a very vital color. There're a lot of reds in this movie, and a lot of blues. A lot of cobalt blue.

PLAYBOY: Why cobalt blue?

DYLAN: It's the color of dissension.

PLAYBOY: Did you study painting?

DYLAN: A lot of the ideas I have were influenced by an old man who had definite ideas on life and the universe and nature—all that matters.

PLAYBOY: Who was he?

DYLAN: Just an old man. His name wouldn't mean anything to you.

He came to this country from Russia in the twenties, started out as a boxer and ended up painting portraits of women.

PLAYBOY: You don't want to mention his name, just to give him a plug?

DYLAN: His first name was Norman. Every time I mention somebody's name, it's like they get a tremendous amount of distraction and irrelevancy in their lives. For instance, there's this lady in L.A. I respect a lot who reads palms. Her name's Tamara Rand. She's for real, she's not a gypsy fortune-teller. But she's accurate! She'll take a look at your hand and tell you things you feel but don't really understand about where you're heading, what the future looks like. She's a surprisingly hopeful person.

PLAYBOY: Are you sure you want to know if there's bad news in your future?

DYLAN: Well, sometimes when the world falls on your head, you know there are ways to get out, but you want to know which way. Usually, there's someone who can tell you how to crawl out, which way to take.

PLAYBOY: Getting back to colors and chords, are there particular musical keys that have personalities or moods the way colors do for you?

DYLAN: Yeah. B major and B-flat major.

PLAYBOY: How would you describe them?

DYLAN: (Pause) Each one is hard to define. Assume the characteristic that is true of both of them and you'll find you're not sure whether you're speaking to them or to their echo.

PLAYBOY: What does a major key generally conjure up for you?

Younger Than That Now

DYLAN: I think any major key deals with romance.

PLAYBOY: And the minor keys?

DYLAN: The supernatural.

PLAYBOY: What about other specific keys?

DYLAN: I find C major to be the key of strength, but also the key of regret. E major is the key of confidence. A-flat major is the key of renunciation.

PLAYBOY: Since we're back on the subject of music, what new songs have you planned?

DYLAN: I have new songs now that are unlike anything I've ever written.

PLAYBOY: Really?

DYLAN: Yes.

PLAYBOY: What are they like?

DYLAN: Well, you'll see. I mean, unlike anything I've ever done. You couldn't even say that *Blood on the Tracks* or *Desire* have led up to this stuff. I mean, it's that far gone, it's that far out there. I'd rather not talk more about them until they're out.

PLAYBOY: When the character Bob Dylan in your movie speaks the words "Rock 'n' roll is the answer," what does he mean?

DYLAN: He's speaking of the sound and the rhythm. The drums and the rhythm are the answer. Get into the rhythm of it and you will lose yourself; you will forget about the brutality of it all. Then you will lose your identity. That's what he's saying.

140

PLAYBOY: Does that happen to you, to the real Bob Dylan?

DYLAN: Well, that's easy. When you're playing music and it's going well, you do lose your identity, you become totally subservient to the music you're doing in your very being.

PLAYBOY: Do you feel possessed?

DYLAN: It's dangerous, because its effect is that you believe that you can transcend and cope with anything. That it is the real life, that you've struck at the heart of life itself and you are on top of your dream. And there's no down. But later on, backstage, you have a different point of view.

PLAYBOY: When you're onstage, do you feel the illusion that death can't get you?

DYLAN: Death can't get you at all. Death's not here to get anybody. It's the appearance of the Devil, and the Devil is a coward, so knowledge will overcome that.

PLAYBOY: What do you mean?

DYLAN: The Devil is everything false, the Devil will go as deep as you let the Devil go. You can leave yourself open to that. If you understand what that whole scene is about, you can easily step aside. But if you want the confrontation to begin with, well, there's plenty of it. But then again, if you believe you have a purpose and a mission, and not much time to carry it out, you don't bother about those things.

PLAYBOY: Do you think you have a purpose and a mission?

DYLAN: Obviously.

PLAYBOY: What is it?

Younger Than That Now

DYLAN: Henry Miller said it: The role of an artist is to inoculate the world with disillusionment.

PLAYBOY: To create rock music, you used to have to be against the system, a desperado. Is settling down an enemy of rock?

DYLAN: No. You can be a priest and be in rock 'n' roll. Being a rock-'n'-roll singer is no different from being a house painter. You climb up as high as you want to. You're asking me, is rock, is the lifestyle of rock 'n' roll at odds with the lifestyle of society in general?

PLAYBOY: Yes. Do you need to be in some way outside society, or in some way an outlaw, some way a . . .

DYLAN: No. Rock 'n' roll forms its own society. It's a world of its own. The same way the sports world is.

PLAYBOY: But didn't you feel that it was valuable to bum around and all that sort of thing?

DYLAN: Yes. But not necessarily, because you can bum around and wind up being a lawyer, you know. There isn't anything definite. Or any blueprint to it.

PLAYBOY: So future rock stars could just as easily go to law school?

DYLAN: For some people, it might be fine. But, getting back to that again, you have to have belief. You must have a purpose. You must believe that you can disappear through walls. Without that belief, you're not going to become a very good rock singer, or pop singer, or folk-rock singer, or you're not going to become a very good lawyer. Or a doctor. You must know why you're doing what you're doing.

PLAYBOY: Why are you doing what you're doing?

DYLAN: [Pause] Because I don't know anything else to do. I'm good at it.

PLAYBOY: How would you describe "it"?

DYLAN: I'm an artist. I try to create art.

PLAYBOY: How do you feel about your songs when you perform them years later? Do you feel your art has endured?

DYLAN: How many singers feel the same way ten years later that they felt when they wrote their song? Wait till it gets to be 20 years, you know? Now, there's a certain amount of act that you can put on, you know, you can get through on it, but there's got to be something to it that is real—not just for the moment. And a lot of my songs don't work. I wrote a lot of them just by gut—because my gut told me to write them—and they usually don't work so good as the years go on. A lot of them do work. With those, there's some truth about every one of them. And I don't think I'd be singing if I weren't writing, you know. I would have no reason or purpose to be out there singing. I mean, I don't consider myself . . . the life of the party. [Laughs]

PLAYBOY: You've given new life to some songs in recent performances, such as "I Pity the Poor Immigrant" in the Rolling Thunder tour.

DYLAN: Oh, yes. I've given new life to a lot of them. Because I believe in them, basically. You know, I believe in them. So I do give them new life. And that can always be done. I rewrote "Lay, Lady, Lay," too. No one ever mentioned that.

PLAYBOY: You changed it to a much raunchier, less pretty kind of song.

DYLAN: Exactly. A lot of words to that song have changed. I recorded it originally surrounded by a bunch of other songs on the *Nashville Skyline* album. That was the tone of the session. Once everything was set, that was the way it came out. And it was fine for that time, but I always had a feeling there was more to the song than that.

PLAYBOY: Is it true that "Lay, Lady, Lay," was originally commissioned for *Midnight Cowboy*?

DYLAN: That's right. They wound up using Freddy Neil's tune.

PLAYBOY: How did it feel doing "Blowin' in the Wind" after all those years during your last couple of tours?

DYLAN: I think I'll always be able to do that. There are certain songs that I will always be able to do. They will always have just as much meaning, if not more, as time goes on.

PLAYBOY: What about "Like a Rolling Stone"?

DYLAN: That was a great tune, yeah. It's the dynamics in the rhythm that make up "Like a Rolling Stone" and all of the lyrics. I tend to base all my songs on the old songs, like the old folk songs, the old blues tunes; they are always good. They always make sense.

PLAYBOY: Would you talk a little about how specific songs come to you?

DYLAN: They come to me when I am most isolated in space and time. I reject a lot of inspiring lines.

PLAYBOY: They're too good?

DYLAN: I reject a lot. I kind of know myself well enough to know that the line might be good and it is the first line that gives you inspiration and then it's just like riding a bull. That is the rest of it. Either you just stick with it or you don't. And if you believe that what you are doing is important, then you will stick with it no matter what.

PLAYBOY: There are lines that are like riding wild bulls?

DYLAN: There are lines like that. A lot of lines that would be better off just staying on a printed page and finishing up as poems. I forget a lot of the lines. During the day, a lot of lines will come to me that I will just say are pretty strange and I don't have anything better to do. I try not to pay too much attention to those wild, obscure lines.

PLAYBOY: You say you get a single line and then you ride it. Does the melody follow after you write out the whole song?

DYLAN: I usually know the melody before the song.

PLAYBOY: And it is there, waiting for that first line?

DYLAN: Yeah.

PLAYBOY: Do you hear it easily?

DYLAN: The melody? Sometimes, and sometimes I have to find it.

PLAYBOY: Do you work regularly? Do you get up every morning and practice?

DYLAN: A certain part of every day I have to play.

PLAYBOY: Has your playing become more complex?

DYLAN: No. Musically not. I can hear more and my melodies now are more rhythmic than they ever have been, but, really, I am still with those same three chords. But, I mean, I'm not Segovia or Montoya. I don't practice 12 hours a day.

PLAYBOY: Do you practice using your voice, too?

Younger Than That Now

DYLAN: Usually, yeah, when I'm rehearsing, especially, or when I'm writing a song, I'll be singing it.

PLAYBOY: Someone said that when you gave up cigarettes, your voice changed. Now we see you're smoking again. Is your voice getting huskier again?

DYLAN: No, you know, you can do anything with your voice if you put your mind to it. I mean, you can become a ventriloquist or you can become an imitator of other people's voices. I'm usually just stuck with my own voice. I can do a few other people's voices.

PLAYBOY: Whose voices can you imitate?

DYLAN: Richard Widmark. Sydney Greenstreet. Peter Lorre. I like those voices. They really had distinctive voices in the early talkie films. Nowadays, you go to a movie and you can't tell one voice from the other. Jane Fonda sounds like Tatum O'Neal.

PLAYBOY: Has your attitude toward women changed much in your songs?

DYLAN: Yeah; in the early period, I was writing more about objection, obsession, or rejection. Superimposing my own reality on that which seemed to have no reality of its own.

PLAYBOY: How did those opinions change?

DYLAN: From neglect.

PLAYBOY: From neglect?

DYLAN: As you grow, things don't reach you as much as when you're still forming opinions.

PLAYBOY: You mean you get hurt less easily?

DYLAN: You get hurt over other matters than when you were 17. The energy of hurt isn't enough to create art.

PLAYBOY: So if the women in your songs have become more real, if there are fewer goddesses—

DYLAN: The goddess isn't real. A pretty woman as a goddess is just up there on a pedestal. The flower is what we are really concerned about here. The opening and the closing, the growth, the bafflement. You don't lust after flowers.

PLAYBOY: Your regard for women, then, has changed?

DYLAN: People are people to me. I don't single out women as anything to get hung up about.

PLAYBOY: But in the past?

DYLAN: In the past, I was guilty of that shameless crime.

PLAYBOY: You're claiming to be completely rehabilitated?

DYLAN: In that area, I don't have any serious problems.

PLAYBOY: There's a line in your film in which someone says to Sara, "I need you because I need your magic to protect me."

DYLAN: Well, the real magic of women is that throughout the ages, they've had to do all the work and yet they can have a sense of humor.

PLAYBOY: That's throughout the ages. What about women now?

DYLAN: Well, here's the new woman, right? Nowadays, you have the concept of a new woman, but the new woman is nothing without a man.

Younger Than That Now

PLAYBOY: What would the new woman say to that?

DYLAN: I don't know what the new woman would say the new woman is the impulsive woman. . . .

PLAYBOY: There's another line in your movie about "the ultimate woman." What is the ultimate woman?

DYLAN: A woman without prejudice.

PLAYBOY: Are there many?

DYLAN: There are as many as you can see. As many as can touch you.

PLAYBOY: So you've run into a lot of ultimate women?

DYLAN: Me, personally? I don't run into that many people. I'm working most of the time. I really don't have time for all that kind of intrigue.

PLAYBOY: Camus said that chastity is an essential condition for creativity. Do you agree?

DYLAN: He was speaking there of the disinvolvement with pretense.

PLAYBOY: Wasn't he speaking of sexual chastity?

DYLAN: You mean he was saying you have to stay celibate to create?

PLAYBOY: That's one interpretation.

DYLAN: Well, he might have been on to something there. It could have worked for him.

PLAYBOY: When you think about rock and the rhythm of the heartbeat is it tied into love in some way?

DYLAN: The heartbeat. Have you ever lain with somebody when your hearts were beating in the same rhythm? That's true love. A man and a woman who lie down with their hearts beating together are truly lucky. Then you've truly been in love, m' boy. Yeah, that's true love. You might see that person once a month, once a year, maybe once a lifetime, but you have the guarantee your lives are going to be in rhythm. That's all you need.

PLAYBOY: Considering that some of your recent songs have been about love and romance, what do you feel about the tendency some people used to have of dividing your work into periods? Did you ever feel it was fair to divide your work, for example, into a political period and a nonpolitical period?

DYLAN: Those people disregarded the ultimate fact that I am a songwriter. I can't help what other people do with my songs, what they make of them.

PLAYBOY: But you were more involved politically at one time. You were supposed to have written "Chimes of Freedom" in the backseat of a car while you were visiting some SNCC people in the South.

DYLAN: That is all we did in those days. Writing in the backseats of cars and writing songs on street corners or on porch swings. Seeking out the explosive areas of life.

PLAYBOY: One of which was politics?

DYLAN: Politics was always one because there were people who were trying to change things. They were involved in the political game because that is how they had to change things. But I have always considered politics just part of the illusion. I don't get involved much in politics. I don't know what the system runs on. For instance, there are people who have definite ideas or who studied all the systems of government. A lot of those people with college-educational backgrounds tended to come in and use up everybody for whatever purposes they had in mind. And, of course, they used music, because music was accessible and we would have done that stuff and written those songs and sung them whether there was any politics or not. I never did renounce a role in politics, because I never played one in politics. It would be comical for me to think that I played a role. Gurdjieff thinks it's best to work out your mobility daily.

PLAYBOY: So you did have a lot of "on the road" experiences?

DYLAN: I still do.

PLAYBOY: Driving around?

DYLAN: I am. interested in all aspects of life. Revelations and realizations. Lucid thought that can be translated into songs, analogies, new information. I am better at it now. Not really written yet anything to make me stop writing. Like, I haven't come to the place that Rimbaud came to when he decided to stop writing and run guns in Africa.

PLAYBOY: Jimmy Carter has said that listening to your songs, he learned to see in a new way the relationship between landlord and tenant, farmer and sharecropper, and things like that. He also said that you were his friend. What do you think of all that?

DYLAN: I am his friend.

PLAYBOY: A personal friend?

DYLAN: I know him personally.

PLAYBOY: Do you like him?

DYLAN: Yeah, I think his heart's in the right place.

PLAYBOY: How would you describe that place?

DYLAN: The place of destiny. You know, I hope the magazine won't take all this stuff and edit—like, Carter's heart's in the right place of destiny, because it's going to really sound . . .

PLAYBOY: No, it would lose the sense of conversation. The magazine's pretty good about that.

DYLAN: Carter has his heart in the right place. He has a sense of who he is. That's what I felt, anyway, when I met him.

PLAYBOY: Have you met him many times?

DYLAN: Only once.

PLAYBOY: Stayed at his house?

DYLAN: No. But anybody who's a governor or a Senate leader or in a position of authority who finds time to invite a folk-rock singer and his band out to his place has got to have . . . a sense of humor . . . and a feeling of the pulse of the people. Why does he have to do it? Most people in those kinds of positions can't relate at all to people in the music field unless it's for some selfish purpose.

PLAYBOY: Did you talk about music or politics?

DYLAN: Music. Very little politics. The conversation was kept in pretty general areas.

PLAYBOY: Does he have any favorite Dylan songs?

DYLAN: I didn't ask him if he had any favorite Dylan songs. He didn't say that he did. I think he liked "Ballad of a Thin Man," really.

Younger Than That Now

PLAYBOY: Did you think that Carter might have been using you by inviting you there?

DYLAN: No, I believe that he was a decent, untainted man and he just wanted to check me out. Actually, as presidents go, I liked Truman.

PLAYBOY: Why?

DYLAN: I just liked the way he acted and things he said and who he said them to. He had a common sense about him, which is rare for a president. Maybe in the old days it wasn't so rare, but nowadays it's rare. He had a common quality. You felt like you could talk to him.

PLAYBOY: You obviously feel you can talk to President Carter.

DYLAN: You do feel like you can talk to him, but the guy is so busy and overworked you feel more like, well, maybe you'd just leave him alone, you know. And he's dealing with such complicated matters and issues that people are a little divided and we weren't divided in Truman's time.

PLAYBOY: Is there anything you're angry about? Is there anything that would make you go up to Carter and say, "Look, you fucker, do this!"?

DYLAN: Right. [Pause] He's probably caught up in the system like everybody else.

PLAYBOY: Including you?

DYLAN: I'm a part of the system. I have to deal with the system. The minute you pay taxes, you're part of the system.

PLAYBOY: Are there any heroes or saints these days?

DYLAN: A saint is a person who gives of himself totally and freely, without strings. He is neither deaf nor blind. And yet he's both. He's the master of his own reality, the voice of simplicity. The trick is to stay away from mirror images. The only true mirrors are puddles of water.

PLAYBOY: How are mirrors different from puddles?

DYLAN: The image you see in a puddle of water is consumed by depth: An image you see when you look into a piece of glass has no depth or life-flutter movement. Of course, you might want to check your tie. And, of course, you might want to see if the makeup is on straight. That's all the way. Vanity sells a lot of things.

PLAYBOY: How so?

DYLAN: Well, products on the market. Everything from new tires to bars of soap. Need is—need is totally overlooked. Nobody seems to care about people's needs. They're all for one purpose. A shallow grave.

PLAYBOY: Do you want your grave unmarked?

DYLAN: Isn't that a line in my film?

PLAYBOY: Yes.

DYLAN: Well, there are many things they can do with your bones, you know. [Pause] They make neckpieces out of them, bury them. Burn them up.

PLAYBOY: What's your latest preference?

DYLAN: Ah—put them in a nutshell.

PLAYBOY: You were talking about vanity and real needs. What needs? What are we missing?

Younger Than That Now

DYLAN: There isn't anything missing. There is just a lot of scarcity.

PLAYBOY: Scarcity of what?

DYLAN: Inspirational abundance.

PLAYBOY: So it's not an energy crisis but an imagination crisis?

DYLAN: I think it's a spiritual crisis.

PLAYBOY: How so?

DYLAN: Well, you know, people step on each other's feet too much. They get on each other's case. They rattle easily. But I don't particularly stress that. I'm not on a soapbox about it, you know. That is the way life is.

PLAYBOY: We asked about heroes and saints and began talking about saints. How about heroes?

DYLAN: A hero is anyone who walks to his own drummer.

PLAYBOY: Shouldn't people look to others to be heroes?

DYLAN: No; when people look to others for heroism, they're looking for heroism in an imaginary character.

PLAYBOY: Maybe that in part explains why many seized upon you as that imaginary character.

DYLAN: I'm not an imaginary character, though.

PLAYBOY: You must realize that people get into a whole thing about you.

DYLAN: I know they used to.

PLAYBOY: Don't you think they still do?

DYLAN: Well, I m not aware of it anymore.

PLAYBOY: What about the 1974 tour? Or the Rolling Thunder tour of 1976?

DYLAN: Well, yeah, you know, when I play, people show up. I'm aware they haven't forgotten about me.

PLAYBOY: Still, people always think you have answers, don't they?

DYLAN: No, listen: If I wasn't Bob Dylan, I'd probably think that Bob Dylan has a lot of answers myself.

PLAYBOY: Would you be right?

DYLAN: I don't think so. Maybe he'd have a lot of answers for him, but for me? Maybe not. Maybe yes, maybe no. Bob Dylan isn't a cat, he doesn't have nine lives, so he can only do what he can do. You know: not break under the strain. If you need someone who raises someone else to a level that is unrealistic, then it's that other person's problem. He is just confronting his superficial self somewhere down the line. They'll realize it, I'm sure.

PLAYBOY: But didn't you have to go through a period when people were claiming you had let them down?

DYLAN: Yeah, but I don't pay much attention to that. What can you say? Oh, I let you down, big deal, OK. That's all. Find somebody else, OK? That's all.

PLAYBOY: You talked about a spiritual crisis. Do you think Christ is an answer?

Younger Than That Now

DYLAN: What is it that attracts people to Christ? The fact that it was such a tragedy, is what. Who does Christ become when he lives inside a certain person? Many people say that Christ lives inside them: Well, what does that mean? I've talked to many people whom Christ lives inside; I haven't met one who would want to trade places with Christ. Not one of his people put himself on the line when it came down to the final hour. What would Christ be in this day and age if he came back? What would he be? What would he be to fulfill his function and purpose? He would have to be a leader, I suppose.

PLAYBOY: Did you grow up thinking about the fact that you were Jewish?

DYLAN: No, I didn't. I've never felt Jewish. I don't really consider myself Jewish or non-Jewish. I don't have much of a Jewish background. I'm not a patriot to any creed. I believe in all of them and none of them. A devout Christian or Moslem can be just as effective as a devout Jew.

PLAYBOY: You say you don't feel Jewish. But what about your sense of God?

DYLAN: I feel a heartfelt God. I don't particularly think that God wants me thinking about Him all the time. I think that would be a tremendous burden on Him, you know. He's got enough people asking Him for favors. He's got enough people asking Him to pull strings. I'll pull my own strings, you know. I remember seeing a *Time* magazine on an airplane a few years back and it had a big cover headline, "IS GOD DEAD?" I mean, that was—would you think that was a responsible thing to do? What does God think of that? I mean, if you were God, how would you like to see that written about yourself? You know, I think the country's gone downhill since that day.

PLAYBOY: Really?

DYLAN: Uh-huh.

PLAYBOY: Since that particular question was asked?

DYLAN: Yeah; I think at that point, some very irresponsible people got hold of too much power to put such an irrelevant thing like that in a magazine when they could be talking about real issues. Since that day, you've had to kind of make your own way.

PLAYBOY: How are we doing, making our own way?

DYLAN: The truth is that we're born and we die. We're concerned here in this life with the journey from point A to point Z, or from what we think is point A to point Z. But it's pretty self-deluding if you think that's all there is.

PLAYBOY: What do you think is beyond Z?

DYLAN: You mean, what do I think is in the great unknown? [Pause] Sounds, echoes of laughter.

PLAYBOY: Do you feel there's some sense of karmic balance in the universe, that you suffer for acts of bad faith?

DYLAN: Of course. I think everybody knows that's true. After you've lived long enough, you realize that's the case. You can get away with anything for a while. But it's like Poe's "The Tell-Tale Heart" or Dostoyevsky's *Crime and Punishment:* Somewhere along the line, sooner or later, you're going to have to pay.

PLAYBOY: Do you feel you've paid for what you got away with earlier?

DYLAN: Right now, I'm about even.

PLAYBOY: Isn't that what you said after your motorcycle accident—" Something had to be evened up"?

Younger Than That Now

DYLAN: Yes.

PLAYBOY: And you meant. . . ?

DYLAN: I meant my back wheel had to be aligned. [Laughter]

PLAYBOY: Let's take one last dip back into the material world. What about an artist's relationship to money?

DYLAN: The myth of the starving artist is a myth. The big bankers and prominent young ladies who buy art started it. They just want to keep the artist under their thumb. Who says an artist can't have any money? Look at Picasso. The starving artist is usually starving for those around him to starve. You don't have to starve to be a good artist. You just have to have love, insight, and a strong point of view. And you have to fight off depravity. Uncompromising, that's what makes a good artist. It doesn't matter if he has money or not. Look at Matisse; he was a banker. Anyway, there are other things that constitute wealth and poverty besides money.

PLAYBOY: What we were touching on was the subject of the expensive house you live in, for example.

DYLAN: What about it? Nothing earthshaking or final about where I live. There is no vision behind the house. It is just a bunch of trees and sheds.

PLAYBOY: We read in the papers about an enormous copper dome you had built.

DYLAN: I don't know what you read in the papers. It's just a place to live for now. The copper dome is just so I can recognize it when I come home.

PLAYBOY: OK, back to less worldly concerns. You don't believe in astrology, do you?

DYLAN: I don't think so.

PLAYBOY: You were quoted recently as having said something about having a Gemini nature.

DYLAN: Well, maybe there are certain characteristics of people who are born under certain signs. But I don't know, I'm not sure how relevant it is.

PLAYBOY: Could it be there's an undiscovered twin or a double to Bob Dylan?

DYLAN: Someplace on the planet, there's a double of me walking around. Could very possibly be.

PLAYBOY: Any messages for your double?

DYLAN: Love will conquer everything—I suppose.

TROUSER PRESS, DECEMBER 12, 1978

Interview with an Icon:
Bob Dylan Grants an Audience

Lynne Allen

If I'd thought about it
I never would have done it
I guess I would 'a let it slide
If I'd 'a lived my life by what others were thinkin'
This heart inside me would 'a died
I was just too stubborn to ever be governed by enforced insanity
Someone had to reach for the risin' star

I guess it was up to me

———•◦•———

BOB DYLAN IS A LEGEND in his own time. Not a full-fledged commercial superstar, for he doesn't make platinum records nor sell out all of his live performances, Dylan is merely a legend, enigmatic and mysterious. Familiar, yet strange. It has been said that Dylan is not half the myth he believes himself to be and that he himself is the mythmonger, selling us his every new phase while, like his descendant in style, David Bowie, he casually discards each old mask with the ease of an actor changing roles. He has also at various times been accused of having sold out, of being too removed, aloof, of not revealing enough, of being cold and calculating, allowing us to see only what he wishes and no more. No matter, in the final analysis he _is_ what he has created. If the '60s were his formative years, the '70s have seen Dylan subject to many changes in his life. From the laid-back family man of *Nashville Skyline* and *New Morning*, Dylan slowly turned and headed back into the more complex reaches of his mind, starting with *Planet Waves*, which signaled the return within, and following with *Blood on the Tracks*, which brought him even closer to his anima, his muse, who finally appeared to him as Isis on *Desire*. (In a dreamscape not unlike Robert Graves' *White Goddess*, who could be found "among pack ice or where the track had faded," Dylan united with his goddess after he "came to the pyramids all imbedded in ice.")

With *Desire* in the stores, Dylan took to the road with his own gypsy troupe. The Rolling Thunder Revue brought to mind the "Indiani Metropolitani," groups of young people who do street theater in Italy. They toured the U.S. playing moderately sized halls, picking up and dropping different performers along the way. *Renaldo & Clara*, Dylan's mammoth and controversial movie, was filmed on the road with Rolling Thunder, during a tumultuous period in which his marriage reportedly took a turn for the worse and his life (along with his newly built dream house) began to slide. Seemingly none the worse for wear and tear, Dylan embarked on the most extensive tour of his career early in 1978. Beginning in Japan, New Zealand, and Australia, it finally wound up matters in the southeastern United States in December of last year. The first time I saw Dylan was in Binghamton, New York, in September 1978. I had always admired him. How could you not? No matter how one views Dylan and/or his music, it's difficult to deny the charismatic mystique that has afforded him widespread recognition and critical acclaim. Personally, I had always responded favorably to whatever courses Dylan had chosen to take, so approaching him live, I was already biased in favor of the man. I was shocked at his appearance. He seemed ragged and worn (which later proved to be deceptive. Makeup, heavy black around the eyes, cast strange shadows over his face under the lights). The music, though, was even more startling. My initial reaction was thoroughly negative, to put it mildly. In comparison to what was then currently happening in rock, the music seemed, bluntly, quite lame. The new arrangements seemed clumsy and awkward, overriding the simplicity that had originally made the songs work. But as I listened closer it rang with a clear resonance. The sound in the hall was exceptional, and the musicians excellent. This was certainly not, as many reviews and reviewers had suggested, "Las Vegas" nor was it disco. It was just Dylan, older, to be sure, scraggly and unkempt as always, even in his new black and white stage suit, his band playing behind him like a miniorchestra in perfect synch. I met Dylan a week later, at a typical record company bash held for him and his band after one of the Madison Square Garden shows. A friend introduced me to him and, sitting at an adjacent table, I had ample opportunity to observe him at close quarters. I sensed no animosity from him, no aggression nor defense; indeed, he seemed rather shy. His expertise at deterring conversation from himself, at keeping the talk light and meaningless, was obvious. He chain-smoked and drank red wine all night. He appeared drunk at times, slurring words and laughing a lot, but it could easily have been an act, a way of retaining his one-upmanship in any situation. Dylan, the enigmatic cynic, the infallible put-on artist remained in control. Three months later, I caught up with the Bob Dylan tour once again, this time, down south in Birmingham, Alabama. Looking disheveled as ever, the Jack of Hearts had once again trumped those in his audience who had been led to believe press reports of his new "slick" image. The tour had almost reached its end and the band was much tighter than they had been earlier. The songs no longer felt stiff, they were flowing now, having settled into their new forms.

Dylan spoke to the crowd a lot that night, introducing songs with brief stories or parables, breathing new life into songs 10, even 15 years old. He ended the show with "Forever Young," which he dedicated to one of his children. "This is our last—look for us," he said, "We may be back. I'm not quite ready to be put out to pasture just yet!" On the way out of town, I left a note for Dylan with the desk clerk of his hotel, saying that I wished to interview him, that I had no ulterior motive at all other than an interest and a desire to talk. I left a number for him to call and headed back home to Atlanta. A week later, backstage at the Omni in Atlanta, an hour before going onstage, Bob Dylan sat alone in his dressing room, strumming an old Martin guitar that had yellowed with age, the wood around the pick-guard chipped from years of use. Dressed in a green flannel shirt, black leather pants and boots, his eyes hidden behind dark aviator shades, he was relaxed and friendly, the antithesis of the guarded creature which the media so often portrays him as. His old black leather jacket lay crumpled up on one of the chairs, a small notebook peeked out of one of the pockets. What appeared to be chicken scratchings made their way across the open page. "I'm always writing something" he explained as he continued to pick a haunting blues melody on the guitar.

I mentioned to him that I had noticed a definite theme running through his more recent albums, culminating on *Desire*. He didn't seem too happy with the idea, though, and emphasized his disagreement with a forceful strum. "That album didn't have a concept. It didn't have that type of concept. Of course I wrote it with somebody else too, but I always kept it kinda on the track of where I thought it should be going. I can look back on it just like anybody else . . . but when that particular album was happening, I didn't know what was happening at the time. We tried it with a lot of different people in the studio, a lot of different types of sound and I even had backup singers on that album for two or three days, a lot of percussion, a lot going on. But as it got down, I got more irritated with all this sound going on and eventually just settled on bass, drums, and violin. "That was new," he stressed. "I didn't take that out as far as I wanted to, I didn't have a chance to do that. I wanted to do more harmonica and violin together but we never got a chance to do that. But, yeah, all that time, those songs like 'Isis' and and all that—gee, I haven't done that for a long time—I used to do that song all the time. . . ." *Desire*, Dylan's collaboration with writer Jacques Levy, was a deeply mystical statement, the violin capturing the free, gypsy spirit so inherent in the songs and later in the whole Rolling Thunder idea. "Yeah, it was that. It definitely was that. Oh you know, we did it all night long, into the morning. I never slept when I made that album, I couldn't sleep. I would have to listen to it again to really answer these questions in a coherent way." "You've left it behind in a way," I said. "No, I haven't left the songs behind. I never leave the songs behind. I might leave the arrangements and the mood behind, but the songs, I never leave them behind." At Newport in 1965, he unleashed his newfound electricity on an unsuspecting audience. Or as he put it in Atlanta, when introducing "Maggie's Farm": "I was invited to Newport in 1965. I had been invited there before and never caused too much fuss, but I was invited in '65 and I went and I played this particular song. Anyway, people booted me out of town, actually, for playing this particular tune and it was hard to believe that this song caused such a disturbance, but it did! It's called "I Ain't Gonna Work on Maggie's Farm No More." Years later, after a seemingly endless flow of changes in direction, he is still meeting with the same type of criticism. Dylan steps in and out of musical forms these days with an unusual ease, echoes of carnival music blend harmoniously with primitive jungle rhythms and Chicago blues, while Dylan the Folksinger and Dylan the Newport Electric Poet still exist. As at Newport, Dylan has not met with much favorable response to his new sound. People are disturbed by the strange changes. The unfamiliarity. He refuses to stagnate, to be pinned down, categorized: "Art is the perpetual motion of illusion," he once observed. And he truly lives his belief. I mentioned a line from "Idiot Wind": "Your chestnut mare shoots through my head and is making me see stars!" (Dylanologist A. J. Weberman claims that equine references in Dylan songs refer to heroin.) Interestingly, "Idiot Wind" was written before Dylan's teaming with Jacques Levy, cowriter (with Roger McGuinn) of "Chestnut Mare" years earlier. "That's right! Yeah!" He laughed delightfully. "I'm sure it's all connected up y'know, way down the line."

"But yeah, I had a couple of years there, where I went out to be by myself quite a bit of the time, and that's where I experienced those kinds of songs, on the *Blood on the Tracks* album . . . I'll do anything to write a song . . ." he laughed. "I used to anyway." *Street Legal* seems to backtrack through all the aforementioned albums. It is an acknowledgment of changes, both internal and external. "You're right. Let's say with a song like 'True Love Tends to Forget . . .'" He lit a cigarette. "The mood I was in on that song is—I mean, that means a lot, if you think about it, y'know. True love tends to forget—it isn't like a possession trip, when you've been wronged, that type of thing—I was trying to get the most out of that. I thought that was my best album." I agreed. "I hear it sometimes on the radio or a record player and I see that it's badly mixed and it doesn't sound very good, but what can you do? I've got, on Columbia Records alone, 21 or 22 albums out. So every time you make an album, you want it to be new, good, and different, but personally, when you look back on them—for me—all my albums are, are just measuring points for wherever I was at at a certain period of time. I went into the studio, recorded the songs as good as I could, and left. Basically, realistically, I'm a live performer and want to play onstage for the people and not make records that may sound really good." I mentioned how the current show had changed each time that I had seen him, and how much tighter the band had become as the tour progressed. "Yeah, well it's never gonna be the same two nights in a row."

Dylan has made many comments in the press recently about the 1980s. In his *Rolling Stone* interview with Jonathan Cott he said, "Anyone who's going to be doing anything will have his or her cards showing. You won't be able to get back in the '80s." What did he mean by that? "I don't know what I meant by that," he chuckled. "Me and Jonathan, every time he does an interview, we just get drunk. I don't think you should show all of your cards all of the time, I didn't mean that." He continued: "It's like, when I started out playing—it's hard to put into words—I don't know what the eighties are going to be like. I imagine a lot of the glue is gonna hold a lot of things together which are sort of scattered now. Appearances of people you know, some wearing blue uniforms with badges, they are probably going to be standing side by side with housewives with their hair up in curlers, wanting the same things. All these different elements are going to—I think—be molded together. I think people are going to be more honest in the '80s." Like the '60s, I wondered? "No, never. I don't think so." He answered adamantly. Dylan remembers the '60s very well. They were years that shaped him, that produced the inspiration for him to create some of the most potent art of the decade. His strange song-poems mirrored the turbulence and chaos of the times. He spoke for an entire generation, it seemed, and then suddenly he wanted no involvement with the movement he had given voice to. Some say it was the motorcycle accident. That it almost killed him, sent him crashing headlong into a nightmare of his own making. Others just say that he fell in love, settled into a more even existence in which politics and protest had no part. Radical critics like Weberman flatly accuse him of "drifting into indifference during a period when resistance was called for."

"I was always more tied up with the Beat Movement," he admits. "I don't know what the hippie movement was all about, that was a media thing, I think, 'Rent a Hippie'—I don't know what that was about. A lot of people, people that I knew, were in the early '60s up 'til '65 or '66. There was a different comradeship. There was drugs, but drugs were something that was just a playful thing or something which wasn't that romanticized. Drugs were always in the folk clubs and in the jazz clubs, but outside of those places I never really saw too many drugs." "The drugs at the end of the '60s were artificial. They were those—ah—L.S., acid, all that stuff made in a laboratory. Well I guess it's all made in a laboratory one way or another. I don't know. I was never involved in the acid scene either." By 1968 the Beatles had released *Sgt. Pepper*. Rock and roll had moved primarily into studios and electronics began to become more and more a part of the music. Acid rock flourished on the West Coast and the new art form was just becoming self-consciously aware of itself with a little help from its friends (often in the form of a little Kool-Aid).

Dylan chose this time to put out the album he had been working on since the cataclysmic accident. *John Wesley Harding* totally contradicted everything happening musically at the time. The deceptively simple folk melodies only served to draw one's attention even closer to the intensity of the lyrical message. Eventually, the '60s came to a close, the Beatles broke up, the war ended in a stale-mate and we stumbled into the '70s in a catatonic daze. The music reflected the times. Rock had a few casualties of its own. Madison Avenue and Wall Street moved in as the voice of the people turned into a multibillion dollar industry. A few couldn't handle it, and destroyed themselves by becoming victims of their own myths. Others, like Jagger and Dylan, survived.

"People are always talking about the '60s and now we are almost into the '80s and everybody wants to know what happened back then. Well," he answered himself, "in the '60s, everything that happened you did because you wanted to. You didn't do it because you thought you should do it or because it was the thing to do. Something inside of you told you you wanted to do it. There was a network all across the country—really. Very small, but very close, I still see those people traveling around y'know, they're still hanging in there. But as far as what happened, it will always be felt just the same as the Civil War was always felt into 1870 and 1880. It was just something which was felt by everyone whether they knew it or not and a lot of people in the '60s started all this which is happening now. They just don't realize it, you know." He put down the guitar, lit another cigarette. "But the '50s gave birth to the '60s too, don't forget, and in the '50s it was even rarer . . . like in the '60s it was people caught up on all the be-bop and the beat movement, or the subterranean culture that was going on, but it was homelike and it gave you identity."

It is interesting that Dylan's material has always dealt with the opposing forces of black and white, whether on a material level—as during the '60s when songs like "The Lonesome Death of Hattie Carroll" clarified the issues of the civil rights movement—or on the spiritual level of his most recent work. Dylan has taken to wearing black and white onstage of late, costuming his entire band in the same. The effect is one of total balance. Yin and yang, darkness and light. "Well, I think I'm more of an extremist. But no, I'm more active than someone who is balancing," he said. "If you play the game all by yourself and you're the only one playing the game, then you want to balance the game, but if you're playing the game with someone else, you've got to ride up when it's time for someone else to ride down." Like a seesaw? "Yeah right, and then you get the same kind of balance, but if you're playing by yourself then you've got to move to the middle." Which you don't do. "No, I'm uncomfortable in the middle, too easily blown down." When questioned about his unusual relationship with his record company—of being able to release any product he wants—he became edgy, his answer accompanied once again by the guitar. [As I am writing this, Bob Dylan is in the process of forming his own record company, Accomplice, to be distributed by CBS.] "CBS doesn't pay me, except for a royalty rate. They don't support these tours for me so they don't have any say. It they supported them, maybe they'd have some say in it." With *Renaldo & Clara*, Dylan took a new approach by filming the characters of his dreams. The film was an unconstructed, symbolic comment, a bold and original epic (its original four-hour length was the major complaint from most of its critics), visually combining the same elements Dylan uses in the written word. The actors and actresses, real people from his life, cast in fantasy roles. American film critics on the whole were not impressed with Dylan's work. They accused him of overindulgence and blamed his "careless treatment" of people close to him for the breakup of his marriage, which followed shortly on the heels of the film's release. The *Village Voice* sent an entire battalion of reviewers to see it and they all came back with negative impressions. However, the film was hailed at last year's Cannes Film Festival as one of the most innovative presentations there, an honor bestowed on Dylan by Europe's most discriminating cinema elite, which must have more than made up for the confused and confusing reviews it received in the US. Filmed by Sam Shepard, Dylan claims *Renaldo* was 10 years in the works but has decided that, "For me, film wouldn't be the right thing to do right now. It's not live enough. You're acting for a camera, a director, you can't really see the results." *Renaldo & Clara* seemed to be spontaneous. "That was great! Yeah, but I can't do that no more. It costs too much money for one, to make your own movie, and then if you make a movie for another man who's putting up the money, then he'll want what he wants."

Younger Than That Now

As the '50s gave way to the '60s, the age of the media superstar was born. James Dean gave way to Elvis Presley who gave way to Bob Dylan, each gigantic myths in their own time. While Elvis found his way into Middle America's heart, the chasm James Dean left wasn't filled until Bob Dylan formed a new link in the ever-growing chain of superantiheroes. When compared to the people he once strived to be like, he denies all similarity of public persona. "It's not as heavy as it probably was to deal with being Elvis Presley. Elvis didn't write any of his songs don't forget, I write all this stuff so I know what I'm saying. I'm behind it so I don't feel like I'm a mystery or anything." Does he consider himself an artist as opposed to a musician or a songwriter? "Well yeah, it's like all the artists have had their periods right, and that they've changed—most people in history that have done anything at all have always been put down—so it don't bother me a bit. I don't care what people say. Whether I'm an artist, or a musician, or a poet, or a songwriter or just anything . . ."

NEW MUSICAL EXPRESS, AUGUST 15, 1981

The Diamond Voice from Within

Neil Spencer

In a rare interview during his 1981 European tour, Bob Dylan talks about his music and religion to Neil Spencer.

HARMONICAS PLAY THE SKELETON KEYS of the rain that drapes Munich in gray drizzle for Bob Dylan's two-day stay in the city.

Our Mercedes taxi splashes its way through sodden streets toward the muzzled gray modernist shapes of the Olympic complex built to house the '74 games and where tonight's show will be staged, in the splendid indoor sports arena, to an audience of several thousand.

Munich is the eleventh stop on a European tour that will take in eight countries and 23 shows, around a third of them in Britain. Being in the business of a ceaseless quest for a Bob Dylan interview, (one of several score, if not hundred), I get to see shows in Paris, London, and Munich where the quest will, to an extent, be realized; a brief backstage encounter being promised by Dylan's management.

This was Dylan's sixth or seventh visit to Europe in his 20-year career, and this time round it was different. A lot has changed since Dylan last trod Albion's shores, not least the social and cultural fabric of Britain itself.

The expected media fanfare came, but it was muted in comparison to that afforded the '78 trip, when Dylan was seen as the consensus of the ongoing "rock" tradition handed down from the 60s; still the enigmatic and unrepentant rebel carrying the standards of alienation, protest, and emotional and spiritual exploration forward into the future.

This time it was Bruce Springsteen's turn to be feted as a visiting American superstar supreme, likewise set at the heart of a rock tradition whose myths are, for a growing number of young Europeans, now despoiled, overtaken by everyday reality or the new myths of punk and postpunk.

The national press, radio, and TV didn't seem to know quite how to respond to the new Christian Bob Dylan; and for them it was a case of better the cozy fantasy scenarios of last-chance power drives down endless American highways than the uncomfortable moral imperatives of Dylan's new kingdom.

Dylan's refusal to bow to the myths of rock—he'd always kept an ambiguous, open relation with "rock" anyway, what with his folk roots, the frequent diversions into country, blues, and anything else that took his fancy—and his insistence on his personal salvation had cost him heavy with critics and fans.

To some of them, any type of born-again Christianity smacked of U.S. president Ronald Reagan's "moral majority," even though Dylan's new songs have consistently spelt out an antiestablishment stance, the protest era rekindled if anything. There again, any spiritual values smack of humbug to a sometimes insensitized youth culture, more caught up with the materialist and consumer values it professes to despise than perhaps it realizes or cares to admit.

Christian or not, in the gritty business of attracting paying customers, there are few artists able to command the allegiance that Dylan still does, and ugly rumors of unsold tickets finally gave way to near-capacity audiences. Around 120,000 saw the British shows.

As at Earl's Court a hard look at the Munich crowd reveals plenty of original Dylan fans, many contemporaries now advancing into affluent middle age. Many more, no doubt, couldn't meet the commitment of tickets, transport, and babysitters. The younger fans that Dylan has always attracted seem more prominent at the Continental shows, where rock tradition and contemporary protest—the German peace and eco movements and their equivalents in France, Benelux, and Scandinavia—have not diverged the way they have in little ol' postindustrial UK.

It hasn't all been "watching the scenery go past the windows" though, as Dylan describes the touring process. A Danish daily paper ran a front page story attacking Dylan, accusing him of paranoia and claiming he kept a veritable squad of Israeli bodyguards on hand to assuage his fear of assassination. Dylan was so incensed by the story he called an impromptu press conference in north Germany where he denied that John Lennon's slaying had provoked any panic in him.

"I might as easily be run over by a truck or something," went the tone of his reply. I never did see more than a couple of security chaps, backstage or front.

Otherwise, Dylan's European jaunt can be safely judged a success. It didn't even rain at the sometimes optimistically staged open-air shows—aides speak of the way it's, ahem, miraculously stopped raining an hour or so before showtime, recalling some of the talk I'd heard around Marley tours ("he had a voice that could really touch you," Dylan says to me later when he crops up in conversation. The two never actually met however.)

Dylan's strategy on this tour has been to present a set that straddles almost his entire career, harking back to his coffeehouse days on numbers like "Barbara Allen," "Girl from the North Country," and featuring a healthy slug of 60s hits—"Like a Rolling Stone," "Tambourine Man," "It's All Over Now Baby Blue"—and reserving pride of place for his postconversion songs, to which he seems to bring an extra vocal commitment.

Younger Than That Now

• • •

His singing this time round was quite astonishing, clearly superior to all his many past styles, from all of which he borrows for the present. With the horn section of 78 now thankfully nudged out—the present group is more supple and understated—the harmonica has found new favor. Indeed, the acoustic and harp spots were among the most affecting of the show. You could almost hear the audience gasp unbelieving joy everytime he picked up his acoustic guitar, feel them tingle whenever Bob whipped a mouth-harp from a pocket and piped that crazy, angular, plaintive harmonica music of his round the hall.

At a time when conventional rock performance is increasingly derided by many musicians and fans, to Dylan it seems that the performance is the crucible of his art, an all-important testing point.

"It's so immediate it changes the whole concept of art to me," he tells me later.

Hearing him draw from that awesome vault of material he's stockpiled over the last twoscore years, it was impossible not to marvel at the sheer volume and quality of his writing. Never did "Masters of War" sound more apt than in the precipitous war-mongering climate of the present. Other songs—"Like a Rolling Stone" being the obvious one—seemed likewise to acquire a new resonance in the light of Dylan's Christian beliefs.

Dylan's new material continues to reflect his Christianity, though the songs of the new LP, *Shot of Love* are less directly devotional in their approach, taking the Christian code as the bedrock of his observations rather than merely preaching, as *Saved* too often did. Dylan's enthusiasm for his new record is only intermittently contagious, but certainly the album boasts some of his finest work in years, particularly the touching melancholic "Grain of Sand" where Dylan's retrospection over his life leads him to state "no inclination to look back on any mistake/ as I hold this chain of events that I must break."

The new songs—which may or may not be called "Angelina" (a title already fabled among fans) and "Caribbean Wind"—he mentioned in my interview sound exciting, promising a fusion of his 60s sound of the *Blonde on Blonde* era and his 80s sensibilities. One aide spoke of the

174

new songs "being as prophetic in their way as the old ones . . . maybe their real time will be someway ahead in the future."

Whatever one may feel about Dylan's conversion—and the ridicule and depth of scorn to which he has been subjected for his beliefs is unfair—it's obvious that we will need some kind of spiritual dimension to our credo if we really are to build the New Jerusalem among the dark, satanic mills.

For all that, I was a little taken aback when the man took exception to having a "Christian label" attached to him when he has so virulently informed everyone of his religious beliefs. People don't constantly refer to Pete Townshend as a Meher Baba follower because he's always kept his beliefs in context. End of sermon.

In the empty lot backstage in the athlete's changing area, Bert, a Dutch Dylanologist from *Oor* magazine, and I are lined up for our brief audience with Dylan.

"Oh God," comes the unmistakable voice through the open door of the dressing room as an aide reminds him of our impending presence and we catch a glimpse of Dylan pulling on a sock.

A minute later and we're shaking hands with the maestro, who seems as nervous as we are, with the air of a man slowly exhaling the potent adrenaline charge of two hours onstage at the hub of 7,000 people's attention.

His stage threads—black trousers, the satin bomber jacket with its curious golden design—lie limply across a chair, Dylan now wearing a sloppy white sweatshirt, jeans, and training shoes. He looks beefier and stronger than all those "wiry little cat" descriptions of history suggest, more sporty; the scene seems almost collegiate. The eyes are large, washed out electric blue, and riveting, still topped by the great burst of locks.

We chat about the show, which Dylan didn't like—"you couldn't hear anything and the audience was kinda strange, you should have been at last night's show"—and about press reaction to the show. Dylan seems to feel the papers gave him a hard time whatever he does with the old songs: "you just can't win."

Younger Than That Now

I remark that "Maggie's Farm" is a popular song in Britain these days, and Dylan and the bassman, who's also present, exchange blank looks before the bassie tumbles "Maggie Thatcher" and they break into laughter, me wondering about the slow association after a week playing down on the farm itself.

He'd heard about The Specials' version but wasn't familiar with it. He mumbles something about "punk waves and new waves" as he packs his stuff, before offering "I like George's song."

"George?"

"Boy, George's song is great."

Oh, George Harrison. (It transpires the two spent some time together on Dylan's stay, inspiring him to play "Here Comes the Sun" at one Earl's Court gig. One wonders whether they discussed Monty Python's "Life of Brian" which Harrison financed.) I mumble something about whether he thinks the old songs seem to get new meaning in the light of changing times and his new beliefs, and Dylan fixes me with a piercing look.

"I'm different," he says. "The songs are the same.

"The songs don't mean that much to me actually," he continues. "I wrote them and I sing them . . . "

There's nothing from *Desire* or *Street Legal* though.

"We could do a completely different set with completely different songs. They're all old songs, even the ones from *Slow Train* are old now."

"I tell you though, I feel very strongly about this show. I feel it has something to offer. No one else does this show, not Bruce Springsteen or anyone."

Was he surprised at the amount of hostility the conversion to Christianity had brought?

"Not surprised at all. I'm just surprised to hear applause every time I play. I appreciate that. You can feel everything that comes off an audience . . . little individual things that are going on. It's a very instant thing."

Outside the tour bus is ticking over and filling up with musicians and road crew, and one of the gospel quartet is doing a soft shoe shuffle in the rain. Tomorrow, comes the word, is a proper interview, at the hotel. Maybe.

I went to see the gypsy, staying in a big hotel in the center of the town, where the occasional appearance of a denim-clad roadie provides colorful contrast to the assembled gray ranks of German businessmen.

Prematch nerves vanish as I trot out onto the turf of Dylan's fourth-floor suite. To one side, a TV flickers without sound. Dylan wanders in wearing a black leather jacket and white jeans, and we start committing words to tape. He talks slowly, his speaking voice deeper than you'd expect from his singing, and not at all like sand and glue. The replies come carefully considered and usually as evasive and noncommittal as we've come to expect over the years.

NS: Someone told me you'd been working with Smokey Robinson. Is that right?

BD: No . . . we were doing a session, along with Ringo and Willy, as he was rehearsing across the street with his new band, a new show. I'd seen him on the street going in so we went out on a break and said hello.

NS: You didn't work with him?

BD: No.

NS: Are you pleased with the new album?

BD: The last time I heard it I was. I haven't heard it since I left for Chicago. Which was at the beginning of June. I was satisfied enough to leave town.

NS: The sound is a lot rawer. A much looser sound.

BD: Well, I had more control over this record . . . That's the type of record I like to make. I just haven't been able to make them.

Younger Than That Now

NS: Why's that?

BD: Well, usually, I've been working quickly in the studio, and for one reason or another I just get locked into whoever's producing, their sound, and I just wanna get it over with.

NS: Who produced this one?

BD: Chuck (Plotkin) and myself produced it. Bumps Blackwell did *Shot of Love* with me, which he helped with a great deal. You remember him?

NS: No, who's that?

BD: Bumps did all the early Little Richard records and Don and Dewey records; he handled all the speciality records.

NS: That's the rockiest track, right? The rest is bluesy, or some of it has a reggae lilt. Do you still like reggae?

BD: There's not much difference between country and reggae when you take away the bass and the drums; they're very similar.

NS: You've always seemed to have one foot in rock'n'roll, Little Richard and all that, and the other in blues, folk, country, traditions . . .

BD: Well, I love it all, whatever might be popular at the moment.

NS: Do you still do everything in a couple of takes?

BD: On this album we did.

NS: I'd heard you like to work in a very spontaneous way.

BD: With this new band we can usually work very quickly with a new tune.

NS: Is it nearer your "mercurial sound" with this band?

BD: Yeah . . . it's a little hard to produce that onstage of course. The only time we were able to do that was with The Band on those Bob Dylan and The Band tours in the 60s. Because the sound back then was so raw and primitive the sound systems wouldn't give us anything else. And when The Beatles played, you could never hear The Beatles. Even The Stones' people were screaming and there wasn't much sound. You could never hear what you were doing.

NS: I have to ask you about the Lenny Bruce song ("Lenny Bruce is Dead"). You said it was very spontaneous.

BD: That was a really quick song for me to write. I wrote that in about five minutes . . . I didn't even know why I was writing it, it just naturally came out. I wasn't, you know, meditating on Lenny Bruce before I wrote it.

NS: It's a very compassionate song.

BD: It is.

NS: It's in the tradition of your songs about folk heroes like "Hurricane," "George Jackson" . . .

BD: I thought "Joey" was a good song. I know no one said much about it, I thought it was one of those songs that came off and you didn't hear that much about it.

NS: Looking at the other songs on the album there are a lot of criticisms of people in high places. Would you say that's true?

BD: (Laughs) Yeah, that's always true I guess . . . I don't really know, y'know. I'm not sure how it hangs together as a concept because there were some real long songs on this album that we recorded, a couple of really long songs, like there was one we did—do you remember "Visions of Johanna"?

Younger Than That Now

NS: Sure.

BD: Well, there was one like that. I'd never done anything like it before. It's got the same kind of thing to it. It seems to be very sensitive and gentle on one level, then on another level the lyrics aren't sensitive and gentle at all. We left that off the album.

We left another thing off the album which is quite different to anything I wrote, that I think in just a musical kind of way you'd like to hear. And in a lyric-content way it's interesting. The way the story line changes from third person to first person and that person becomes you, then these people are there and they're not there. And then the time goes way back and then it's brought up to the present. And I thought it was really effective, but that again is a long song and when it came to putting the songs on the album we had to cut some, so we cut those. Now what we have left is an album which seems to make its kind of general statement, but it's too soon to say what that general statement is.

NS: There's a reference to "the politics of sin" on "Dead Man."

BD: Yeah, well that's what sin is, politics. It just came to me when I was writing that's the way it is . . . the diplomacy of sin. The way they take sin, and put it in front of people . . . the way that they say this is good and that's bad, you can do this and you can't do that, the way sin is taken and split up and categorized and put on different levels so it becomes more of a structure of sin, or, "these sins are big ones, these are little ones, these can hurt this person, these can hurt you, this is bad for this reason, and that is bad for another reason." The politics of sin; that's what I think of it.

NS: Do you still feel politics is part of the illusion?

BD: I've never really been into politics, mostly I guess because of the world of politics. The people who are into politics as a profession, you know, it's . . . the art of politics hasn't changed much over the years.

Were there politics in Roman times? And are there politics in communist countries? I'm sure there are.

NS: You feel what the world is facing is more of a spiritual crisis?

BD: Oh yeah, definitely. Definitely. People don't know who the enemy
is. They think the enemy is something they can see, and the reality of
the enemy is a spirtual being they can't see, and it influences all they
can see and they don't go to the top, the end line of the real enemy—
like the enemy who's controlling who you think who's your enemy.

NS: Who's that?

BD: What, who you think your enemy is?

NS: Yes.

BD: You would think the enemy is someone you could strike at and
that would solve the problem, but the real enemy is the devil. That's
the real enemy, but he tends to shade himself and hide himself and put
it into people's minds that he's really not there and he's really not so
bad, and that he's got a lot of good things to offer too. So there's this
conflict going, to blind the minds of men.

NS: A conflict in all of us?

BD: Yeah, he puts the conflict there, without him there'd be no conflict.

NS: Maybe that struggle is necessary?

BD: Well, that's a whole other subject . . . yes, I've heard that said too.

NS: When you said "strengthen the things that remain" (from "When
You Gonna Wake Up") what were you thinking of?

Younger Than That Now

BD: Well, the things that remain would be the basic qualities that don't change, the values that do still exist. It says in the bible, "resist not evil, but overcome evil with good." And the values that can overcome evil are the ones to strengthen.

NS: People feel that fighting oppression is more important than spiritual interests.

BD: That's wrong. The struggle against oppression and injustice is always going to be there, but the devil himself is the one who creates it. You can come to know yourself, but you need help in doing it.

But the only one who can overcome all that is the great creator himself. If you can get his help you can overcome it. To do that you must know something about the nature of the creator. What Jesus does for an ignorant man like myself is to make the qualities and characteristics of God more believable to me, 'cause I can't beat the devil. Only God can. He already has. Satan's working everywhere. You're faced with him constantly. If you can't see him he's inside you making you feel a certain way. He's feeding you envy and jealousy, he's feeding you oppression, hatred . . .

NS: Do you feel the only way to know the creator is through Christ?

BD: I feel the only way . . . let me see. Of course you can look on the desert and wake up to the sun and the sand and the beauty of the stars and know there is a higher being, and worship that creator.

But being thrown into the cities you're faced more with man than with God. We're dealing here with man, y'know, and in order to know where man's at you have to know what God would do if he was man. I'm trying to explain to you in intellectual mental terms, when it actually is more of a spiritual understanding than something which is open to debate.

NS: You can't teach people things they don't experience for themselves . . .

BD: Most people think that if God became a man he would go up on a mountain and raise his sword and show his anger and his wrath or his love and compassion in one blow. And that's what people expected the Messiah to be—someone with similar characteristics, someone to set things straight, and here comes a Messiah who doesn't measure up to those characteristics and causes a lot of problems.

NS: Someone who put the responsibility back on us?

BD: Right.

NS: From your songs like "Dead Man" and "When He Returns" it's obvious you believe the second coming is likely in our lifetimes.

BD: Possibly. Possibly at any moment. It could be in our lifetimes. It could be a long time. This earth supposedly has a certain number of years which I think is 7,000 years; 7,000 or 6,000.

We're in the last cycle of it now. Going back to the first century there's like 3,000 years before that and 4,000 after it, one of the two, the last thousand would be the millenium years.

I think that everything that's happened is like a preview of what's going to happen.

NS: How strict is your interpretation of Christianity? The original Christians seems to have a different faith and belief that got lost.

BD: I'm not that much of a historian about Christianity. I know it's been changed over the years but I go strictly according to the gospels.

NS: Have you seen the gnostic gospels?

BD: Some place I have. I don't recall too much about them but I've seen them.

NS: Are you going to make any more movies?

Younger Than That Now

BD: If we can get a story outline we will, I'd like to.

NS: *Renaldo & Clara* was very symbolist, and your songs on *Street Legal* were full of Tarot imagery. Have those interests left you now?

BD: Those particular interests have, yes.

NS: Do you think that "occult" interests like the Tarot are misleading?

BD: I don't know. I didn't get into the Tarot cards all that deeply. I do think they're misleading for people though. You're fixed on something which keeps a hold on you. If you can't or don't understand why you're feeling this way at that moment, with those cards you come up with a comfortable feeling that doesn't have any necessary value.

NS: You were also interested in Judaism at one point. You visited Israel and the Wailing Wall in Jerusalem. Do you feel that your interests at that time are compatible with your present beliefs?

BD: There's really no difference between any of it in my mind. Some people say they're Jews and they never go to a synagogue or anything. I know some gangsters who say they're Jews. I don't know what that's got to do with anything. Judaism is really the laws of Moses. If you follow the laws of Moses you're automatically a Jew I would think.

NS: You've always had a strong religious theme in your songs even before you became a Christian.

BD: (Angrily) I don't really want to walk around with a sign on me saying "Christian."

NS: It might appear that way to a lot of people . . .

BD: Yeah, but a lot of people want to hang a sign on you for whatever. It's like Mick Jagger said, "They wanna hang a sign on you."

NS: In a *Playboy* interview three years ago you said you agreed with Henry Miller's saying that "the purpose of the artist is to inoculate the world with disillusionment." Do you still agree with that?

BD: (Laughs) That's pretty good for Henry Miller . . . maybe that would be good for what he wanted to do. Maybe that's the purpose of his art.

NS: Not yours?

BD: Well, what I do is more of an immediate thing; to stand up on stage and sing—you get it back immediately. It's not like writing a book or even making a record. And with a movie—it's so difficult to get anything back working on a movie, you never know what you're doing and the results never come in until usually years afterwards. What I do is so immediate it changes the nature, the concept, of art to me. I don't know what it is. It's too immediate. It's like the man who made that painting there (points to painting on wall of hotel room) has no idea we're sitting here now looking at it or not looking at it or anything . . . performing is more like a stage play.

NS: You haven't painted your masterpiece yet then?

BD: No. I don't know if I ever will, I've given up thinking about it though.

SUNDAY TIMES, JULY 1, 1984

"Jesus Who's Got Time to Keep Up with the Times?"

Mick Brown

THIS WEEK BOB DYLAN COMES to Britain. The folksinger-cum-folk hero of the 1960s has not always had a good reception here. In 1965 purists attacked him for "going electric." In 1981 his newfound evangelism left many of his fans cold. What should they expect this time? Last week Mick Brown had an exclusive interview.

Bob Dylan tugged at a cigarette, stroked the beginnings of an untidy beard and gazed pensively at the stream of traffic passing down the Madrid street. "What you gotta understand," he said at length, "is that I do something because I feel like doing it. If people can relate to it, that's great; if they can't, that's fine too. But I don't think I'm gonna be really understood until maybe 100 years from now. What I've done, what I'm doing, nobody else does or has done."

The messianic tone grew more intense. "When I'm dead and gone maybe people will realize that, and then figure it out. I don't think anything I've done has been evenly mildly hinted at. There's all these interpreters around, but they're not interpreting anything except their own ideas. Nobody's come close."

Younger Than That Now

But a lot of people, it seems, still want to. Bob Dylan may no longer sell records in the consistently enormous quantities he once did—a fact to which he will allow a tinge of regret—but his capacity to hold his audience in thrall seems undiminished.

By the time Bob Dylan arrives in Britain this week for performances at St. James's Park, Newcastle, on Tuesday and Wembley Stadium on Saturday, he will already have performed to almost half a million people throughout Europe—half a million people singing the chorus of "Blowin' In The Wind," an esperanto that is as much a testament to Dylan's abiding influence and charisma as the insatiable interest of the world's press in his activities.

This interest is equaled only by Dylan's determination to keep his own counsel whenever possible. As Bill Graham, the tour's garrulous American promoter and Dylan's closest adviser, keeps reminding you, Bob "is not your everyday folksinger."

All the German magazine *Stern* had wanted to do was touch base for five minutes in return for a front cover. Dylan declined. The press conference that he had been persuaded to hold in Verona, attended by 150 excitable European journalists, had been a fiasco: photographers barred, and the first question from the floor—"What are your religious views nowadays?"—met by Dylan irritably brushing the table in front of him, as if to sweep aside that and all other questions to follow.

"I mean, nobody cares what Billy Joel's religious views are, right?" he tells me with a wry smile. "what does it matter to people what Bob Dylan is? But it seems to, right? I'd honestly like to know why it's important to them."

One expects many things of Bob Dylan, but such playful ingenuousness is not one of them.

Dylan protects himself well, not with bodyguards but with a smokescreen of privacy and elusiveness of the sort that encourages speculation and myth. Meeting him involves penetrating a frustrating maze of "perhapses" and "maybes," of cautions and briefings—suggestive of dealing with fine porcelain—culminating in a telephone call summoning you to an anonymous cafeteria filled with Spanish families who give not a second glance to the figure in a Hawaiian shirt and straw hat who at last comes ambling through the door.

He is surprisingly genial, youthful for his 43 years, lean, interested and alert, who treats the business of being Bob Dylan with an engagingly aw-shucks kind of bemusement.

It was in striking contrast to the apparition Dylan had presented the previous night, onstage in front of 25,000 people in a Madrid football stadium, his black smock coat, high boots and hawkish profile suggesting some avenging backwoods preacher.

The emphasis in his performance has shifted from the overtly evangelical songs heard in Dylan's last visit to Britain three years ago. Now it spans every phase of his 21-year career. The themes of social protest, personal love, and religious faith have never been more of a piece. Dylan remains what he has always been, an uncompromising moralist. And to hear songs such as "Masters Of War," "A Hard Rain's A Gonna Fall" (about nuclear war), and "Maggie's Farm" (about rebellious labor) invested with fresh nuances of meaning, not to say vitriol, is to realize that, while the sentiments may have become unfashionable in popular music, they are no less pertinent. Nobody else is writing songs like Bob Dylan. Nobody ever did.

"For me, none of the songs I've written has really dated," he says. "They capture something I've never been able to improve on, whatever their statement is. A song like 'Maggie's Farm'—I could feel like that just the other day, and I could feel the same tomorrow. People say they're 'nostalgia,' but I don't know what that means really. A Tale of Two Cities was written 100 years ago; is that nostalgia? This term 'nostalgia,' it's just another way people have of dealing with you and putting you some place they think they understand. It's just another label."

Labels exercise Bob Dylan greatly. People have been trying to put them on him since he started, he says, "and not one of them has ever made any sense."

The furor about his religious beliefs puzzled him most of all, "like I was running for pope or something." When the word first spread that he had eschewed Judaism and embraced Christianity, and he toured America in 1979 singing overtly religious songs, the most hostile reception came not from rock audiences but when he played university campuses, "and the so-called intellectual students showed their true monstrous selves."

"Born-again Christians" is just another label, he says. He had attended bible school in California for three months, and the book was never far from his side, but the idea that faith was a matter of passing through one swing door and back out another struck him as ridiculous. "I live by a strict disciplinary code, you know, but I don't know how moral that is or even where it comes from really. These things just become part of your skin after a while; you get to know what line not to step over—usually because you stepped over it before and were lucky to get back."

Was he an ascetic? Dylan lit another cigarette and asked what the word meant. "I don't think so. I still have desires, you know, that lead me around once in a while. I don't do things in excess, but everybody goes through those times. They either kill you, or make you a better person."

By this time in the conversation it did not seem awkward to ask: did he believe in evil?

"Sure I believe in it. I believe that ever since Adam and Eve got thrown out of the garden that the whole nature of the planet has been heading in one direction—towards apocalypse. It's all there in the Book of Revelations, but it's difficult talking about these things to most people because most people don't know what you're talking about, or don't want to listen.

"What it comes down to is that there's a lot of different gods in the world against the god—that's what it's about. There's a lot of different gods that people are subjects of. There's the god of mammon. Corporations are gods. Governments? No, governments don't have much to do with it anymore, I don't think. Politics is a hoax. The politicians don't have any real power. They feed you all this stuff in the newspapers about what's going on, but that's not what's really going on.

190

"But then again, I don't think that makes me a pessimistic person. I'm a realist. Or maybe a surrealist. But you can't beat your head against the wall forever."

He had never, he said, been a utopian: that was always a foreign term to him, something to do with moving to the country, living communally, and growing rice and beans. "I mean, I wanted to grow my own rice and beans—still do—but I never felt part of that movement."

But he could still look back on the 1960s with something approaching affection. "I mean, the Kennedys were great-looking people, man, they had style." He smiles. "America is not like that anymore. But what happened, happened so fast that people are still trying to figure it out. The TV media wasn't so big then. It's like the only thing people knew was what they knew; then suddenly people were being told what to think, how to behave, there's too much information.

'"It just got suffocated. Like Woodstock—that wasn't about anything. It was just a whole new market for tie-dyed T-shirts. It was about clothes. All those people are in computers now."

This was beyond him. He had never been good with numbers, and had no desire to stare at a screen. "I don't feel obliged to keep up with the times. I'm not going to be here that long anyway. So I keep up with these times, then I gotta keep up with the 90s. Jesus, who's got time to keep up with the times?"

It is at moments such as this that Dylan—once, misleadingly perhaps, characterized as a radical—reveals himself as much of a traditionalist; an adherent of Biblical truths; a firm believer in the family and the institution of marriage—despite his own divorce from his wife, Sara; a man disenchanted with many of the totems and values of modern life, mass communications, the vulgarity of popular culture, the "sameness" of everything. Personally he had been reading Cicero, Machiavelli, and John Stuart Mill. Contemporary literature? "Oh yeah, I read a detective story, but I can't remember what it was called."

"At least in the 1960s it seemed there was room to be different.

Younger Than That Now

For me, my particular scene, I came along at just the right time, and I understood the times I was in. If I was starting out right now I don't know where I'd get the inspiration from, because you need to breathe the right air to make the creative process work. I don't worry about it so much for me; I've done it; I can't complain. But the people coming up, the artists and writers, what are they gonna do, because these are the people who change the world."

Nowadays, he admits, he finds writing harder than ever. A song like "Masters of War" he would dispatch in 15 minutes, and move onto the next one without a second thought. "If I wrote a song like that now I wouldn't feel I'd have to write another one for two weeks. There's still things I want to write about, but the process is harder. The old records I used to make, by the time they came out I wouldn't even want them released because I was already so far beyond them."

Much of his time nowadays is spent traveling. He was in Jerusalem last autumn for his son Jesse's bar-mitzvah—"his grand-mother's idea," he smiles. Israel interests him from "a biblical point of view," but he had never felt that atavistic Jewish sense of home-coming. In fact he lives principally on his farm in Minnesota, not far from the town of Hibbing where he spent his adolescence. Then there is the domed house in Malibu, California, originally built to accommodate his five children—good schools nearby, he says—but which he has seldom used since his divorce, and a 63ft sailing boat with which he cruises the Caribbean "when I can't think of anything else to do."

He had never contemplated retirement: the need to make money was not a factor—he is a wealthy man—but the impulse to continue writing was. "There's never really been any glory in it for me," he says. "Being seen in the places and having everybody put their arms around you, I never cared about any of that. I don't care what people think. For me, the fulfilment was always in just doing it. That's all that really matters."

As the conversation had progressed, more and more people had realized who the man in the straw hat was. A steady stream had made their way to his table, scraps of paper in hand. Dylan had signed them all, with a surprisingly careful deliberation—almost as if he was practicing—but his discomfort at being on view was becoming more apparent. As peremptorily as he arrived, Bob Dylan made his excuses and left.

The Bono Vox Interview

Bono Vox

Slane Castle *and* Hot Press: *two of the enduring institutions of modern Irish popular culture.* Hot Press, *Ireland's first rock culture magazine, was just six years old when, in 1981, the legendary Irish band Thin Lizzy headlined the first ever rock festival in the natural amphitheatre of Slane Castle, a stately pile of land sweeping down to the river Boyne, about 50 miles from Dublin. That Lizzy concert was notable too for the appearance further down the bill of a then rising young Dublin four-piece by the name of U2. One year later, in the summeer of 1982, Slane Castle's place on the international rock festival map as confirmed with an appearance by the Rolling Stones in front of a crowd estimated at 80,000 strong. Since then, the field below the Castle has played host to many of the biggest names in rock, including Bruce Springsteen, Queen, REM, Guns N' Roses, David Bowie, and, perhaps most memorable of all, U2 themselves, who returned home as world-conquering heroes to play two massive shows at the venue in 2001. But back in 1984, that level of success was still ahead of U2 when Bob Dylan arrived in Ireland to headline that year's Slane Festival. A friend of* Hot Press, *as well as one of it's cover stars, since U2's inception, frontman*

Younger Than That Now

Bono willingly donned a guest reporter's hat to file this account of a backstage meeting with Dylan and Van Morrison, two veterans of the sixties who had briefly collaborated on stage that day during Dylan's performance. And who, clearly, as the transcript reveals, had some words of wisdom for a young singer who would himself go on to become one of the most recognizable rock icons of the 80s, 90s, and the new millennium.

------*·*------

BONO: You have been to Ireland before, haven't you?

DYLAN: Yeah, I was in Belfast and in Dublin, and we traveled around a little bit too.

BONO: Have you ever spent any time here? Have you ever been here on holiday?

DYLAN: Yeah, well, when I was here, we traveled by car, so we stayed in different places—but Irish music has always been a great part of my life because I used to hang out with the Clancy Brothers. They influenced me tremendously.

BONO: Yeah, they have so much balls as a sound, you know, when they sing, it's like punk rock.

Dylan: Yeah, they were playing clubs as big as this room right here and the place—you couldn't put a pin in it, it would be so packed with people.

BONO: You could smell their breath?

DYLAN: Yeah!

BONO: I bet you could. They blow you over with their lungs! God, I'd love to sing like that.

DYLAN: Yeah, I spent years with them running around, 61, 62, 63.

BONO: Greenwich Village?

DYLAN: All over the place, I played on the same bill with them once.

BONO: Get their autographs? (laughs)

DYLAN: No, I didn't get their autograph. But you know one of the things I recall from that time is how great they all were—I mean there is no question, but that they were great. But Liam Clancy was always my favorite singer, as a ballad singer. I just never heard anyone as good, and that includes Barbara Streisand and Pearl Bailey.

BONO: You got to be careful here!

DYLAN: He's just a phenomenal ballad singer.

BONO: Yeah, you know what I envy of you is that my music, and the music of U2 is like, it's in space somewhere. There is no particular musical roots or heritage that we plug into. In Ireland there is a tradition, but I've never plugged into it. It's like as if we're caught in space. There's a few groups now who are caught in space . . .

DYLAN: Well, you have to reach back.

BONO: We never did play a 12 bar.

DYLAN: You have to reach! There's another group I used to listen to called the McPeake Family. I don't know if you ever heard of them?

BONO: The McPeake Family! I'd love to have heard of them, with a name like that.

DYLAN: They are great. Paddy Clancy recorded them. He had a label called Tradition Records, and he used to bring back these records; they recorded for Prestige at the time, and Tradition Records, his company. They were called The McPeake family. They were even more rural than the Clancy Brothers. The Clancy Brothers had always that touch of commerciality to them—you didn't mind it, but it was still there, whereas the McPeake Family sang with harps. The old man, he played the harp—and it was that (gestures) big—and the drums.

BONO: Were they a real family?

DYLAN: Yeah, they were a real family; if you go to a record store and as for a McPeake Family record, I don't know, I'm sure you could still get them in a lot of places.

BONO: Have you heard of an Irish group that are working now in this middle ground between traditional and contemporary music called Clannad? Clannad is Gaelic for family, and they've made some very powerful pieces of music, including a song called "Theme From Harry's Game," it's from a film, and it knocked over everyone in Europe. It didn't get played in the US. It's just vocal and they used some low bass frequencies in it as well—it's just beautiful. They're a family, they come from Donegal, and have worked from that same base of traditional music.

DYLAN: There's a group you have here, what's it called, Plankston?

BONO: Planxty.

DYLAN: They're great!

BONO: Another rock'n'roll band!

DYLAN: Yeah, but when I think of what's happening—I think they're great.

BONO: There's another group called De Dannan. The name De Dannan has something to do with with the lost tribes of Dan. You heard of the disappearing tribe of Dan? They say they came from Ireland.

DYLAN: Yeah, I've heard that, I've heard that.

BONO: I'm not a musicologist or expert in this area, but it would appear that this is true. Also, you know they say the Irish musical scale has no roots in Europe whatsoever, rather it comes from Africa and India. The Cartesian people, the Egyptian people, what gave them supremacy in the Middle East was the sail they developed. I forget what they call it, I forget the name of the sail, but this sail allowed them to become successful seafarers and traders and they dominated as a result of their reading, and that same sail which was used on those boats, is used on the West of Ireland.

DYLAN: Is that right?

BONO: Bob Quinn made a film called *Atlanteans* in which this theory was elaborated. He suggests that the book of Kells, which is a manuscript, part of it has it's roots in Coptic script, not in Europe. It's not a European thing at all—it's linked from Africa, Spain, Brittany, and Ireland, because that was a sea route. I'm not an expert. I shouldn't be talking about it really. But it's of interest when you think of it.

DYLAN: Sure it is.

BONO: I might be able to send you over some tapes of that actually.

DYLAN: I'd like to have them. You know Planxty? I also like Paul Brady a lot.

BONO: Yeah, he's great. He's a real songwriter. Tell me—have you ever approached a microphone, not with words, but just to sing? I had to do this as a necessity once when some lyrics of mine were stolen—and I learnt to sing on the microphone just singing and working the words into it later. I find when I put a pen in my hand it gets in the way! Do you have words first?

DYLAN: I do at certain times.

BONO: In Portland, Oregon a number of years ago two pretty girls walked in the dressing room, smiled, and walked out with some of our songs, in a briefcase.

DYLAN: I used to have that happen to me all the time, except they used to take clothes!

BONO: Is that right?

DYLAN: They used to take all my best clothes, but never took my songs.

BONO: After that we had to go in to record our second LP, *October*, without any songs—there was a lot of pressure. Having to sing under that stress without any words, I found out a lot of things about myself that I didn't even know were there. I'd wondered, had some of the things that have come out of you ever been a surprise to you?

DYLAN: That usually happens at concerts or shows I'm doing, more than recording studios. Also, I never sit around, I usually play . . . I'll play my guitar, rather than just have something to say, to express myself. I can express it better with my guitar.

BONO: I wondered had the songs that you were writing ever frightened you in some way?

DYLAN: Oh yeah, I've written some songs that did that. The songs that I wrote for the *Slow Train* album did that. I wrote those songs. I didn't plan to write them, but I wrote them anyway. I didn't like writing them, I didn't want to write them. I didn't figure . . . I just didn't want to write them songs at that period of time. But I found myself writing these songs and after I had a certain amount of them, I thought I didn't want to sing them, so I had a girl sing them for me at the time, and what I wanted to do was . . . she's a great singer. . . .

BONO: Who is this?

DYLAN: A girl I was singing with at the time, Carolyn Dennis her name was. I gave them all to her and had her record them, and not even put my name on them. But I wanted the songs out; I wanted them out, but *I* didn't want to do it because I knew that it wouldn't be perceived in that way. It would just mean more pressure. I just did not want that at that time.

BONO: But are you a troublemaker? Is there something in you that wants trouble that an album like *Slow Train* stirs up? Do you wanna fight? Do you wanna box!?

DYLAN: I don't know! I mean, I wanna piss people off once in a while, but boxing or fighting—it would be an exercise to do it. You know, I love to do it, but not with anything at stake.

BONO: Chess, do you play chess?

DYLAN: Yeah, I play chess. Are you a chess player?

BONO: I am a chess player.

DYLAN: I'm not that good actually.

BONO: I'll challenge you to a game of chess.

DYLAN: I don't have it right now actually, I just don't have one on me, but the next time you see me!

Younger Than That Now

BONO: Oh, you can get these little ones you know, that you can carry around.

DYLAN: Yeah, I take them on tour all the time, but nobody in the band will play me.

BONO: Really?

DYLAN: Yeah, they say it's an ego trip. They say I want to win, I don't want to win, I just like to play.

BONO: When you put out a record that causes trouble—is it part of an overall plan, or do you just do it?

DYLAN: No, I don't ever put out a record to cause trouble—if it causes trouble, it causes trouble, that's apart from me. If it causes trouble, that's other people's problem. It's not my problem. I'm just not going to put out a record that I just feel—you know, if I feel like I'm inspired to make a statement, I'll make that statement. But what happens after I do it, I don't care about that.

BONO: What's your opening game?

DYLAN: My opening game, you mean king's pawn up two—and all that? I don't know.

BONO: You just takes it as it comes.

DYLAN: Yeah. I don't really play that seriously.

BONO: Well, I thought I did until I played Adam's brother Sebastian— he was only about 13 years old and he beat me!

DYLAN: Somebody may have a chess game here.

BONO: I'd love to play.

[Searching for a chess board . . . enter Van Morrison]

BONO: You haven't used any synthesizers on your records so far?

DYLAN: No, I've never used those machines.

BONO: The Fairlight Music Computer—have you heard of that?

DYLAN: Fairlight?

BONO: Van, what do you think of electronic music?

MORRISON: I like the music Brian Eno plays.

BONO: He speaks very highly of you. He's producing our record right now.

MORRISON: Say hello.

BONO: (to Bob) Do you know Brian Eno?

DYLAN: Brian Eno? I don't know Brian Eno, but I know some of his work.

BONO: When you're working with a producer, do you give him the lee-way to challenge you?

DYLAN: Yeah, if he feels like it. But usually we just go into the studio and sing a song, and play the music, and have, you know . . .

BONO: Have you had somebody in the last five years who said, "That's crap, Bob"?

DYLAN: Oh, they say that all the time!

Younger Than That Now

BONO: Mark Knopfler, did he say that?

DYLAN: I don't know, they spend time getting their various songs right, but with me, I just take a song into the studio and try to rehearse it, and then record it, and then do it. It's a little harder now though to make a good record—even if you've got a good song and a good band. Even if you go in and record it live, it's not gonna sound like it used to sound, because the studios now are so modern, and overly developed, that you can take anything good and you can press it and squeeze it and squash it, and constipate it and suffocate it. You do a great performance in the studio and you listen back to it because the speakers are all so good, but, ah, no!

BONO: All technology does is—you go into a dead room with dead instruments and you use technology to give it life that it doesn't have, and then it comes out of the speakers and you believe it. What I've been trying to do is find a room that has life in itself.

DYLAN: Yeah.

BONO: A "living" room.

DYLAN: The machines though, can even take the life out of that room, I've found. You can record in St. Peter's Cathedral, you know, and they still make it sound like, eh, . . .

BONO: Somebody's backyard.

DYLAN: Yeah.

DYLAN: That's a good idea. I'd love to record in a cathedral.

DYLAN: You know the studios in the old days were all much better, and the equipment so much better, there's no question about it in my mind. You just walked into a studio, they were just big rooms, you just sang, you know, you just made records; and they sounded like the way they sounded there. That stopped happening in the late sixties, for me anyway. I noticed the big change. You go into a studio now and they got rugs on the floor, settees and pinball machines and videos and sandwiches coming every ten minutes. It's a big expensive party and you're lucky if you come out with anything that sounds decent.

BONO: Yeah, records haven't got better, have they?

DYLAN: No, you go in now, you got your producer, you got your engineer, you got your assistant engineer, usually your assistant producer, you got a guy carrying the tapes around. I mean, you know, there's a million people go into recording just an acoustic song on your guitar. The boys turn the machines on and it's a great undertaking.

BONO: There's a system called Effanel which Mick Fleetwood from Fleetwood Mac brought to Africa. It was built for him because he wanted to get some real African drummin' for "Tusk." We've used that system. It comes in a light suitcase, very small, no bullshit studio, and it just arrives, you can literally bring it to your living room.

MORRISON: I think all the same they'll go back to 2-track eventually.

BONO: There's a guy called Conny Plank, who lives in Germany. He's a producer I think. He produced Makem and Clancy and some Irish traditional bands, also orchestral and funnily enough a lot of the new electronic groups, DAF, Ultravox, and so on. He used to record orchestras by just finding a position in the room where they were already balanced and he applies this in his thinking, in recording modern music: he finds a place in the room where it's already mixed.

MORRISON: I don't know, when I started we didn't think about that! You didn't even think about recording . . . (laughs)

BONO: You didn't even think!

Younger Than That Now

MORRISON: You didn't even know what was on the cards. One day you were in the room, they turned the tape on. After about eight hours or so, they'd say, "OK, tea break, it's over."

DYLAN: Yeah, next song, next song!

MORRISON: And that was that—it was an album.

DYLAN: Yeah, you'd make an album on three days or four days and it was over—if that many! It's that long now . . . it takes four days to get a drum sound.

BONO: Do you know the Monty Python team, they're comedians, British comedians, "Monty Python and the Holy Grail." They have a sketch that reminds me of you guys—sitting back talking of days gone by: "You tell that to the young people of today and they'd never believe you." But you can't go backwards, you must go forward. You try to bring the values that were back there, you know, the strength, and if you see something that was lost, you got to find a new way to capture that same strength. Have you any idea of how to do that? I think you've done it by the way . . . I think "Shot Of Love," that opening track has that.

DYLAN: I think so too. You're one of the few people to say that to me about that record, to mention that record to me.

BONO: That has *that* feeling.

DYLAN: It's a great record, it suits just about everybody.

BONO: The sound from that record makes me feel like I'm in the same room as the other musicians. I don't feel like they're over *there*. Some of our records, I feel like they're over there because we got into this cinema type sound, not bland like FM sound, but we got into this very broad sound. Now we're trying to focus more of a punch, and that's what we are after, this intimacy. . . . I've never interviewed any-body before, by the way. I hate being interviewed myself.

MORRISON: You're doing a good job!

BONO: Is this OK? Good! What records do you listen to?

DYLAN: What records do I listen to? New records? I don't know, just the old records really. Robert Johnson. I still listen to those records that I listened to when I was growing up—they really changed my life. They still change my life. They still hold up, you know. The Louvain Brothers, Hank Williams, Muddy Waters, Howlin' Wolf, Charlie Patton, I always liked to listen to him.

BONO: I just bought Woody Guthrie's *Bound For Glory*. I'm just a beginner when it comes to America. I mean, it's changed me. When you go to the US, coming from this country, it's more than a different continent. . . .

MORRISON: It's shell shock.

BONO: Yeah, coming from troubled Ireland, it's the real shell shock! I'm just getting acquainted with American music and literature. Do you still see Allen Ginsberg?

DYLAN: I run across Allen from time to time, yeah, Gregory Corsos's back now, he's doing some readings, I think he's just published a new book.

BONO: I've just been reading this book *Howl*.

DYLAN: Oh, that's very powerful. That's another book that changed me. *Howl, On the Road, Dharma Bums*.

MORRISON: (to Bono) Have you read *On the Road*?

Younger Than That Now

BONO: Yes I have, I'm just starting that. You have a reference in one of your songs to John Donne, "Rave On John Donne." Have you read his poetry?

MORRISON: I was reading it at the time.

DYLAN: (to Bono) You heard the songs—Brendan Behan's songs?

BONO: Yeah.

DYLAN: "Royal Canal," you know "Royal Canal"?

MORRISON: His brother wrote it. His name is Dominic.

DYLAN: Oh, Dominic wrote "Royal Canal"?

BONO: You know Brendan's son hangs out around here in Dublin. He's a good guy, I believe.

DYLAN: I know the solo lyrics to "Royal Canal." I used to sing it all the time.

BONO: How does it go?

DYLAN: (sings) "The hungry feeling came over me stealing, as the mice were squalling in my prison cell."

BONO: That's right, yeah!

DYLAN: (continues) "That old triangle went jingle jangle, all along the banks of the Royal Canal."

BONO: That's right, when did you read that?

DYLAN: (there's no way stopping him now) "In the female prison there's seventy women. It's all over there that I want to dwell. And that old triangle goes jingle jangle, all along the banks of the Royal Canal."

BONO: Have you been to the Royal Canal?

DYLAN: No I used to sing that song though. Every night.

BONO: Our music—as I was saying earlier—it doesn't have those roots.

MORRISON: Yeah, there was a break in the lineage. I sussed that out when I went to see Thin Lizzy years ago, the first night in L.A. and I was watching at the back of the stage and I realized that the music was a complete cut in the connection between the end of the sixties and the middle of the seventies—a severing of the traditional lineage of groups.

BONO: I like to know more about roots music. I'm hungry for a past.

MORRISON: You know you should listen to some of that stuff.

BONO: I will. I've been listening to some gospel music, you know, like the Swan Silvertones, and stuff like that.

DYLAN: That's US stuff though.

MORRISON: US stuff, but the British stuff you should listen to, you know, like some of the old stuff, like the Yardbirds.

BONO: Yeah, I've got some of their tapes recently, some real good tapes.

DYLAN: You can still hear the McPeakes. The next generation may not be able to though. Who knows? I would hate to think that. Listen we're gonna have to get ready to play. Are you gonna stay for the show?

BONO: Certainly, that's what I'm here for actually.

DYLAN: To record it, ha!

LOS ANGELES TIMES, NOVEMBER 17, 1985

Bob Dylan:
Still A-Changin'

Robert Hilburn

MAYBE IT'S BECAUSE HE DID NOT give interviews at all for years, or maybe it is just that he is the most important songwriter of the modern pop era, but I cannot imagine passing up the chance to talk to Bob Dylan—even if strings are attached.

The interview invitation from Columbia Records suggested that Dylan only wanted to discuss his latest album: *Empire Burlesque*, the studio collection from last summer and *Biograph*, the ambitious retrospective set that just hit the stores.

Dylan himself quickly cut the strings. He showed little interest in those subjects as he sat on a chair in the backyard of his Malibu home.

"The new releases?" Dylan asked almost sheepishly, "I hope you don't make this look like some carny trying to hawk his own records. I don't know if you even want to hit on the records. When people think of me, they are not necessarily going to buy the latest record, anyway. They may buy a record from years ago. Besides I don't think interviews sell records."

So why did Dylan agree to a

series of interviews, including his first formal network TV interview (for *20/20*)?

"I really haven't had that much connection or conversation (over the years) with the people at Columbia" he said, referring to his record label for most of two decades. "Usually I turn in my records, and they release them. But they really like this record (*Empire Burlesque*), so they asked me to do some videos and a few interviews to draw attention to it."

"But that doesn't mean I want to sit around and talk about the record. I haven't even listened to it since it came out. I'd rather spend my time working on new songs or listen to other people's records. Have you heard the new Hank Williams album, the collection of old demo tapes? It's great."

About the project, Dylan said: "Columbia wanted to put out (a retrospective) album on me a few years ago. They had pulled out everything (from earlier albums) that could be classified as love songs and had it on one collection. I didn't care one way or another, but I had a new record coming out, so I asked them not to do it then."

"I guess it's OK for someone who has never heard of me and is looking for a crash course or something. But I've got a lot of stuff that is lying around all over the place in cassette recorders that I'd put out if I was putting the set together."

One thing about *Biograph* that does please Dylan is a 36-page booklet written by Cameron Crowe, who wrote numerous *Rolling Stone* magazine profiles and the book and then the screenplay *Fast Times at Ridgemont High*. The *Biograph* text is a brief, affectionate look at Dylan's life with generous quotes from the songwriter.

Dylan, 44, is not being open just to the press these days. For years he has tended to be isolated even when doing a benefit concert— avoiding photographers and, often, other artists backstage by arriving just before showtime and leaving quickly after the last number.

At September's Farm Aid benefit at the University of Illinois, however, he was almost leisurely hanging out with Tom Petty, whose band backed him on the show, and chatting with other performers including Randy Newman, Lou Reed, and Emmylou Harris. Normally camera-shy, Dylan did not even turn away when a TV crew and a few photographers pointed their lenses at him as he sat on steps outside his dressing room trailer.

One reason for the naturalness, a backstage observer joked at Farm Aid, was that Dylan wanted to prove—after his disastrously spacey performance with the Stones' Keith Richard and Ron Wood at Live Aid —that he still had his faculties.

"Yeah," Dylan grumped about July's Live Aid concert in Philadelphia, "They screwed around with us. We didn't even have any (sound) monitors out there. When they threw in the grand finale at the last moment, they took all the settings off and set the stage up for the 30 people who were standing behind the curtain. We couldn't even hear our own voices (out front), and when you can't hear, you can't play; you don't have any timing. It's like proceeding on radar."

Dylan's Malibu home, on a bluff overlooking the ocean, is quite secluded and a guard shack at the only entrance to the property keeps the curious away. The atmosphere is rural. A dirt driveway runs through the property, and lots of small animals, including chickens and a few large dogs roam around.

On this cool afternoon, Dylan was wearing the same outfit that he has always seemed to be wearing in recent years: jeans looking as if they were ready for the hamper, a wrinkled T-shirt, and motorcycle boots. Except for Europe last year, he has not toured much in the 80s. Still he is on the road so much—Minnesota, New York, London, or some more isolated exotic places—that he does not really call any place home.

"I'm just not the kind of person who seems to be able to settle down," he said as two dogs edged against his chair. "If I'm in L.A. for say, two months, I'll be in the studio for maybe a month out of that time, putting down ideas for songs."

"On the other days I'm usually recuperating from being in the studio. I usually stay in a long time, all night, part of the day. Then I'll go off to New York or London and do the same thing. I'm going to London soon to work on some stuff with Dave Stewart."

Stewart, one half of the Eurythmics, joined Dylan on guitar on the "Emotionally Yours" video.

Younger Than That Now

Dylan expects to concentrate on performance videos because he has not been pleased with concert clips based upon his songs—either the arty "Jokerman" video or more conventional narrative of "Tight Connection to My Heart."

He would probably just as soon not do videos at all, but realizes their importance in the marketplace.

"It used to be that people would buy a record if they liked what they heard on the radio, but video has changed a lot of that," he said. "If someone comes along now with a new song, people talk about 'Well, what does it look like?' It is like 'I saw this new song.'"

One continuing question for Dylan is his much-publicized "born-again" Christian phase. He has said he does not like the term "born-again," and his music has moved away from the aggressive dogma of the *Slow Train Coming* album. But Dylan still refuses to define his exact religion.

"I fell like pretty soon I am going to write about that," he said. "I feel like I got something to say but more than you can say in a few paragraphs in a newspaper."

He did smile at the mention of the hostile reactions generated during his "born-again" Christian tours of 1979 and 1980. "If you make people jump on any level, I think it is worthwhile, because people are so asleep."

Beyond music, Dylan's special interest these days is art. He maintains an artist's studio behind his Malibu house and showed off his character sketches, with the nervous excitement of a proud parent. He hopes to put them in a book and write something to go with each drawing. Dylan is also thinking about a book of short stories. "That may sound presumptuous," he said, "but there are a lot of things, I'd like to say that I can't say in songs."

On his continued energy he said: "It's kinda funny. When I see my name anywhere, it's (often) the '60s this or the '60s that. I can't figure out sometimes if people think I'm dead or alive."

This man who has been hounded, dissected, idolized, and ridiculed over the years, stepped outside the studio. The sun had set and the dogs raced over to him. He paused—as if searching for a summary statement.

"I've had some personal ups and downs, but usually things have been pretty good for me," he finally said. "I don't feel old," but I remember in my 20s (when) I'd think about people in their 30s as old. The thing I really notice now is time."

"Things used to go a lot slower. The days now go by so very fast. But I've never felt numb (about life). There is something about the chords, the sound of them that makes you feel alive. As long as you can play music, I believe you'll feel alive."

SPIN, DECEMBER 1985

Bob Dylan Not Like a Rolling Stone Interview

Scott Cohen

Don't Ask Me Nothin' About Nothin', I Just Might Tell You The Truth Bob Dylan, in perhaps his most revealing interview in years, proves there's nothing more mysterious than a normal musical genius.

Who's Who, What's What, and Why

In this issue we publish what is possibly Bob Dylan's most candid interview ever. Scott Cohen spent several days with Dylan in California and then stayed in constant touch with him for the following two weeks as they added to the story. Starting on page 36, it is the largest interview we've ever run.

*Don't Ask Me
Nothin' About Nothin'
I Might Just Tell
You The Truth*

BOB DYLAN, POET LAUREATE, PROPHET in a motorcycle jacket. Mystery tramp. Napoleon in rags.

Younger Than That Now

A Jew. A Christian. A million contradictions. A complete unknown, like a rolling stone. He's been analyzed, classified, categorized, crucified, defined, dissected, detected, inspected, and rejected, but never figured out. He blew into mythology in 1961 with a guitar, harmonica, and corduroy cap, a cross between Woody Guthrie and Little Richard. He was like the first punk folksinger. He introduced the protest song to rock. He made words more important than melody, more important than the beat. His smoky, nasal voice and sexy phrasings are unique. He can write surreal songs with a logic all their own—like a James Rosenquist painting or a Rimbaud prose poem—and simple, straight-from-the-heart ballads with equal ease. He can take the dark out of the nighttime and paint the daytime black. He probably could have been the biggest sex symbol since Elvis, had he chosen to. Then Mick Jagger came along. The Stones, the Beatles, Jim Morrison, Janis Joplin, Jimi Hendrix, all paid him their due. The radical Weathermen took their name from him. He caused a riot at the 1965 Newport Folk Festival when he went on-stage and played electric rock. The folk faction thought he sold out. Later, during the height of "flower power," when everyone was getting into Eastern religion, Dylan went to Jerusalem, to the Wailing Wall, wearing a yarmulke. A decade later he was a born-again Christian, or so it seemed, putting out gospel records. People discovered that he really wasn't where it's at. It's not like Dylan suddenly got less political or more spiritual. Biblical references have always been in his songs. People have been calling him a visionary for years. Who knows? Suppose a spiritual revolution is going on and rock 'n' roll's just a prelude to something else. Who would make a better prophet than Dylan? Sometimes, what looks large from a distance, close up ain't never that big. Dylan's like one of his lines. He lives pretty simply, in a nice house on secluded property on the California coast, with a bunch of chickens, horses, and dogs. The fact that he's more visible now and doing ordinary things, like the Grammies, videos, even this interview, doesn't make him any less mysterious. It adds to it.

You Want to Talk to Me, Go Ahead and Talk
A lot of people from the press want to talk to me, but they never do,

and for some reason there's this great mystery, if that's what it is. They put it on me. It sells newspapers, I guess. News is a business. It really has nothing to do with me personally, so I really don't keep up with it. When I think of mystery, I don't think about myself. I think of the universe, like why does the moon rise when the sun falls? Caterpillars turn into butterflies? I really haven't remained a recluse. I just haven't talked to the press over the years because I've had to deal with personal things and usually they take priority over talking about myself. I stay out of sight if I can. Dealing with my own life takes priority over other people dealing with my life. I mean, for instance, if I got to get the landlord to fix the plumbing, or get some guy to put up money for a movie, or if I just feel I'm being treated unfairly, then I need to deal with this by myself and not blab it all over to the newspapers. Other people knowing about things confuses the situation, and I'm not prepared for that. I don't like to talk about myself. The things I have to say about such things as ghetto bosses, salvation and sin, lust, murderers going free, and children without hope—messianic kingdom-type stuff, that sort of thing—people don't like to print. Usually I don't have any answers to the questions they would print, anyway.

Who would you want to interview?
A lot of people who aren't alive: Hank Williams, Apollinaire, Joseph from the Bible, Marilyn Monroe, John F. Kennedy, Mohammed, Paul the Apostle, maybe John Wilkes Booth, maybe Gogol. I'd like to interview people who died leaving a great unsolved mess behind, who left people for ages to do nothing but speculate. As far as anybody living goes, who's there to interview? Castro? Gorbachev? Reagan? The Hillside Strangler? What are they going to tell you? The destiny of the world's wealthiest man, that don't interest me. I know what his reward is. Anybody who's done work that I admire, I'd rather just leave it at that. I'm not that pushy about finding out how people come up with what they come up with, so what does that leave you with? Just the daily life of somebody. You know, like, "How come you don't eat fish?" That really wouldn't give me answers to what I'm wondering about.

Younger Than That Now

Dark Sunglasses
I started out with Batman and Robin-type sunglasses. I always thought the best kind of sunglasses are the motorcycle helmets with the black plastic masks on them. That way, nobody can recognize the back of your head either. With sunglasses, you buy them off the rack, if they fit, and put them on. Shoes are tougher. You go into a store, try this pair on, that pair on. I feel I have to buy something if I put it on. What I'm looking for is a pair of glasses that can see through walls, whether they're sunglasses or not.

Isn't it hard to wear dark glasses after all these years?
Late at night it is, when I'm driving. I don't wear them all the time. I've gone through periods when I wear them, but I don't know why. I'm nearsighted, so I wear them for that reason.

Highway 61 Revisited
People ask me about the '60s all the time. That's the first thing they want to know. I say, if you want to know about the '60s, read *Armies of the Night* by Norman Mailer, or read Marshall McLuhan or Abraham Maslow. A lot of people have written about the '60s in an exciting way and have told the truth. The singers were just a part of it. I can't tell them that much. Certain things I can remember very clearly. Others are a kinda blur, but where I was and what was happening I can focus in on if I'm forced to. Of course, there are people who can remember in vivid detail. Ginsberg has that talent and Kerouac had that talent to a great degree. Kerouac never forgot anything, so he could write anything because he could just remember.

My Back Pages
Miles Davis is my definition of cool. I loved to see him in the small clubs playing his solo, turn his back on the crowd, put down his horn and walk off the stage, let the band keep playing, and then come back and play a few notes at the end. I did that at a couple of shows. The audience thought I was sick or something. Lily St. Cyr (the stripper), Dorothy Dandridge, Mary Magdalen, that's my definition of hot. My

first pop hero was Johnny Ray. I saw him late '78. I think he was playing club lounges. He hasn't had a hit for a while. Maybe he needs a new record company. I hope the guy's still alive. People forget how good he was. The only person I can think of who didn't return a phone call of mine was Walter Yetnikoff (president of CBS) the summer before last. I placed it personally, direct dial, long distance, at 3 o'clock in the morning. The last record I bought was Lucille Bogan. She was a blues singer who I had heard of, but not her records. I don't buy too many contemporary records. I didn't go down to the record store and buy the record personally. I know someone who works in a record store in town and I called and asked him to set it aside. No, I didn't actually pick it up, somebody else did. The first expensive thing I bought with my first big paycheck was a '65 baby-blue Mustang convertible. But a guy who worked for me rolled it down a hill in Woodstock and it smashed into a truck. I got 25 bucks for it. The name on my driver's license is Bob Dylan. It was legally changed when I went to work for Folk City a few thousand years ago. They had to get my name straight for the union. I never watch sports on TV, although I did see John McEnroe beat Jimmy Connors at Wimbledon when I was over in England last year. There was a TV set backstage and I had gotten there early and I paid attention to the whole thing. Usually I don't stay with something that long. I used to play hockey when I was growing up. Everyone sort of learns how to skate and play hockey at an early age (in Minnesota). I usually played forward, sometimes center. My cousin was a goalie at the University of Colorado. I didn't play too much baseball, because my eyes were kind of bad and the ball would hit me when I wasn't looking. I never played much basketball, unless I played with my kids. Football I never played at all, not even touch football. I really don't like to hurt myself. I have a good understanding with all the women who have been in my life, whether I see them occasionally or not. We're still always best of friends.

Tangled Up in Blue
I once read a book of Nathaniel Hawthorne's letters to some girl, and they were extremely private and personal, and I didn't feel there was

any of myself in those letters, but I could identify with what he was saying. A lot of myself crosses over into my songs. I'll write something and say to myself, I can change this, I can make this not so personal, and at other times I'll say, I think I'll leave this on a personal level, and if somebody wants to peek at it and make up their own minds about what kind of character I am, that's up to them. Other times I might say, well, it's too personal, I think I'll turn the corner on it, because why do I want somebody thinking about what I'm thinking about, especially if it's not to their benefit.

Tales of Yankee Power

The best songs are the songs you write that you don't know anything about. They're an escape. I don't do too much of that because maybe it's more important to deal with what's happening rather than to put yourself in a place where all you can do is imagine something. If you can imagine something and you haven't experienced it, it's usually true that someone else has actually gone through it and will identify with it. I actually think about Poe's stories, "The Tell-Tale Heart," "The Pit and the Pendulum." Certainly, if you look at his life, he really didn't experience any of that stuff. But some fantastic stories came out of his imagination. Like, "Here I am stuck in this job I can't get out of. I'm working as a civil servant, what am I going to do next? I hate this existence." So what does he do? He sits in his attic and writes a story and all the people take it to mean he's a very weird character. Now, I don't think that's an illegitimate way to go about things, but then you got someone like Herman Melville who writes out of experience—*Moby Dick* or *Confidence Man*. I think there's a certain amount of fantasy in what he wrote. Can you see him riding on the back of a whale? I don't know. I've never been to college and taken a literary course. I can only try to answer these questions, because I'm supposed to be somebody who knows something about writing, but the actual fact is, I don't really know that much about it. I don't know what there is to know about it, anyway. I began writing because I was singing. I think that's an important thing. I started writing because things were changing all the time and a certain song needed to be written. I started writing them because I wanted to sing them. If they had been written, I wouldn't have started to write them. Anyway, one thing led to another and I just kept on writing my own songs, but I stumbled into it, really. It was nothing I had prepared myself for, but I did sing a lot of songs before I wrote any of my own. I think that's important too.

Did you ever send your poems to any poetry magazines?
No, I didn't start writing poetry until I was out of high school. I was 18 or so when I discovered Ginsberg, Gary Snyder, Phillip Whalen, Frank O'Hara, and those guys. Then I went back and started reading the French guys, Rimbaud and Francois Villon; I started putting tunes to their poems. There used to be a folk music scene and jazz clubs just about every place. The two scenes were very much connected, where the poets would read to a small combo, so I was close up to that for a while. My songs were influenced not so much by poetry on the page but by poetry being recited by the poets who recited poems with jazz bands.

The Real You at Last
Sometimes the "you" in my songs is me talking to me. Other times I can be talking to somebody else. If I'm talking to me in a song, I'm not going to drop everything and say, alright, now I'm talking to you. It's up to you to figure out who's who. A lot of times it's "you" talking to "you." The "I," like in "I and I," also changes. It could be I, or it could be the "I" who created me. And also, it could be another person who's saying "I." When I say "I" right now, I don't know who I'm talking about.

All I Really Want to Do
As long as I continue to make records and play, which I'm not through doing yet, I have to go along with what the scene is at the time. I'm not a Pete Seeger. I've actually done that every once in a while, where I have led two thousand, three thousand people through songs, but I haven't done it like Pete Seeger. He's a master at that, leading a mass of people in four-part harmony to a song not even in their language. I think he could appeal to people as much as Sting could, because he

could make them feel like they matter and make sense to themselves and feel like they're contributing to something. Seeing Tears for Fears is like being a spectator at a football game. Pete is almost like a tribal medicine man, in the true sense of the word. Rock 'n roll performers aren't. They're just kind of working out other people's fantasies.

Bob Dylan's 115th Dream

I signed a record contract with John Hammond, Sr., of Columbia Records in 1961. It was a big moment. I had been rejected by a lot of folk companies—Folkways, Tradition, Prestige, Vanguard. It was meant to be, actually. If those other companies had signed me, I would have recorded folk songs, and I don't think they would have stayed with me. Most of those companies went out of business, anyway. Dream #116: The *Freewheelin'* album. The girl on the cover with me is Suze Rotolo, my roommate at the time.

Newport, 1965

The first time I played electric before a large group of people was at the Newport Folk Festival, but I had a hit record out (*Bringing It All Back Home*), so I don't know how people expected me to do anything different. I was aware that people were fighting in the audience, but I couldn't understand it. I was a little embarrassed by the fuss, because it was for the wrong reasons. I mean, you can do some really disgusting things in life and people will let you get away with it. Then you do something that you don't think is anything more than natural and people react in that type of riotous way, but I don't pay too much attention to it.

Motorpsycho Nitemare

In 1966 I had a motorcycle accident and ended up with several broken vertebrae and a concussion. That put me down for a while. I couldn't go on doing what I had been. I was pretty wound up before that accident happened. It set me down so I could see things in a better perspective. I wasn't seeing anything in any kind of perspective. I probably would have died if I had kept on going the way I had been.

Gospel Plow

In 1979 I went out on tour and played no song that I had ever played before live. It was a whole different show, and I thought that was a pretty amazing thing to do. I don't know any other artist who has done that, has not played whatever they're known for. The *Slow Train* record was out and I had the songs to the next record and then I had some songs that never were recorded. I had about 20 songs that never had been sung live before, and nobody seemed to pick up on that. They were seeing me as if they were dropping into some club I was playing in and were to witness something that really wasn't for publicity purposes. Yet it got all kinds of negative publicity. The only thing that bothered me about it was that the negative publicity was so hateful that it turned a lot of people off from making up their own minds, and financially that can hurt if you got a show on the road. The first time we went out on that tour, we had something like eight weeks booked. Two of the weeks were in San Francisco. In the review in the paper, the man did not understand any of the concepts behind any part of the show, and he wrote an anti-Bob Dylan thing. He probably never liked me anyway, but just said that he did. A lot of them guys say stuff like, "Well, he changed our lives before, how come he can't do it now?" Just an excuse really. Their expectations are so high, nobody can fulfill them. The can't fulfill their own expectations, so they expect other people to do it for them. I don't mind being put down, but intense personal hatred is another thing. It was like an opening-night critic burying a show on Broadway. This particular review got picked up and printed in all the newspapers of the cities we were going to play to even before tickets went on sale, and people would read this review and decide they didn't want to see the show. So it hurt us at the box office, and it took a while to work back from there. I thought the show was pretty relevant for what was going on at the time.

Positively 4th Street

Outside of a song like "Positively 4th Street," which is extremely one-dimensional, which I like, I don't usually purge myself by writing anything about any type of quote, so-called, relationships. I don't have the kinds of relationships that are built on any kind of false pretense, not to say that I haven't. I've had just as many as anybody else, but I haven't had them in a long time. Usually everything with me and anybody is up front. My-life-is-an-open-book sort of thing. And I choose to be involved with the people I'm involved with. They don't choose me.

Heart of Gold

The only time it bothered me that someone sounded like me was when I was living in Phoenix, Arizona, in about '72 and the big song at the time was "Heart of Gold." I used to hate it when it came on the radio. I always liked Neil Young, but it bothered me every time I listened to "Heart of Gold." I think it was up at number one for a long time, and I'd say, "Shit, that's me. If it sounds like me, it should as well be me." There I was, stuck on the desert someplace, having to cool out for a while. New York was a heavy place. Woodstock was worse, people living in trees outside my house, fans trying to batter down my door, cars following me up dark mountain roads. I needed to lay back for a while, forget about things, myself included, and I'd get so far away and turn on the radio and there I am, but it's not me. It seemed to me somebody else had taken my thing and had run away with it, you know, and I never got over it. Maybe tomorrow.

Has Anybody Seen My Love?

"Tight Connection to My Heart" is a very visual song. I want to make a movie out of it. I don't think it's going to get done. I think it's going to go past on the way, but of all the songs I've ever written, that might be one of the most visual. Of all the songs I've written, that's the one that's got characters that can be identified with. Whatever the fuck that means. I don't know, I may be trying to make it more important than it is, but I can see the people in it. Have you ever heard that song "I'm a Rambler, I'm a Gambler," . . . "I once had a sweetheart, age was 16, she was the Flower of Belton and the Rose of Saline"? Same girl, maybe older. I don't know, maybe it should stay a song. In most of my songs, I know who it is that I'm singing about and to. Lately, since '78, that's been true and hasn't changed. The stuff before '78, those people have kinda disappeared, '76, '75, '74. If you see me live, you won't hear me sing too many of those songs. There's a certain area of songs, a certain period that I don't feel that close to. Like the songs on the *Desire* album, that's kind of a fog to me. But since '78 the characters have all been extremely real and are still there. The ones I choose to talk about and relate to are the ones I find some kind of greatness in.

Million Dollar Bash

I know going on the Grammies is not my type of thing, but with Stevie (Wonder) it seemed like an interesting idea. I wasn't doing anything that night. I didn't feel I was making any great statement. For me, it was just going down to the place and changing my clothes.

Idiot Wind

Videos are out of character for me, too. The latest ones I've done with Dave Stewart are all right. The other ones, I don't know, I was just ordered around. I didn't pay much attention to those videos. You have to make them if you make records. You just have to. But you have to play live. You can't hide behind videos. I think once this video thing peaks out, people will get back to see who performs live and who don't.

X-Rated

I don't think censorship applies to me. It applies more to Top 40 artists. People who have hit records might have to be concerned with that, but I don't have those kinds of records that I'd have to be concerned about what I say. I'm just going to write any old song I feel like writing. The way I feel about it, I don't buy any of those records, anyway. I don't even like most of that music. I couldn't care at all if the records you hear on the radio are X-rated or R-rated. I don't think it's right, however, I'm opposed to it. I think every single song that you hear can be seen in another point of view from what it is. People have been reading stuff into my songs for years. I'd probably be the first one with a letter on their record.

Younger Than That Now

Which letter?

F and B, Fire and Brimstone. But I don't know about the B, that could stand for Boring. Certainly a lot of stuff today would fall into that category.

Rainy Day Women

I've always been drawn to a certain kind of woman. It's the voice more than anything else. I listen to the voice first. It's that sound I heard when I was growing up. It was calling out to me. When everything was blank and void, I would listen for hours to the Staple Singers. It's that sort of gospel singing sound. Or that voice on the Crystal's record, "Then He Kissed Me," Clydie King, Memphis Minnie, that type of thing. There's something in that voice, that whenever I hear it, I drop everything, whatever it is.

What happens when the body doesn't match the voice?

A body is a body. A woman could be deaf, dumb, crippled, and blind and still have soul and compassion. That's all that matters to me. You can hear it in the voice.

I Forgot More Than You'll Ever Know

I never had that much to do with Edie Sedgwick. I've seen where I have had, and read that I have had, but I don't remember Edie that well. I remember she was around, but I know other people who, as far as I know, might have been involved with Edie. Uh, she was a great girl. An exciting girl, very enthusiastic. She was around the Andy Warhol scene, and I drifted in and out of that scene, but then I moved out of the Chelsea Hotel. We, me and my wife, lived in the Chelsea Hotel on the third floor in 1965 or '66, when our first baby was born. We moved out of that hotel maybe a year before *Chelsea Girls*, and when *Chelsea Girls* came out, it was all over for the Chelsea Hotel. You might as well have burned it down. The notoriety it had gotten from that movie pretty much destroyed it. I think Edie was in *Chelsea Girls*. I had lost total touch with her by that time, anyway. It may just have been a time when there was just a lot of stuff happening. Ondine, Steve Paul's Scene,

Cheetah. That's when I would have known Edie if I would have known her, and I did know her, but I don't recall any type of relationship. If I did have one, I think I'd remember.

I Threw It All Away

I once traded an Andy Warhol "Elvis Presley" painting for a sofa, which was a stupid thing to do. I always wanted to tell Andy what a stupid thing I done, and if he had another painting he would give me, I'd never do it again.

Another Side of Bob Dylan

I never read Freud. I've never been attracted to anything he has said, and I think he's started a lot of nonsense with psychiatry and that business. I don't think psychiatry can help or has helped anybody. I think it's a big fraud (pun not intended) on the public. Billions of dollars have changed hands that could be used for far better purposes. A lot of people have trouble with their parents up until they're 50, 60, 70 years old. They can't get off their parents. I never had that kind of problem with my parents. Like John Lennon, "Mother": "Mother, you had me but I never had you." I can't imagine that. I know a lot of people have. There are a lot of orphans in the world, for sure. But that's not been my experience. I have a strong identification with orphans, but I've been raised by people who feel that fathers, whether they're married or not, should be responsible for their children, that all sons should be taught a trade, and that parents should be punished for their children's crimes. Actually, I was raised more by my grandmother. She was a fantastic lady. I love her so much, and I miss her a lot. But, getting back to the other thing, it all needs to be shaken up, and it will be. I never had any barriers to get across that were that clear to me, that I had to bust down to anything I truly loved. If I had any advantage over anybody at all, it's the advantage that I was all alone and could think and do what I wanted to. Looking back on it, it probably has a lot to do with growing up in northern Minnesota. I don't know what I would have been if I was growing up in the Bronx or Ethiopia or South America or even California. I think everybody's environment affects him in that way. Where I grew up . . . it's been a long time since. I forgot about it once I went east. I couldn't remember very much about it even then. I remember even less about it now. I don't have any long great story to tell about when I was a kid that would let anybody know how it is that I am what I am.

Patti Smith says you were Rimbaud in a previous incarnation
I don't know if she's right or wrong, but Patti Smith, then, of course, knows a lot of deep details that I might not be aware of. She might be clued in to something that's a little beyond me. I know at least a dozen women who tell me they were the Queen of Sheba. And I know a few Napoleons and two Joan of Arcs and one Einstein.

All Along the Watchtower
There weren't too many Jews in Hibbing, Minnesota. Most of them I was related to. The town didn't have a rabbi, and it was time for me to be bar mitzvahed. Suddenly a rabbi showed up under strange circumstances for only a year. He and his wife got off the bus in the middle of winter. He showed up just in time for me to learn this stuff. He was an old man from Brooklyn who had a white beard and wore a black hat and black clothes. They put him upstairs of the cafe, which was the local hangout. It was a rock 'n' roll cafe where I used to hang out, too. I used to go up there every day to learn this stuff, either after school or after dinner. After studying with him an hour or so, I'd come down and boogie. The rabbi taught me what I had to learn, and after he conducted this bar mitzvah, he just disappeared. The people didn't want him. He didn't look like anybody's idea of a rabbi. He was an embarrassment. All the Jews up there shaved their heads and, I think, worked on Saturday. And I never saw him again. It's like he came and went like a ghost. Later I found out he was Orthodox. Jews separate themselves like that. Orthodox, Conservative, Reform, as if God calls them that. Christians, too. Baptists, Assembly of God, Methodists, Calvinists. God has no respect for a person's title. He don't care what you call yourself.

A Puff of Smoke

I've never been able to understand the seriousness of it all, the seriousness of pride. People talk, act, live as if they're never going to die. And what do they leave behind? Nothing. Nothing but a mask.

Knockin' on Heaven's Door

Whenever anybody does something in a big way, it's always rejected at home and accepted someplace else. For instance, that could apply to Buddha. Who was Buddha? An Indian. Who are Buddhists? Chinese, Japanese, Asian people. They make up the big numbers in Buddhism. It's the same way with Jesus being a Jew. Who did he appeal to? He appeals to people who want to get into heaven in a big way. But some day the true story will reveal itself, and by that time, people will be ready for it, because it's just going in that direction. You can come out and say it all now, but what does it matter? It's going to happen anyway. Vanities of vanities, that's all it is.

They're Not Showing Any Lights Tonight

I went to Bible school at an extension of this church out in the Valley in Reseda, California. It was affiliated with the church, but I'm not a believer in that born-again type thing. Jesus told Nicodemus, "A man must be born again." And Nicodemus said, "How can I go through my mother's womb?" and Jesus said, "You must be born of the spirit." And that's where that comes from, that born-again thing. People have put a heavy trip on it. People can call you what they want. The media make up a lot of these words for the definition of people. I mean, who's a person anymore? Everything's done for the media. If the media don't know about it, it's not happening. They'll take the littlest thing and make it spectacular. They're in the business of doing that. Everything's a business. Love, truth, beauty. Conversation is a business. Spirituality is not a business, so it's going to go against the grain of people who are trying to exploit other people. God doesn't look at people and say, "That's a banker, that's a dentist, that's an oil-well driller."

Younger Than That Now

What's the messianic complex?

All that exists is spirit, before, now, and forever more. The messianic thing has to do with this world, the flesh world, and you got to pass through this to get to that. The messianic thing has to do with the world of mankind, like it is. This world is scheduled to go for 7,000 years. Six thousand years of this, where man has his way, and 1,000 years when God has His way. Just like a week. Six days work, one day rest. The last thousand years is called the Messianic Age. Messiah will rule. He is, was, and will be about God, doing God's business. Drought, famine, war, murder, theft, earthquake, and all other evil things will be no more. No more disease. That's all of this world. What's gonna happen is this: you know when things change, people usually know, like in a revolution, people know before it happens who's coming in and who's going out. All the Somozas and Batistas will be on their way out, grabbing their stuff and whatever, but you can forget about them. They won't be going anywhere. It's the people who live under tyranny and oppression, the plain, simple people, that count, like the multitude of sheep. They'll see that God is coming. Somebody representing Him will be on the scene. Not some crackpot lawyer or politician with the mark of the beast, but somebody who makes them feel holy. People don't know how to feel holy. They don't know what it's about or what's right. They don't know what God wants of them. They'll want to know what to do and how to act. Just like you want to know how to please any ruler. They don't teach that stuff like they do math, medicine, and carpentry, but now there will be a tremendous calling for it. There will be a run on godliness, just like now there's a run on refrigerators, headphones, and fishing gear. It's going to be a matter of survival. People are going to be running to find out about God, and who are they going to run to? They're gonna run to the Jews, 'cause the Jews wrote the book, and you know what? The Jews ain't gonna know. They're too busy in the fur business and in the pawnshops and in sending their kids to some atheist school. They're too busy doing all that stuff to know. People who believe in the coming of the Messiah live their lives right now as if he was here. That's my idea of it, anyway. I know people are going to say to themselves, "What the fuck is this guy talking about?" But it's all there in black and white, the written and unwritten word. I don't have to defend this. The scriptures back me up. I didn't ask to know this stuff. It just came to me at different times from experiences throughout my life. Other than that, I'm just a rock 'n' roller, folk poet, gospel-blues-protestest guitar player. Did I say that right?

Blowin' in the Wind

Politics have changed. The subject matter has changed. In the '60s there was a lot of people coming out of schools who were taught politics by professors who were political thinkers, and those people spilled over into the streets. What politics I ever learned, I learned in the streets, because it was part of the environment. I don't know where somebody would hear that now. Now everybody wants their own thing. There's no unity. There's the Puerto Rican Day parade, Polish Day, German Week, the Mexican parades. You have all these different types of people all waving their own flags, and there's no unity between all these people. In the '60s, there wasn't any separation. That's the difference between then and now that I can see. Everybody now is out for their own people and their own selves, and they should be 'cause they look around and see everything's unbalanced.

The Times They Are a-Changing

The times still are a-changing, every day. I'm trying to slow down every day, because the times may be a-changing, but they're going by awfully fast. "When I was a child, I spoke as a child, I thought as a child. When I became a man, I put away childish things."

ROLLING STONE (AUSTRALIA),
JANUARY 16, 1986

Gates of Eden Revisited:
A Conversation with Bob Dylan

Toby Creswell

IT DOESN'T REALLY MATTER NOW whether Bob Dylan is a funda-
mentalist Christian, any more than it mattered whether he was going
to the Synagogue when he recorded *Blood on the Tracks* ten years ago.
Amongst all the crucial lines that Dylan has sung, one sticks out—"He
not busy being born is busy dying." Dylan, of all the great creators of
his generation, has been busy being born over a series of almost thirty
albums, each of which has added to all that had come before.

However, there have been some constants. There has always
been a sense of engagement with the external world.
When Dylan gave up writing specific protest songs in
1964, he began writing songs about hypocrisy, prejudice, injustice, malice, exploitation, and cruelty.
Those concerns are still the subject of his songs. At
the same time he was writing love songs like "Love
Minus Zero/No Limit," which is a tender and complete statement of affection that is also a
religious statement. Dylan has sung of
both sacred and profane love
throughout his career, sometimes
concentrating on one, sometimes
on the other. Then there was the

electric bite of pure rock & roll as portrayed on "Subterranean Home-sick Blues," a song that Dylan notes, on the five-album *Biograph* retro-spective, was recorded in one take.

All these are still elements of Dylan's current work. His choice of Tom Petty and the Heartbreakers as a backing band suggests that he still after that fire in his rock & roll. Moreover, the news that he is working with Dave Stewart of the Eurythmics suggests that he still sees himself as contemporary.

Given all of that and the quality of the last album, *Empire Burlesque*, the presence of the Heartbreakers on Dylan's Australian tour promises us an extraordinary series of concerts.

CBS has just issued the *Biograph* box set: ten sides of Dylan from *Bob Dylan* to *Shot of Love*. It is an awesome body of work, unequalled in rock & roll, even the outtakes and the unfinished songs like "Jet Pilot" which later became "Tombstone Blues."

As somebody who has listened to Bob Dylan for twenty years, I jumped at the chance of an interview. But what do you say over the telephone to someone whom you have grown up with? My friend Danny said you usually talk about how the family is doing. What do you ask Bob Dylan, though?

TC: This tour you'll be playing with the Heartbreakers, the first time you've played with a band since the Band tour a decade ago. It must be good to get back to that format.

BD: We don't really know what the format is going to be yet. It's a lot easier, though, because as band members they sort of think as one person. When you put people together who've never played together before, there's so many different people; it takes years for people to play together like the Tom Petty Band. We were all raised on the same sort of music.

TC: You played with the Heartbreakers for Farm Aid. You seem to have been doing rather a lot of those shows lately.

BD: These things pop up every once in a while. I don't think it'll become a regular thing. This year these seem to have been a couple of those kind of shows.

TC: It seems that these shows have become such huge events that they tend to overshadow the issues.

BD: I know what you mean. That can happen. The atmosphere is like a carnival. But by raising that kind of money, they must be getting these problems into the minds of a lot of people who wouldn't have had it on their minds before, and that's a good thing.

TC: You have said in the past that the function of art is to lead you to God. There were the three gospel albums: *Slow Train Coming, Saved,* and *Shot of Love,* but your last two records have taken a different slant.

BD: Well, it all depends where you come at it from. I come at things from different sides to get a different perspective on what it is I'm trying to focus in on. Maybe all my songs are focusing on the same thing. I don't know; maybe I'm just coming in from all sides.

TC: The difference between the gospel records and the recent stuff seems to be that earlier you were laying down the law.

BD: Every so often you have to have the law laid down so that you know what the law is. Then you can do whatever you please with it. I haven't heard those albums in quite a while; you're probably right.

TC: You have said recently that you didn't think rock & roll still existed in its pure form, that it was no longer viable. Would you put yourself in with that?

BD: I don't think I put myself in that category. I'm not coming up anymore, you know what I mean? I probably was speaking about the industry itself. I listen to it but mostly I don't pay much attention to modern music. It's everywhere, in places that maybe it shouldn't be. There comes a time to shut off the radio, there's a time to turn off the tube, but the way it's projected into society there's not much of a chance that you can get to do that. There are very few people I know who play the real old-style music. When it first appeared, as I remember it, it was an escape from everything that was going on, which was mainly lies, so when music came it was a direction to pull you in that was out of this myth. But now nobody wants to get pulled out of the myth because they don't recognize it as being a myth. That's what it's like here anyway. They like where they're at, they like what's going on, and music is just an extension of that, so they like it, too. It's nothing different, it doesn't pull you anywhere.

TC: So what's the solution?

BD: Turn it off. It's a decision people have to make. That's what the sixties and the fifties were all about. There are other ways to operate, to survive. There's got to be some type of light, some type of brightness outside of everything that you're given on a mass consumer level. What I can see is the mass monster. I don't know what it's like in Australia, but in America it's everywhere. It's invaded your home, your bed, it's in your closet. It's come real close to kicking over life itself. Unless you're able to go into the woods, the back country, and even there it reaches you. It seems to want to make everybody the same. People who are different are looked at as being a little bit crazy or a little bit odd. It's hard to stand outside of all that and remain sane. Even outrageousness gets to be in fashion. Anything you can think of to do, someone is going to come along and market it. I think it's going to change. I don't think it can stay like this forever, that's for sure. I think it's going to change but for the moment it's hard to find anything that's really hot.

TC: *Empire Burlesque* seems a very straightforward record by comparison with some of your earlier work. Is simplicity something you are striving for?

BD: I strive for something that feels right to me. It could be a lot of different kinds of moods and phrasings, or lines that might not seem to be too connected at the time with the music. They're all connected. A lot of times people will take the music out of my lyrics and just read them as lyrics. That's not really fair because the music and the lyrics I've always felt are pretty closely wrapped up. You can't separate one from the other that simply. A lot of time the meaning is more in the way a line is sung, and not just in the line.

TC: These last few years have been very prolific for you.

BD: Yeah, I've been trying to find different things that are offshoots of the things I would normally do. I feel like something might open up in the next couple of months in different areas. There's a bunch of songs I want to write that I haven't been able to get close to. I almost know what they are but the information that I need is not really available to me so I have to go out and get it and I haven't done that. I expected to have a little more of that on *Empire Burlesque* but I just didn't do it. They are the true story type things, real things that have happened that I would like to comment on. I need to talk to the people involved but I haven't followed through yet. I hope to have some of that stuff on the next album I do.

TC: Were you pleased with the way *Empire Burlesque* turned out?

BD: Yes, for what it was I thought it was really good. I think the next record is going to sound even better. I'm not too experienced at having records sound good. I don't know how to go about doing that, though I thought I got pretty close last time with Arthur Baker. I think next time, working with Dave Stewart here, the stuff we're doing has been happening a lot easier, quicker, so I think it's going to sound a lot more together than the last record.

TC: You recorded that album yourself and gave it to Arthur Baker to mix?

Younger Than That Now

BD: Pretty much so. I just went out and recorded a bunch of stuff all over the place and then when it was time to put this record together I brought it all to him and he made it sound like a record. Usually I stay out of that side of the finished record.

TC: Why?

BD: I'm not good at it. There are guys that don't mind sitting in the control booth for days and days. I'm just not like that; I'm a one-mix man. I can't tell the difference after that.

TC: Your music often seems to get ignored as compared with the emphasis that's placed on the lyrics, but they're have been some really nice instrumental passages like "Pat Garrett and Billy the Kid," for example.

BD: Yes, I just did a bunch of tracks with Dave Stewart that have no lyrics, and you don't even miss the lyrics, really. They're just different chord patterns that make up a melody. My records usually don't have a lot of guitar solos or anything like that on them. The vocals mean a lot and the rhythm means a lot, that's about it.

TC: Your voice seems to have changed a lot over the years.

BD: Maybe it has, I don't know.

TC: It sounded different to me, particularly after *Street Legal* when you started using girl singers.

BD: I'm not aware of any significant difference, really. I've always heard that sound (female backing) with my music. I just hear it in there, it's just like another way of putting horns in. That sound has always been one of my favorites, just that vocal part, because I don't do anything with solo-type work—it's all part of the overall effect, it's more just playing the song and getting the structure of it right. The vocal parts are like another instrument but not a solo instrument. Apart from that, I just like the gospel sound.

TC: Seeing the latest videos and the "We are the World" video, you seem to have less of the legend around your neck, you seem freed of the burden of being Bob Dylan.

BD: I don't think I ever carried that around except for 1974, when I did that tour with the Band. That was pretty much of a heavy tour because of the notoriety and the legendary quality of the people involved. I had to step into Bob Dylan's shoes for that tour. Since that time, I never thought about it. I wouldn't do half the things I do if I was thinking about having to live up to a Bob Dylan myth.

TC: Do you feel that you've been guided to where you are?

BD: You're always guided to where you are, but you have the choice to mess it up. Sooner or later everything that goes around comes around. So, yeah, I feel like I've been guided to wherever it is I'm at right now, but I don't know whatever it is I'm supposed to be doing. I might have something else to do. I can't figure out what it would be, though, because I like doing what I do. Who's to say? There's a lot of luck involved, a lot of circumstance. You can't do anything alone, though. You've always got to have somebody supporting you or nobody would get anywhere.

TC: Do you think that with time comes wisdom?

BD: With experience. Things don't really change, just attitudes.

TC: You've been doing videos with Dave Stewart. What do you think of the video age?

BD: I don't think much about it at all. It's not going to go away. Everyplace you look, you're drowning in it. You can't turn on your

TV without seeing music videos. It's like the unions. Unions in the early thirties were all communist organizations and now they're big business.

TC: It's got to the point where everybody seems to be using rock & roll for their own ends. In America, you have politicians associating themselves with rock & roll songs.

BD: Absurd isn't it. The rock & roll songs they're quoting from don't deserve to be quoted from like that. You couldn't do that with the early stuff, Little Richard and Chuck Berry—what politician is going to quote Chuck Berry? Who's going to quote Carl Perkins or Gene Vincent or any of those guys? It was outside then.

TC: Today it's image rather than content. People hold up an image of a star and hope to attach themselves to that image.

BD: That's absolutely correct. It's destroying the fabric of our minds and all we can do is complain about it, so we just have to shut it out. You just have to cut it off and not let it get into your framework because that's the only way you're going to escape it. You can't meet it head on. You've probably got a little more space to breathe over there, but here it's heavy. There's not many places you can go where you're not reminded of the current cultural ambitions of people who are on their way to be stars.

TC: When you started out you must have wanted to be a star in some way?

BD: I wanted to be a star in my own mind, I wanted to be my own star. I didn't want to be a star for people I didn't really identify with. For me what I did was a way of life, it wasn't an occupation.

TC: Has it been all it was cracked up to be?

BD: Yes and no. I'm still doing it , you know. It seems to be what I've done more years than I haven't done it, but I'm just going to keep on doing it till it runs out. Yes, it was all it was cracked up to be, because I never strayed from it. Maybe I would've gone down if I'd gone into being a movie star or if I'd started believing what other people said of me or if I'd started to think I was this person that everybody was talking about. I know there are a lot of people that did go down. They started believing what the newspapers said about them. I never believed it one way or another, so for me, I don't really feel much of a change. I feel very little change between now and ten years ago, twenty years ago. I don't feel like I've traveled that far or done that much.

TC: You mentioned the unions earlier and I was thinking of the song "Union Sundown," on *Infidels* which is a very specific commentary. Do you still feel a need to make that type of comment?

BD: Oh, yes, that comes with the territory.

TC: There seems to be two types of songs you've written, those which are here and now, and a lot that seem to focus on the eternals.

BD: Well, that's the important thing, if you lose that, you start getting into stuff that is mindless and meaningless. Usually there's a voice that goes on, there's some kind of warning point if that ever happens, but mostly what this kind of music is about is your ability to feel things. There's a lot of stuff going on that you hear that you know nobody felt nothing about; you can hear it in the spirit. So much stuff gets thrown at you with no feeling behind it because nobody feels anything anymore. But there are a lot of good things going on that I don't understand. A lot of music that's coming out is way beyond me. There are some people who are really gifted musicians, I mean in a classical sense, and they're coming out with a lot of different stuff that is being thought out and preplanned.

Younger Than That Now

TC: There does seem to be an attempt by people, like Miami Steve on the *Sun City* record, to say things about apartheid and about what is happening in America today.

BD: Yes, he's highly committed to that.

TC: It seems like a very difficult struggle.

BD: Well, it is a very difficult struggle, because most people don't want to hear that.

TC: There's a lot of red-baiting going on again.

BD: That's been going on since the fifties.

TC: The cold war seems to be coming back.

BD: I don't think it ever went away, you know. It just lays low for a while. People need something to hate, you've got to hate something. As soon as your old enough, people try to make you hate something or somebody. Blacks are a little easier, Communists you can't really see. The early Christians were like Communists. The Roman Empire treated the Early Christians the same way as the Western world treats the Communists.

TC: So it doesn't really change?

BD: No, things don't, it's just got a different name on it. There's always someone you're told you've got to step on so you can rise up a little higher.

TC: Your kids are grown up now. What's the perspective like as a father?

BD: It gives you a perspective on what kids are doing. I don't think kids are any different from what they ever were, really. It's like my daddy once said, when he was twelve years old he asked his dad something and he didn't think his dad knew too much about what he was talking about. When he got to twenty-five, he asked him the same question and he got the same answer and he was amazed how his father got to be so smart.

The SongTalk Interview

Paul Zollo

"I've made shoes for everyone, even you, while I still go barefoot"
  —from "I and I" By Bob Dylan

SONGWRITING? WHAT DO I KNOW about songwriting? Bob Dylan asked, and then broke into laughter. He was wearing blue jeans and a white tank-top T-shirt, and drinking coffee out of a glass. "It tastes better out of a glass," he said grinning. His blonde acoustic guitar was leaning on a couch near where we sat. Bob Dylan's guitar. His influence is so vast that everything that surrounds takes on enlarged significance: Bob Dylan's moccasins. Bob Dylan's coat.

"And the ghost of 'lectricity howls in the bones of
   her face
Where these visions of Johanna have now taken my
   place.
The harmonicas play the skeleton
   keys and the rain
And these visions of Johanna are
   now all that remain"
   —from "Visions of Johanna"

Younger Than That Now

• • •

Pete Seeger said, "All songwriters are links in a chain," yet there are few artists in this evolutionary arc whose influence is as profound as that of Bob Dylan. It's hard to imagine the art of songwriting as we know it without him. Though he insists in this interview that "somebody else would have done it," he was the instigator, the one who knew that songs could do more, that they could take on more. He knew that songs could contain a lyrical richness and meaning far beyond the scope of all previous pop songs, and they could possess as much beauty and power as the greatest poetry, and that by being written in rhythm and rhyme and merged with music, they could speak to our souls.

Starting with the models made by his predecessors, such as the talking blues, Dylan quickly discarded old forms and began to fashion new ones. He broke all the rules of songwriting without abandoning the craft and care that holds songs together. He brought the linguistic beauty of Shakespeare, Byron, and Dylan Thomas, and the expansiveness and beat experimentation of Ginsberg, Kerouac, and Ferlinghetti, to the folk poetry of Woody Guthrie and Hank Williams. And when the world was still in the midst of accepting this new form, he brought music to a new place again, fusing it with the electricity of rock and roll. "Basically, he showed that anything goes," Robbie Robertson said. John Lennon said that it was hearing Dylan that allowed him to make the leap from writing empty pop songs to expressing the actuality of his life and the depths of his own soul. "Help" was a real call for help, he said, and prior to hearing Dylan it didn't occur to him that songs could contain such direct meaning. When he asked Paul Simon how he made the leap in his writing from fifties rock & roll songs like "Hey Schoolgirl" to writing "Sound of Silence" he said, "I really can't imagine it could have been anyone else besides Bob Dylan."

> *"Yes, to dance beneath the diamond sky*
> *with one hand waving free,*
> *silhouetted by the sea,*
> *circled by the circus sands,*

With all memory and fate
driven deep beneath the waves,
Let me forget about today until tomorrow."
—from "Mr. Tambourine Man"

There's an unmistakable elegance in Dylan's words, an almost biblical beauty that he has sustained in his songs throughout the years. He refers to it as a "gallantry" in the following, and pointed to it as the single thing that sets his songs apart from others. Though he's maybe more famous for the freedom and expansiveness of his lyrics, all of his songs possess this exquisite care and love for the language. As Shakespeare and Byron did in their times, Dylan has taken English, perhaps the world's plainest language, and instilled it with a timeless, mythic grace.

"Ring them bells, sweet Martha, for the poor man's son
Ring them bells so the world will know that God is one
Oh, the shepherd is asleep
where the willows weep
and the mountains are filled with lost sheep"
—from "Ring Them Bells"

As much as he has stretched, expanded and redefined the rules of songwriting, Dylan is a tremendously meticulous craftsman. A brutal critic of his own work, he works and reworks the words of his songs in the studio and even continues to rewrite certain ones even after they've been recorded and released. "They're not written in stone," he said. With such a wondrous wealth of language at his fingertips, he discards imagery and lines other songwriters would sell their souls to discover. The Bootleg Series, a recently released collection of previously unissued recordings, offers a rare opportunity to see the revisions and regrouping his songs go through. "Idiot Wind" is one of his angriest songs ("You don't hear a song like that every day," he said), which he recorded on *Blood on the Tracks* in a way that reflects this anger, emphasizing lines of condemnation like "one day you'll be in the ditch, flies buzzin' around your eyes, blood on your saddle." On The Bootleg Series , we get an alternate approach to the song, a quiet, tender reading of the same lines that makes the inherent disquiet of the song even more disturbing, the tenderness of Dylan's delivery adding a new level of genuine sadness to lines like "people see me all the time and they just can't remember how to act." The peak moment of the song is the penultimate chorus when Dylan addresses America: "Idiot wind, blowing like a circle around my skull, from the Grand Coulee Dam to the Capitol." On the Bootleg version, this famous line is still in formation: "Idiot wind, blowing every time you move your jaw, from the Grand Coulee Dam to the Mardi Gras." His song "Jokerman" also went through a similar evolution, as a still unreleased bootleg of the song reveals. Like "Idiot Wind," the depth and intensity of the lyric is sustained over an extraordinary amount of verses, yet even more scenes were shot that wound up on the cutting room floor, evidence of an artist overflowing with the abundance of creation:

> "It's a shadowy world
> skies are slippery gray
> A woman just gave birth to a prince today
> and dressed him in scarlet
> He'll put the priest in his pocket,
> put the blade to the heat
> Take the motherless children off the street
> And place them at the feet of a harlot" \
> —from "Jokerman" on Infidels

> "It's a shadowy world
> skies are slippery gray
> A woman just gave birth to a prince today
> and she's dressed in scarlet
> He'll turn priests into pimps
> and make all men bark
> Take a woman who could have been Joan of Arc
> and turn her into a harlot"
> —from "Jokerman" on Outfidels, a bootleg

Often Dylan lays abstraction aside and writes songs as clear and telling as any of Woody Guthrie's narrative ballads, finding heroes and anti-heroes in our modern times as Woody found in his. Some of these subjects might be thought of as questionable choices for heroic treatment, such as underworld boss Joey Gallo, about whom he wrote the astounding song, "Joey." It's a song that is remarkable for its cinematic clarity; Dylan paints a picture of a life and death so explicit and exact that we can see every frame of it, and even experience Gallo's death as if we were sitting there watching it. And he does it with a rhyme scheme and a meter that makes the immediacy of the imagery even more striking:

> "One day they blew him down
> in a clam bar in New York
> He could see it coming through the door
> as he lifted up his fork.
> He pushed the table over to protect his family
> Then he staggered out into the streets
> of Little Italy."
> —from "Joey"

"Yes, well, what can you know about anybody?" Dylan asked, and it's a good question. He's been a mystery for years, "kind of impenetrable, really," Paul Simon said, and that mystery is not penetrated by this interview or any interview. Dylan's answers are often more enigmatic than the questions themselves, and like his songs, they give you a lot to think about while not necessarily revealing much about the man. In person, as others have noted, he is Chaplinesque. His body is smaller and his head bigger than one might expect, giving the effect of a kid wearing a Bob Dylan mask. He possesses one of the world's most striking faces; while certain stars might seem surprisingly normal and unimpressive in the flesh, Dylan is perhaps even more startling to confront than one might expect. Seeing those eyes, and that nose, it's clear it could be no one else than he, and to sit at a table with him and face those iconic features is no less impressive than suddenly finding yourself sitting face-to-face with William Shakespeare. It's a face we associate with an enormous, amazing body of work, work that has changed the world. But it's not really the kind of face one expects to encounter in everyday life.

Though Van Morrison and others have called him the world's greatest poet, he doesn't think of himself as a poet. "Poets drown in lakes," he said to us. Yet he's written some of the most beautiful poetry the world has known, poetry of love and outrage, of abstraction and clarity, of timelessness and relativity. Though he is faced with the evidence of a catalogue of songs that would contain the whole careers of a dozen fine songwriters, Dylan told us he doesn't consider himself to be a professional songwriter. "For me it's always been more confessional than professional," he said in distinctive Dylan cadence. "My songs aren't written on a schedule." Well, how are they written, we asked? This is the question at the heart of this interview, the main one that comes to mind when looking over all the albums, or witnessing the amazing array of moods, masks, styles and forms all represented on the recently released Bootleg Series. How has he done it? It was the first question asked, and though he deflected it at first with his customary humor, it's a question we returned to a few times. "Start me off somewhere," he said smiling, as if he might be left alone to divulge the secrets of his songwriting, and our talk began.

SONGTALK: Okay, Arlo Guthrie recently said, "Songwriting is like fishing in a stream; you put in your line and hope you catch something. And I don't think anyone downstream from Bob Dylan ever caught anything."

DYLAN: [Much laughter]

ST: Any idea how you've been able to catch so many?

DYLAN:[Laughs] It's probably the bait.[More laughter]

ST: What kind of bait do you use?

DYLAN: Uh . . . bait . . . You've got to use some bait. Otherwise you sit around and expect songs to come to you. Forcing it is using bait.

ST: Does that work for you?

DYLAN: Well, no. Throwing yourself into into a situation that would demand a response is like using bait. People who write about stuff that hasn't really happened to them are inclined to do that.

ST: When you write songs, do you try to consciously guide the meaning or do you try to follow subconscious directions?

DYLAN: Well, you know, motivation is something you never know behind any song, really. Anybody's song, you never know what the motivation was. It's nice to be able to put yourself in an environment where you can completely accept all the unconscious stuff that comes to you from your inner workings of your mind. And block yourself off to where you can control it all, take it down. Edgar Allan Poe must have done that. People who are dedicated writers, of which there are some, but mostly people get their information today over a television set or some kind of a way that's hitting them on all their senses. It's not just a great novel anymore. You have to be able to get the thoughts out of your mind.

ST: How do you do that?

DYLAN: Well, first of all, there's two kinds of thoughts in your mind: there's good thoughts and evil thoughts. Both come through your mind. Some people are more loaded down with one than another. Nevertheless, they come through. And you have to be able to sort them out, if you want to be a songwriter, if you want to be a good song singer. You must get rid of all that baggage. You ought to be able to sort out those thoughts, because they don't mean anything, they're just pulling you around, too. It's important to get rid of all them thoughts. Then you can do something from some kind of surveillance of the situation. You have some kind of place where you can see but it can't affect you. Where you can bring something to the matter, besides just take, take, take, take, take. As so many situations in life are today. Take, take, take, that's all that it is. What's in it for me? That syndrome which started in the Me Decade, whenever that was. We're still in that. It's still happening.

ST: Is songwriting for you more a sense of taking something from someplace else?

DYLAN: Well, someplace else is always a heartbeat away. There's no rhyme or reason to it. There's no rule. That's what makes it so attractive. There isn't any rule. You can still have your wits about you and do something that gets you off in a multitude of ways. As you very well know, or else you yourself wouldn't be doing it.

ST: Your songs often bring us back to other times, and are filled with mythic, magical images. A song like "Changing Of The Guard" seems to take place centuries ago, with lines like "They shaved her head/she was torn between Jupiter and Apollo/a messenger arrived with a black nightingale. . . ." How do you connect with a song like that?

DYLAN:[Pause] A song like that, there's no way of knowing, after the fact, unless somebody's there to take it down in chronological order, what the motivation was behind it. [Pause] But on one level, of course, it's no different from anything else of mine. It's the same amount of metric verses like a poem. To me, like a poem. The melodies in my mind are very simple, they're very simple, they're just based on music we've all heard growing up. And that and music which went beyond that, which went back further, Elizabethan ballads and whatnot . . . To me, it's old. [Laughs] It's old. It's not something, with my minimal amount of talent, if you could call it that, minimum amount . . . To me somebody coming along now would definitely read what's out there if they're seriously concerned with being an artist who's going to still be an artist when they get to be Picasso's age. You're better off learning some music theory. You're just better off, yeah, if you want to write songs. Rather than just take a hillbilly twang, you know, and try to base it all on that. Even country music is more orchestrated than it used to be. You're better off having some feel for music that you don't have to carry in your head, that you can write down. To me those are the people who . . . are serious about this craft. People who go about it that way. Not people who just want to pour out their insides and they got to get a big idea out and they want to tell the world about this, sure, you can do it through a song, you always could. You can use a song for anything, you know. The world don't need any more songs.

ST: You don't think so?

DYLAN: No. They've got enough. They've got way too many. As a matter of fact, if nobody wrote any songs from this day on, the world ain't gonna suffer for it. Nobody cares. There's enough songs for people to listen to, if they want to listen to songs. For every man, woman, and child on earth, they could be sent, probably, each of them, a hundred records, and never be repeated. There's enough songs. Unless someone's gonna come along with a pure heart and has something to say. That's a different story. But as far as songwriting, any idiot could do it. If you see me do it, any idiot could do it. [Laughs] It's just not that difficult of a thing. Everybody writes a song just like everybody's got that one great novel in them. There aren't a lot of people like me. You just had your interview with Neil [Young], John Mellencamp . . . Of course, most of my ilk that came along write their own songs and play them. It wouldn't matter if anybody ever made another record. They've got enough songs. To me, someone who writes really good songs is Randy Newman. There's a lot of people who write good songs. As songs. Now Randy might not go out onstage and knock you out, or knock your socks off. And he's not going to get people thrilled in the front row. He ain't gonna do that. But he's gonna write a better song than most people who can do it. You know, he's got that down to an art. Now Randy knows music. He knows music. But it doesn't get any better than "Louisiana" or "Cross Charleston Bay" ["Sail Away"]. It doesn't get any better than that. It's like a classically heroic anthem theme. He did it. There's quite a few people who did it. Not that many people in Randy's class. Brian Wilson. He can write melodies that will beat the band. Three people could combine on a song and make it a great song. If one person would have written the same song, maybe you would have never heard it. It might get buried on some . . . rap record. [Laughs]

ST: Still, when you've come out with some of your new albums of songs, those songs fit that specific time better than any songs that had already been written. Your new songs have always shown us new possibilities.

DYLAN: It's not a good idea and it's bad luck to look for life's guidance to popular entertainers. It's bad luck to do that. No one should do that. Popular entertainers are fine, there's nothing the matter with that but as long as you know where you're standing and what ground you're on, many of them, they don't know what they're doing either.

ST: But your songs are more than pop entertainment . . .

DYLAN: Some people say so. Not to me.

ST: No?

DYLAN: Pop entertainment means nothing to me. Nothing. You know, Madonna's good. Madonna's good, she's talented, she puts all kind of stuff together, she's learned her thing . . . But it's the kind of thing which takes years and years out of your life to be able to do. You've got to sacrifice a whole lot to do that. Sacrifice. If you want to make it big, you've got to sacrifice a whole lot. It's all the same, it's all the same. [Laughs]

ST: Van Morrison said that you are our greatest living poet. Do you think of yourself in those terms?

256

DYLAN: [Pause] Sometimes. It's within me. It's within me to put myself up and be a poet. But it's a dedication. [Softly] It's a big dedication. [Pause] Poets don't drive cars. [Laughs] Poets don't go to the supermarket. Poets don't empty the garbage. Poets aren't on the PTA. Poets, you know, they don't go picket the Better Housing Bureau, or whatever. Poets don't . . . Poets don't even speak on the telephone. Poets don't even talk to anybody. Poets do a lot of listening and . . . and usually they know why they're poets! [Laughs] Yeah, there are . . . what can you say? The world don't need any more poems, it's got Shakespeare. There's enough of everything. You name it, there's enough of it. There was too much of it with electricity, maybe, some people said that. Some people said lightbulb was going too far. Poets live on the land. They behave in a gentlemanly way. And live by their own gentlemanly code. [Pause] And die broke. Or drown in lakes. Poets usually have very unhappy endings. Look at Keats' life. Look at Jim Morrison, if you want to call him a poet. Look at him. Although some people say that he is really in the Andes.

ST: Do you think so?

DYLAN: Well, it never crossed my mind to think one way or the other about it, but you do hear that talk. Piggyback in the Andes. Riding a donkey.

ST: People have a hard time believing that Shakespeare really wrote all of his work because there is so much of it. Do you have a hard time accepting that?

DYLAN: People have a hard time accepting anything that overwhelms them.

ST: Might they think that of you, years from now, that no one man could have produced so much incredible work?

DYLAN: They could. They could look back and think nobody produced it. [Softly] It's not to anybody's best interest to think about how they will be perceived tomorrow. It hurts you in the long run.

ST: But aren't there songs of your own that you know will always be around?

DYLAN: Who's gonna sing them? My songs really aren't meant to be covered. No, not really. Can you think of . . . Well, they do get covered, but it's covered . They're not intentionally written to be covered, but okay, they do.

ST: Your songs are much more enjoyable to sing and play than most songs . . .

DYLAN: Do you play them on piano or guitar?

ST: Both.

DYLAN: Acoustic guitar?

ST: Mostly.

DYLAN: Do you play jazz? It never hurts to learn as many chords as you can. All kinds. Sometime it will change the inflection of a whole song, a straight chord, or, say, an augmented seventh chord.

ST: Do you have favorite keys to work in?

DYLAN: On the piano, my favorite keys are the black keys. And they sound better on guitar, too. Sometimes when a song's in a flat key, say B flat, bring it to the guitar, you might want to put it in A. But . . . that's an interesting thing you just said. It changes the reflection. Mainly in mine the songs sound different. They sound . . . when you take a black key song and put it on the guitar, which means you're playing in A flat, not too many people like to play in those keys. To me it doesn't matter.

[Laughs] It doesn't matter because my fingering is the same anyway. So there are songs that, even without the piano, which is the dominant sound if you're playing in the black keys—why else would you play in that key except to have that dominant piano sound?—the songs that go into those keys right from the piano, they sound different. They sound deeper. Yeah. They sound deeper. Everything sounds deeper in those black keys. They're not guitar keys, though. Guitar bands don't usually like to play in those keys, which kind of gives me an idea, actually, of a couple of songs that could actually sound better in black keys.

ST: Do keys have different colors for you?

DYLAN: Sure. Sure. [Softly] Sure.

ST: You've written some great A minor songs. I think of "One More Cup Of Coffee"—

DYLAN: Right. B minor might sound even better.

ST: How come?

DYLAN: Well, it might sound better because you're playing a lot of open chords if you're playing in A minor. If you play in B minor, it will force you to play higher. And the chords . . . you're bound, someplace along the line, because there are so many chords in that song, or seem to be anyway, you're bound someplace along the line to come down to an open chord on the bottom. From B. You would hit E someplace along the line. Try it in B minor. [Laughs] Maybe it will be a hit for you. A hit is a number one song, isn't it? Yeah.

ST: When you sit down to write a song, do you pick a key first that will fit a song? Or do you change keys while you're writing?

DYLAN: Yeah. Yeah. Maybe like in the middle of the thing. There are ways you can get out of whatever you've gotten into. You want to get out of it. It's bad enough getting into it. But the thing to do as soon as you get into it is realize you must get out of it. And unless you get out of it quickly and effortlessly, there's no use staying in it. It will just drag you down. You could be spending years writing the same song, telling the same story, doing the same thing. So once you involve yourself in it, once you accidentally have slipped into it, the thing is to get out. So your primary impulse is going to take you so far. But then you might think, well, you know, is this one of these things where it's all just going to come? And then all of the sudden you start thinking. And when my mind starts thinking, "What's happening now? Oh, there's a story here," and my mind starts to get into it, that's trouble right away. That's usually big trouble. And as far as never seeing this thing again. There's a bunch of ways you can get out of that. You can make yourself get out of it by changing key. That's one way. Just take the whole thing and change key, keeping the same melody. And see if that brings you any place. More times than not, that will take you down the road. You don't want to be on a collision course. But that will take you down the road. Somewhere. And then if that fails, and that will run out, too, then you can always go back to where you were to start. It won't work twice, it only works once. Then you go back to where you started. Yeah, because anything you do in A, it's going to be a different song in G. While you're writing it, anyway. There's too many wide passing notes in G [on the guitar] not to influence your writing, unless you're playing barre chords.

ST: Do you ever switch instruments, like from guitar to piano, while writing?

DYLAN: Not so much that way. Although when it's time to record something, for me, sometimes a song that has been written on piano with just lyrics here in my hand, it'll be time to play it now on guitar. So it will come out differently. But it wouldn't have influenced the writing of the song at all. Changing keys influences the writing of the song. Changing keys on the same instrument. For me, that works. I think for somebody else, the other thing works. Everything is different.

ST: I interviewed Pete Seeger recently—

DYLAN: He's a great man, Pete Seeger.

ST: I agree. He said, "All songwriters are links in a chain." Without your link in that chain, all of songwriting would have evolved much differently. You said how you brought folk music to rock music. Do you think that would have happened without you?

DYLAN: Somebody else would have done it in some other kind of way. But, hey, so what? So what? You can lead people astray awfully easily. Would people have been better off? Sure. They would have found somebody else. Maybe different people would have found different people, and would have been influenced by different people.

ST: You brought the song to a new place. Is there still a new place to bring songs? Will they continue to evolve?

DYLAN: [Pause] The evolution of song is like a snake with its tail in its mouth. That's evolution. That's what it is. As soon as you're there, you find your tail.

ST: Would it be okay with you if I mentioned some lines from your songs out of context to see what response you might have to them?

DYLAN: Sure. You can name anything you want to name, man.

ST: "I stand here looking at your yellow railroad/in the ruins of your balcony . . . [from "Absolutely Sweet Marie"].

DYLAN: [Pause] Okay. That's an old song. No, let's say not even old. How old? Too old. It's matured well. It's like wine. Now, you know, look, that's as complete as you can be. Every single letter in that line. It's all true. On a literal and on an escapist level.

Younger Than That Now

ST: And is it truth that adds so much resonance to it?

DYLAN: Oh yeah, exactly. See, you can pull it apart and it's like, "Yellow railroad?" Well, yeah. Yeah, yeah. All of it.

ST: "I was lying down in the reeds without any oxygen/I saw you in the wilderness among the men/I saw you drift into infinity and come back again . . ." [from "True Love Tends To Forget"].

DYLAN: Those are probably lyrics left over from my songwriting days with Jacques Levy. To me, that's what they sound like. Getting back to the yellow railroad, that could be from looking someplace. Being a performer you travel the world. You're not just looking off the same window everyday. You're not just walking down the same old street. So you must make yourself observe whatever. But most of the time it hits you. You don't have to observe. It hits you. Like "yellow railroad" could have been a blinding day when the sun was bright on a railroad someplace and it stayed on my mind. These aren't contrived images. These are images which are just in there and have got to come out. You know, if it's in there it's got to come out.

ST: "And the chains of the sea will be busted in the night . . ." [from "When The Ship Comes In"].

DYLAN: To me, that song says a whole lot. Patti Labelle should do that. You know? You know, there again, that comes from hanging out at a lot of poetry gatherings. Those kind of images are very romantic. They're very gothic and romantic at the same time. And they have a sweetness to it, also. So it's a combination of a lot of different elements at the time. That's not a contrived line. That's not sitting down and writing a song. Those kind of songs, they just come out. They're in you so they've got to come out.

ST: "Standing on the water casting your bread/while the eyes of the idol with the iron head are glowing . . ." [from "Jokerman"].

DYLAN: [Blows small Peruvian flute] Which one is that again?

ST: That's from "Jokerman."

DYLAN: That's a song that got away from me. Lots of songs on that album [*Infidels*] got away from me. They just did.

ST: You mean in the writing?

DYLAN: Yeah. They hung around too long. They were better before they were tampered with. Of course, it was me tampering with them. [Laughs] Yeah. That could have been a good song. It could've been.

ST: I think it's tremendous.

DYLAN: Oh, you do? It probably didn't hold up for me because in my mind it had been written and rewritten and written again. One of those kinds of things.

ST: "But the enemy I see wears a cloak of decency . . ." [from "Slow Train"].

DYLAN: Now don't tell me . . . wait . . . Is that "When You Gonna Wake Up"?

ST: No, that's from "Slow Train."

DYLAN: Oh, wow. Oh, yeah. Wow. There again. That's a song that you could write a song to every line in the song. You could.

ST: Many of your songs are like that.

DYLAN: Well, you know, that's not good either. Not really. In the long run, it could have stood up better by maybe doing just that, maybe taking every line and making a song out of it. If somebody had the willpower. But that line, there again, is an intellectual line. It's a line, "Well, the enemy I see wears a cloak of decency," that could be a lie. It just could be. Whereas "Standing under your yellow railroad," that's not a lie. To Woody Guthrie, see, the airwaves were sacred. And when he'd hear something false, it was on airwaves that were sacred to him. His songs weren't false. Now we know the airwaves aren't sacred but to him they were. So that influenced a lot of people with me coming up. Like, "You know, all those songs on the Hit Parade are just a bunch of shit, anyway." It influenced me in the beginning when nobody had heard that. Nobody had heard that. You know, "If I give my heart to you, will you handle it with care?" Or "I'm getting sentimental over you." Who gives a shit! It could be said in a grand way, and the performer could put the song across, but come on, that's because he's a great performer not because it's a great song. Woody was also a performer and songwriter. So a lot of us got caught up in that. There ain't anything good on the radio. It doesn't happen. Then, of course, the Beatles came along and kind of grabbed everybody by the throat. You were for them or against them. You were for them or you joined them, or whatever. Then everybody said, Oh, popular song ain't so bad, and then everyone wanted to get on the radio. [Laughs] Before that it didn't matter. My first records were never played on the radio. It was unheard of! Folk records weren't played on the radio. You never heard them on the radio and nobody cared if they were on the radio. Going on into it further, after the Beatles came out and everybody from England, rock and roll still is an American thing. Folk music is not. Rock and roll is an American thing, it's just all kind of twisted. But the English kind of threw it back, didn't they? And they made everybody respect it once more. So everybody wanted to get on the radio. Now nobody even knows what radio is anymore. Nobody likes it that you talk to. Nobody listens to it. But, then again, it's bigger than it ever was. But nobody knows how to really respond to it. Nobody can shut it off. [Laughs] You know? And people really aren't sure whether they want to be on the radio or whether they don't want to be on the radio. They might want to sell a lot of records, but people always did that. But being a folk performer, having hits, it wasn't important. Whatever that has to do with anything . . . [Laughs]

ST: Your songs, like Woody's, always have defied being pop entertainment. In your songs, like his, we know a real person is talking, with lines like "You've got a lot of nerve to say you are my friend."

DYLAN: That's another way of writing a song, of course. Just talking to somebody that ain't there. That's the best way. That's the truest way. Then it just becomes a question of how heroic your speech is. To me, it's something to strive after.

ST: Until you record a song, no matter how heroic it is, it doesn't really exist. Do you ever feel that?

DYLAN: No. If it's there, it exists.

ST: You once said that you only write about what's true, what's been proven to you, that you write about dreams but not fantasies.

DYLAN: My songs really aren't dreams. They're more of a responsive nature. Waking up from a dream is . . . when you write a dream, it's something you try to recollect and you're never quite sure if you're getting it right or not.

ST: You said your songs are responsive. Does life have to be in turmoil for songs to come?

DYLAN: Well, to me, when you need them, they appear. Your life doesn't have to be in turmoil to write a song like that but you need to be outside of it. That's why a lot of people, me myself included, write songs when one form or another of society has rejected you. So that you can truly write about it from the outside. Someone who's never been out there can only imagine it as anything, really.

Younger Than That Now

ST: Outside of life itself?

DYLAN: No. Outside of the situation you find yourself in. There are different types of songs and they're all called songs. But there are different types of songs just like there are different types of people, you know? There's an infinite amount of different kinds, stemming from a common folk ballad verse to people who have classical training. And with classical training, of course, then you can just apply lyrics to classical training and get things going on in positions where you've never been in before. Modern twentieth century ears are the first ears to hear these kind of Broadway songs. There wasn't anything like this. These are musical songs. These are done by people who know music first. And then lyrics. To me, Hank Williams is still the best songwriter.

ST: Hank? Better than Woody Guthrie?

DYLAN: That's a good question. Hank Williams never wrote "This Land Is Your Land." But it's not that shocking for me to think of Hank Williams singing "Pastures of Plenty" or Woody Guthrie singing "Cheatin' Heart." So in a lot of ways those two writers are similar. As writers. But you mustn't forget that both of these people were performers, too. And that's another thing which separates a person who just writes a song . . . People who don't perform but who are so locked into other people who do that, they can sort of feel what that other person would like to say, in a song and be able to write those lyrics. Which is a different thing from a performer who needs a song to play onstage year after year.

ST: And you always wrote your songs for yourself to sing—

DYLAN: My songs were written with me in mind. In those situations, several people might say, "Do you have a song laying around?" The best songs to me—my best songs—are songs which were written very quickly. Yeah, very, very quickly. Just about as much time as it takes to write it down is about as long as it takes to write it. Other than that, there have been a lot of ones that haven't made it. They haven't survived. They could . They need to be dragged out, you know, and looked at again, maybe.

ST: You said once that the saddest thing about songwriting is trying to reconnect with an idea you started before, and how hard that is to do.

DYLAN: To me it can't be done. To me, unless I have another writer around who might want to finish it . . . outside of writing with the Traveling Wilburys, my shared experience writing a song with other songwriters is not that great. Of course, unless you find the right person to write with as a partner . . . [Laughs] . . . you're awfully lucky if you do, but if you don't, it's really more trouble than it's worth, trying to write something with somebody.

ST: Your collaborations with Jacques Levy came out pretty great.

DYLAN: We both were pretty much lyricists. Yeah, very panoramic songs because, you know, after one of my lines, one of his lines would come out. Writing with Jacques wasn't difficult. It was trying to just get it down. It just didn't stop. Lyrically. Of course, my melodies are very simple anyway so they're very easy to remember.

ST: With a song like "Isis" that the two of you wrote together, did you plot that story out prior to writing the verses?

DYLAN: That was a story that [Laughs] meant something to him. Yeah. It just seemed to take on a life of its own, [Laughs] as another view of history. [Laughs] Which there are so many views that don't get told. Oh history, anyway. That wasn't one of them. Ancient history but history nonetheless.

ST: Was that a story you had in mind before the song was written?

DYLAN: No. With this "Isis" thing, it was "Isis" . . . you know, the name sort of rang a bell but not in any kind of vigorous way. So therefore, it was name-that-tune time. It was anything. The name was familiar. Most people would think they knew it from somewhere. But it seemed like just about any way it wanted to go would have been okay, just as long as it didn't get too close. [Laughs]

ST: Too close to what?

DYLAN: [Laughs] Too close to me or him.

ST: People have an idea of your songs freely flowing out from you, but that song and many others of yours are so well-crafted; it has as ABAB rhyme scheme which is like something Byron would do, interlocking every line—

DYLAN: Oh, yeah. Oh, yeah. Oh, sure. If you've heard a lot of free verse, if you've been raised on free verse, William Carlos Williams, e.e. cummings, those kind of people who wrote free verse, your ear is not going to be trained for things to sound that way. Of course, for me it's no secret that all my stuff is rhythmically oriented that way. Like a Byron line would be something as simple as "What is it you buy so dear/with your pain and with your fear?" Now that's a Byron line, but that could have been one of my lines. Up until a certain time, maybe in the twenties, that's the way poetry was. It was that way. It was . . . simple and easy to remember. And always in rhythm. It had a rhythm whether the music was there or not.

ST: Is rhyming fun for you?

DYLAN: Well, it can be, but, you know, it's a game. You know, you sit around . . . you know, it's more like it's mentally . . . mentally . . . it gives you a thrill. It gives you a thrill to rhyme something you might think, "Well, that's never been rhymed before." But then again, people have taken rhyming now, it doesn't have to be exact anymore. Nobody's going to care if you rhyme "represent" with "ferment," you know. Nobody's gonna care.

ST: That was a result of a lot of people of your generation for whom the craft elements of songwriting didn't seem to matter as much. But in your songs the craft is always there, along with the poetry and the energy—

DYLAN: My sense of rhyme used to be more involved in my song-writing than it is . . . Still staying in the unconscious frame of mind, you can pull yourself out and throw up two rhymes first and work it back. You get the rhymes first and work it back and then see if you can make it make sense in another kind of way. You can still stay in the unconscious frame of mind to pull it off, which is the state of mind you have to be in anyway.

ST: So sometimes you will work backwards, like that?

DYLAN: Oh, yeah. Yeah, a lot of times. That's the only way you're going to finish something. That's not uncommon, though.

ST: Do you finish songs even when you feel that maybe they're not keepers?

DYLAN: Keepers or not keepers . . . you keep songs if you think they're any good, and if you don't . . . you can always give them to somebody else. If you've got songs that you're not going to do and you just don't like them . . . show them to other people, if you want. Then again, it all gets back to the motivation. Why you're doing what you're doing. That's what it is. [Laughs] It's confrontation with that . . . goddess of the self. God of the self or goddess of the self? Somebody told me that the goddess rules over the self. Gods don't concern themselves with such earthly matters. Only goddesses . . . would stoop so low. Or bend down so low.

ST: You mentioned that when you were writing "Every Grain Of Sand" that you felt you were in an area where no one had ever been before—

Younger Than That Now

DYLAN: Yeah. In that area where Keats is. Yeah. That's a good poem set to music.

ST: A beautiful melody.

DYLAN: It's a beautiful melody, too, isn't it? It's a folk derivative melody. It's nothing you can put your finger on, but, you know, yeah, those melodies are great. There ain't enough of them, really. Even a song like that, the simplicity of it can be . . . deceiving. As far as . . . a song like that just may have been written in great turmoil, although you would never sense that. Written but not delivered. Some songs are better written in peace and quiet and delivered in turmoil. Others are best written in turmoil and delivered in a peaceful, quiet way. It's a magical thing, popular song. Trying to press it down into everyday numbers doesn't quite work. It's not a puzzle. There aren't pieces that fit. It doesn't make a complete picture that's ever been seen. But, you know, as they say, thank God for songwriters.

ST: Randy Newman said that he writes his songs by going to it every day, like a job—

DYLAN: Tom Paxton told me the same thing. He goes back with me, way back. He told me the same thing. Everyday he gets up and he writes a song. Well, that's great, you know, you write the song and then take your kids to school? Come home, have some lunch with the wife, you know, maybe go write another song. Then Tom said for recreation, to get himself loose, he rode his horse. And then pick up his child from school, and then go to bed with the wife. Now to me that sounds like the ideal way to write songs. To me, it couldn't be any better than that.

ST: How do you do it?

DYLAN: Well, my songs aren't written on a schedule like that. In my mind it's never really been seriously a profession . . . It's been more confessional than professional. Then again, everybody's in it for a different reason.

ST: Do you ever sit down with the intention of writing a song, or do you wait for songs to come to you?

DYLAN: Either or. Both ways. It can come . . . some people are . . . It's possible now for a songwriter to have a recording studio in his house and record a song and make a demo and do a thing. It's like the roles have changed on all that stuff. Now for me, the environment to write the song is extremely important. The environment has to bring something out in me that wants to be brought out. It's a contemplative, reflective thing. Feelings really aren't my thing. See, I don't write lies. It's a proven fact: Most people who say I love you don't mean it. Doctors have proved that. So love generates a lot of songs. Probably more so than a lot. Now it's not my intention to have love influence my songs. Any more than it influenced Chuck Berry's songs or Woody Guthrie's or Hank Williams'. Hank Williams, they're not love songs. You're degrading them songs calling them love songs. Those are songs from the Tree of Life. There's no love on the Tree of Life. Love is on the Tree of Knowledge, the Tree of Good and Evil. So we have a lot of songs in popular music about love. Who needs them? Not you, not me. You can use love in a lot of ways in which it will come back to hurt you. Love is a democratic principle. It's a Greek thing. A college professor told me that if you read about Greece in the history books, you'll know all about America. Nothing that happens will puzzle you ever again. You read the history of Ancient Greece and when the Romans came in, and nothing will ever bother you about America again. You'll see what America is. Now, maybe, but there are a lot of other countries in the world besides America . . . [Laughs] Two. You can't forget about them. [Laughter]

ST: Have you found there are better places in the world than others to write songs?

DYLAN: It's not necessary to take a trip to write a song. What a long, strange trip it's been, however. But that part of it's true, too. Environment is very important. People need peaceful, invigorating environments.

Younger Than That Now

Stimulating environments. In America there's a lot of repression. A lot of people who are repressed . They'd like to get out of town, they just don't know how to do it. And so, it holds back creativity. It's like you go somewhere and you can't help but feel it. Or people even tell it to you, you know? What got me into the whole thing in the beginning wasn't songwriting. That's not what got me into it. When "Hound Dog" came across the radio, there was nothing in my mind that said, "Wow, what a great song, I wonder who wrote that?" It didn't really concern me who wrote it. It didn't matter who wrote it. It was just . . . it was just there. Same way with me now. You hear a good song. Now you think to yourself, maybe, "Who wrote it?" Why? Because the performer's not as good as the song, maybe. The performer's got to transcend that song. At least come up to it. A good performer can always make a bad song sound good. Record albums are filled with good performers singing filler stuff. Everybody can say they've done that. Whether you wrote it or whether somebody else wrote it, it doesn't matter. What interested me was being a musician. The singer was important and so was the song. But being a musician was always first and foremost in the back of my mind. That's why, while other people were learning . . . whatever they were learning. What were they learning way back then?

ST: "Ride, Sally, Ride"?

DYLAN: Something like that. Or "Run, Rudolph, Run." When the others were doing "Run, Rudolph, Run," my interests were going more to Leadbelly kind of stuff, when he was playing a Stell 12-string guitar. Like, how does the guy do that? Where can one of these be found, a 12-string guitar? They didn't have any in my town. My intellect always felt that way. Of the music. Like Paul Whiteman. Paul Whiteman creates a mood. Bing Crosby's early records. They created a mood, like that Cab Calloway, kind of spooky horn kind of stuff. Violins, when big bands had a sound to them, without the Broadway glitz. Once that Broadway trip got into it, it became all sparkly and Las Vegas, really. But it wasn't always so. Music created an environment. It doesn't happen anymore. Why? Maybe technology has just booted it out and there's no need for it. Because we have a screen which supposedly is three-dimensional. Or comes across as three-dimensional. It would like you to believe it's three-dimensional. Well, you know, like old movies and stuff like that that's influenced so many of us who grew up on that stuff. [Picks up Peruvian flute] Like this old thing, here, it's nothing, it's some kind of, what is it? . . . Listen: [Plays a slow tune on the flute] Here, listen to this song. [Plays more] Okay. That's a song. It don't have any words. Why do songs need words? They don't. Songs don't need words. They don't.

ST: Do you feel satisfied with your body of work?

DYLAN: Most everything, yeah.

ST: Do you spend a lot of time writing songs?

DYLAN: Well, did you hear that record that Columbia released last year, *Down In The Groove*? Those songs, they came in pretty easy.

ST: I'd like to mention some of your songs, and see what response you have to them.

DYLAN: Okay.

ST: "One More Cup Of Coffee" [from *Desire*]

DYLAN: [Pause] Was that for a coffee commercial? No . . . It's a gypsy song. That song was written during a gypsy festival in the south of France one summer. Somebody took me there to the gypsy high holy days which coincide with my own particular birthday. So somebody took me to a birthday party there once, and hanging out there for a week probably influenced the writing of that song. But the "valley below" probably came from someplace else. My feeling about the song was that the verses came from someplace else. It wasn't about anything, so this "valley below" thing became the fixture to hang it on. But "valley below" could mean anything.

Younger Than That Now

ST: "Precious Angel" [*from Slow Train Comin'*]

DYLAN: Yeah. That's another one, it could go on forever. There's too many verses and there's not enough. You know? When people ask me, "How come you don't sing that song anymore?" It's like it's another one of those songs: it's just too much and not enough. A lot of my songs strike me that way. That's the natural thing about them to me. It's too hard to wonder why about them. To me, they're not worthy of wondering why about them. They're songs. They're not written in stone. They're on plastic.

ST: To us, though, they are written in stone, because Bob Dylan wrote them. I've been amazed by the way you've changed some of your great songs—

DYLAN: Right. Somebody told me that Tennyson often wanted to rewrite his poems when he saw them in print.

ST: "I and I" [*from Infidels*]

DYLAN: [Pause] That was one of them Caribbean songs. One year a bunch of songs just came to me hanging around down in the islands, and that was one of them.

ST: "Joey" [*from Desire*]

DYLAN: To me, that's a great song. Yeah. And it never loses its appeal.

ST: And it has one of the greatest visual endings of any song.

DYLAN: That's a tremendous song. And you'd only know that singing it night after night. You know who got me singing that song? [Jerry] Garcia. Yeah. He got me singing that song again. He said that's one of the best songs ever written. Coming from him, it was hard to know which way to take that. [Laughs] He got me singing that song again with them [The Grateful Dead]. It was amazing how it would, right from the get go, it had a life of its own, it just ran out of the gate and it just kept on getting better and better and better and better and it keeps on getting better. It's in its infant stages, as a performance thing. Of course, it's a long song. But, to me, not to blow my own horn, but to me the song is like a Homer ballad. Much more so than "A Hard Rain," which is a long song, too. But, to me, "Joey" has a Homeric quality to it that you don't hear everyday. Especially in popular music.

ST: "Ring Them Bells" [from *Oh Mercy*]

DYLAN: It stands up when you hear it played by me. But if another performer did it, you might find that it probably wouldn't have as much to do with bells as what the title proclaims. Somebody once came and sang it in my dressing room. To me. [Laughs] To try to influence me to sing it that night. [Laughter] It could have gone either way, you know. Elliot Mintz: Which way did it go?

DYLAN: It went right out the door. [Laughter] It went out the door and didn't come back. Listening to this song that was on my record, sung by someone who wanted me to sing it . . . There was no way he was going to get me to sing it like that. A great performer, too.

ST: "Idiot Wind" [from *Blood On The Tracks*]

DYLAN: "Idiot Wind." Yeah, you know, obviously, if you've heard both versions you realize, of course, that there could be a myriad of verses for the thing. It doesn't stop. It wouldn't stop. Where do you end? You could still be writing it, really. It's something that could be a work continually in progress. Although, on saying that, let me say that my lyrics, to my way of thinking, are better for my songs than anybody else's. People have felt about my songs sometimes the same way as me. And they say to me, your songs are so opaque that, people tell me, they have feelings they'd like to express within the same framework. My response, always, is go ahead, do it, if you feel like it. But it never comes off. They're not as good as my lyrics. There's just something about my lyrics that just have a gallantry to them. And that might be all they have going for them. [Laughs] However, it's no small thing.

NEWSWEEK, MARCH 20, 1995

A Primitive's Portfolio

Malcolm Jones, Jr.

THE ONE SURE THING ABOUT Bob Dylan is that there is no sure thing. In a musical career stretching over more than three decades, he has proven time and again that he owns the most bottomless bag of tricks in the business. With changeling grace, he has embraced folk music, rock and roll, country, and gospel; on his last two albums, pop music's most singular singer-songwriter covered folk songs written and sung before he was born. It's the same with his public pronounce-ments. In interviews over the years, he has been baleful, apoc-alyptic, charming, abrasive, squirrelly and profound, depending on his mood. When he sat down two weeks ago for an exclusive interview with *Newsweek* to talk about his latest project, a book of his drawings, he wore the guise of plain old Bob, earnest, articulate, self-deprecating and darn near kitten-cuddly.

"My favorite artists are people like Donatello or Caravaggio or Titioan, all those over-whelming guys," he says. "I wouldn't even know where to begin to approach that kind of mastery." Of his own work, he is content to say, "The purpose of my drawings is very undefined. They're very personal drawings, I guess like someone would knit a sweater, y'know?" It takes a while to get used to this kind of talk from the man whose music elevated scorn to an art form. But then, this isn't Dylan the musician, this is Dylan the artist promoting *Drawn Blank* (Random House, $30), a collection of pencil, charcoal, and pen-and ink drawings. Every Dylan fan has known for years that he dabbled in art. He did the cover paintings for the Band's debut album *Music From Big Pink*, and his own *Self Portrait*, and in the '80s, his sketches /adorned the album jacket art of *Infidels* and *Empire Burlesque*. But with this book he's laid his artistic bid on the line.

Asked where the idea came from, Dylan says it came from his publisher. David Rosenthal, Dylan's editor at Random House, says the idea came from Dylan's people. Dylan denies he had much to do with putting the book together; he submitted drawings and they did the rest. But Rosenthal says Dylan was "deeply, deeply involved." The only thing that's clear is that the man who sang "It's always been my nature to take chances" is walking on untried ground and doing damage control with every step.

He needn't worry so hard. There's nothing in this book to rival Rembrandt, and the selection might have been more rigorously culled (captions would be nice too). But the best of the work displays a becoming spareness of line and a loopy but engaging sense of composition. Hotel rooms, street scenes, big diesel trucks, Dylan doesn't do pretty. He's content to take the world as he finds it, and whatever is, is interesting.

"I don't concoct drawings out of my head. It's all out there somewhere and that's the only way I can work or get any satisfaction out of doing it," he says, sitting in an empty Manhattan recording studio where, well into a Saturday night, he's been rehearsing his band for a European tour. With his black-and-gray checked shirt hanging out over black slacks, black boots and his every-day-is-a-bad-hair-day hair framing a motel tan, the 53-year-old Dylan looks every inch the rock-and-roll eminence gone a tad long in the tooth. Setting fire to a filtered Camel, he continues, "These drawings, they kind of go with my primitive style of music." Both are based in reality, and in both music making l and drawing he aims to lose himself. "It's almost like meditating. I feel like I'm renewed after I make a drawing."

A lot of Dylan's art, his portraits particularly, resemble the drawings high school kids do for fun on the covers of their notebooks. The difference is that while most people grow up and shy away from art, Dylan persists. Like his music, where professional polish has never been the point, his drawings epitomize the amateur's creed, that homemade, hand-hewn stuff is always the best.

Dylan's fascination with reality does not extend to the virtual variety. Though his life and work recently provided the subject matter for a CD-ROM package entitled *Bob Dylan: Highway 61 Interactive*, he has not yet seen it. "I'm just rooted back there in the '50s, and what's got me this far keeps me going," he says with a grin. "I know people who've got that online thing and games and things, but I find it too inhibiting to sit in front of a screen. On any level I don't even like to sit and watch TV too much. I feel I'm being manipulated."

"Greed": Dylan called his latest, Grammy-winning album *World Gone Wrong*, and meant every word of it. Two songs are by the late Georgia bluesman Willie McTell, a musician whose passing he mourned in one of his greatest songs, "Blind Willie McTell" ("Power and greed and corruptible seed / Seem to be all that there is") and whose work, for Dylan, symbolizes a level of craft fast vanishing. "If you're looking for depth," he says, "you gotta go back." McTell's songs, most written in the '20s, '30s, and '40s, are touchstones to reality for Dylan. "To be around a long time, a musician has got to learn what he can trust. These songs are based on reality, like these drawings. These were real things that happened."

Dylan's increasing fascination with the legacy of the past extends to his own early work. "I've been working on some songs for 20 years, always moving toward some kind of perfection," even though "I know it's never going to happen." (The latest incarnation of those songs will appear next month in an album of Dylan's much-lauded MTV "Unplugged" concert.) But art for him has always been about subversive change. As a result, he can't abide those fans who want him to continue performing his old songs exactly the way he recorded them. "I'd rather live in the moment than some kind of nostalgia trip, which I feel is a drug, a real drug that people are mainlining. It's outrageous. People are mainlining nostalgia like it was morphine. I don't want to be a drug dealer." Chuckling at his own joke, the man who has made a career out of reinventing himself stands up to go find more cigarettes and coffee and get back to work.

FORT LAUDERDALE SUN SENTINEL,
SEPTEMBER 29, 1995

A Midnight Chat with Bob Dylan

John Dolen

WHEN BOB DYLAN CALLS, it's nearly midnight. When he speaks it is with a clear, distinctive voice. Even though he's at the end of his day, having just returned to a Fort Lauderdale hotel after a band rehearsal, he is contemplative, enigmatic, even poetic.

The Southern leg of his current tour cranks into high gear tonight with the first of two concerts at the Sunrise Musical Theatre. The tour, which has been in progress for more than a year, has earned rave reviews from critics in New York, San Francisco, Dublin. In a nearly hour-long interview with Arts & Features Editor John Dolen, the first in-depth interview he has given to a newspaper this year, Dylan talks about his songs, the creative process and the free gig at the Edge in Fort Lauderdale last Saturday.

Q: Like many others, over the years I've spent thousands of hours listening to your albums. Even now, not a month goes by without me reaching for *Blonde on Blonde, Highway 61 Revisited, Slow Train Coming, Street Legal, Oh Mercy.* Do you sit back and look at all these albums and say, hey, that's pretty good?

Younger Than That Now

A: You know, it's ironic, I never listen to those records. I really don't notice them anymore except to pick songs off of them here and there to play. Maybe I should listen to them. As a body of work, there could always be more. But it depends. Robert Johnson only made one record. His body of work was just one record. Yet there's no praise or esteem high enough for the body of work he represents. He's influenced hundreds of artists. There are people who put out 40 or 50 records and don't do what he did.

Q: What was the record?

A: He made a record called *King of the Delta Blues Singers*. In '61 or '62. He was brilliant.

Q: Your performance at the Rock and Roll Hall of Fame concert in Cleveland earlier this month drew a lot of great notices. Is that important to you? What's your feeling about that institution?

A: I never visited the actual building, I was just over at the concert, which was pretty long. So I have no comment on the interior or any of the exhibits inside.

Q: But how do you feel about the idea of a rock hall of fame itself?

A: Nothing surprises me anymore. It's a perfect time for anything to happen.

Q: At the Edge show Saturday, you did a lot of covers, including some old stuff, like "Confidential." Was that a Johnny Ray song?
A: It's by Sonny Knight. You won't hear that again.

Q: Oh, was that the reason for your "trying to turn bullshit into gold" comment at the show? Were these covers just something for folks at the Edge? Does that mean you aren't going to be doing more material like that on your tour, including the Sunrise shows?

A: It will be the usual show we're used to doing on this tour now, songs most people will have heard already.

Q: In the vein of non-Dylan music, what does Bob Dylan toss on the CD or cassette player these days?

A: Ever heard of John Trudell? He talks his songs instead of singing them and has a real good band. There's a lot of tradition to what he is doing. I also like Kevin Lynch. And Steve Forbert.

Q: Are there new bands you think are worth bringing to attention?

A: I hear people here and there and I think they're all great. In most cases I never hear of them again. I saw some groups in London this summer. I don't know their names.

Q: At this stage of your career, when you've earned every kind of honor and accolade that a person can get, what motivates you?

A: I've had it both ways. I have had good and bad accolades. If you pay any attention to them at all, it makes you pathological. It makes us pathological, to read about ourselves. You try not to pay attention or you try to discard it as soon as possible.

Q: For some writers the motivation is that burden, that you have to get what's inside of you out and down on paper. How is it with you?

A: Like that, exactly. But if I can't make it happen when it comes, you know, when other things intrude, I usually don't make it happen. I don't go to a certain place at a certain time every day to build it. In my case, a lot of these songs, they lay around imperfectly . . .

Q: As a songwriter, what's the creative process? How does a song like "All Along the Watchtower" come about?

Younger Than That Now

A: There's three kinds of ways. You write lyrics and try to find a melody. Or, if you come up with a melody, then you have to stuff the lyrics in there some kinda way. And then the third kind of a way is when they both come at the same time. Where it all comes in a blur: The words are the melody and the melody is the words. And that's the ideal way for somebody like myself to get going with something. "All Along the Watchtower" was that way. It leaped out in a very short time. I don't like songs that make you feel feeble or indifferent. That lets a whole lot of things out of the picture for me.

Q: How did you feel when you first heard Jimi Hendrix's version of "All Along the Watchtower"?

A: It overwhelmed me, really. He had such talent, he could find things inside a song and vigorously develop them. He found things that other people wouldn't think of finding in there. He probably improved upon it by the spaces he was using. I took license with the song from his version, actually, and continue to do it to this day.

Q: "Angelina," off The Bootleg Series, is such a great song, but no matter how hard I try I can't figure out the words; any clues for me?

A: I never try to figure out what they're about. If you have to think about it, then it's not there.

Q: A song that always haunted me was "Senor," from *Street Legal*. Have you played that at all in the last few years?

A: We play that maybe once every third, fourth, or fifth show.

Q: In the 70s, after years abroad, I remember the incredible elation I felt coming back to the States and hearing your Christian songs, a validation of experiences I had been through in Spain. I remember the lines.

You talk about Buddha
You talk about Muhammad
But you never said a word about
the one who came to die for us instead. . . .

Those were fearless words. How do you feel about those words and the
songs your wrote during that period now?

A: Just writing a song like that probably emancipated me from other
kinds of illusions. I've written so many songs and so many records that
I can't address them all. I can't say that I would disagree with that line.
On its own level it was some kind of turning point for me, writing that.

Q: With the great catalog you have and with the success this year with
the *MTV Unplugged* disc, why does this concert tour have such a heavy
guitar and drums thing going?

A: It's not the kind of music that will put anybody to sleep.

Q: The other night at the Edge you left the harmonicas on the stand
without touching them, any reason for that?

A: They are such a dynamo unto themselves. I pick them up when I feel
like it.

Q: You've made several passes through here in the past 10 years. Your
thoughts on South Florida?

A: I like it a lot, who wouldn't. There's a lot to like.

Q: Now there is Bob Dylan on CD-ROM, Bob Dylan on the Internet
and all that stuff. Are some people taking you too seriously?

A: It's not for me to say. People take everything seriously. You can get
too altruistic on yourself because of the brain energy of other people.

Younger Than That Now

Q: Across the Atlantic is a fellow named Elvis Costello, who, after you, takes a lot of shelf space in my stereo. Both of you are prolific, turn out distinctive albums each time, have great imagery, have a lot to say, and so on. Is there any reason that in all the years I've never seen your names or faces together?

A: It's funny you should mention that. He just played four or five shows with me in London and Paris. He was doing a lot of new songs, playing them by himself. He was doing his thing. You so had to be there.

Q: Is America better or worse than, say, in the days of "The Times They Are A-Changin' "?

A: I see pictures of the '50s, the '60s, and the '70s and I see there was a difference. But I don't think the human mind can comprehend the past and the future. They are both just illusions that can manipulate you into thinking there's some kind of change. But after you've been around awhile, they both seem unnatural. It seems like we're going in a straight line, but then you start seeing things that you've seen before. Haven't you experienced that? It seems we're going around in circles.

Q: When you look ahead now, do you still see a Slow Train Coming?

A: When I look ahead now, it's picked up quite a bit of speed. In fact, it's going like a freight train now.

USA TODAY, SEPTEMBER 28, 1997

At the Heart of Dylan

Edna Gunderson

SANTA MONICA, CALIFORNIA—HEARTACHE. The word literally and figuratively defines Bob Dylan in 1997. After surviving a life-threatening cardiac infection, he is resuming his storied career with a powerful album about lost love and dwindling hope.

Time Out of Mind, in stores Tuesday, examines mortality and heart-break in 11 raw and potent tracks. Though finished long before Dylan was hospitalized, the lyrics carry added resonance in light of his illness.

Disciples will ruminate over lines like "When you think you've lost everything, you find you can lose a little more," "It's not dark yet but it's getting there" and "I was on anything but a roll."

At 56, nearly four decades after his first public appearances, Dylan is on a roll. A chorus of praise greets *Time Out of Mind:* A+ in *Entertainment Weekly,* **** in *Rolling Stone,* "his best sustained work since the mid-1970s," raves the *New York Times.* He's *Newsweek's* cover boy. On Saturday, he played for the pope. In December, he'll become the first rock star anointed a Kennedy Center honoree.

Younger Than That Now

Dylan, slim and natty in a black shirt, slacks, and patent leather loafers, seems anything but morose during a rare interview. His clear blue eyes, ready smile, and animated demeanor suggest good health and high spirits. He is quick to discourage analysts who'd dismantle his songs for clues about death and despair.

"I don't think they should or could be interpreted that way, if at all," he says, his back to a hotel window that frames the Pacific sunset. "You can't interpret a Hank Williams song. He's done the interpretation and the performance, and that's it. Now it's for the listener to decide if it moves him or not. That's something you don't even decide. That happens to you unconsciously.

"I let the songs fly, and people respond. Whether they make a valid interpretation or look at it with a false eye, I'm not concerned with that."

Nor is the ferociously private Dylan willing to expound on *Time*'s tales of shattered romance, except to acknowledge that the songs are drawn from personal experience.

"I can identify with other people and situations, but I tend not to," he says. "I would rather recall things from my own life, and I don't have to force myself. . . . Just being in certain environments triggers a response in my brain, a certain feeling I want to articulate. For some reason, I am attracted to self-destruction. I know that personal sacrifice has a great deal to do with how we live or don't live our lives.

"These songs are not allegorical," Dylan stresses. "I have given that up. . . . Philosophical dogma doesn't interest me."

Pop's most scrutinized yet inscrutable artist doesn't deny his mercurial nature or his disdain for the labels of rebel, poet, and prophet. Though he radically transformed folk, rock, and the singer/songwriter genre in the '60s, he refuses to clone seminal works and adopts a humble stance.

"I don't consider myself a songwriter in the sense of Townes Van Zandt or Randy Newman," he says. "I'm not Paul Simon. I can't do that. My songs come out of folk music and early rock 'n' roll, and that's it. I'm not a classical lyricist, I'm not a meticulous lyricist. I don't write melodies that are clever or catchy. It's all very traditionally documented."

The most influential songwriter of modern times recognizes that his mass appeal has waned.

"I'm under the impression that people aren't really paying attention to my records," he says. "I'm aware that I don't sell records like I did in the '80s or the '70s, and that's OK as long as I can play, and the right crowd is going to come and see it properly. I don't follow what records are at the top of the charts. I ceased doing that a long, long time ago."

He does, however, take notice of rising son Jakob, whose band the Wallflowers, No. 31 after 64 weeks on *Billboard*'s chart, commercially outranks his dad's '90s output.

"I'm proud of his accomplishments," Dylan says. "He's still young, and he's come a long way in a short time. I worried about him when he started out. I just didn't want to see him get roughed up. This business can throw you into deep water."

The murkiest depths? Celebrity. "It mortifies me to even think that I am a celebrity," Dylan says. "I'm not one, and I never want to be one. I lead a very insular existence. It's different onstage, because those people look at me as a performer.

"By being a celebrity, you lose your anonymity. It short-circuits your creative powers when people come up and interrupt your train of thought. They consider you completely approachable. And you can't be rude to people, so basically you shut yourself down. I know I do. I shut myself down when people come up and want to shake my hand or want to talk. That's just dead time."

Dylan avoids the press, loathes photo sessions, and steadily releases records with scant promotion.

Time contains his first batch of originals since 1990's *Under the Red Sky*. Since then, he has released a boxed set of rarities, his third greatest hits album, an *MTV Unplugged*, and two collections of vintage folk and blues, 1992's *Good as I Been to You* and 1993's *World Gone Wrong*.

Making *Time* was a liberating experience for Dylan, who can feel burdened by the weight of his legend. The classics he performs onstage "are proven to be true and strong, otherwise I couldn't sing them night after night," he says. "It's not like I can eclipse that.

"I'm not looking to do that, but to record new songs, they have to be in that arena, and that's why it took a long time. I was constantly thinking, will these songs stand up to what I'm playing night after night?"

Dylan considers his early records roughly sketched prototypes that later matured onstage. Produced by Daniel Lanois last January in a Miami studio, the new songs were captured live with sidemen schooled in low-tech production.

"This record is not a blueprint," Dylan says. "This is it. This is the way these songs should go, every single last one. This record went through evolutions. What you hear comes through that whole maze, that labyrinth of fire that it takes to perfect the arrangement and structure.

"There is nothing contemporary about it. There is no trickery. We went back to the way a primitive record was made, before the advent of technology. It's almost a revolutionary concept these days."

The man who shocked the folk rank and file by plugging in now worries that high-watt noise is eradicating traditional American music.

"You see all this electricity speaking, all this wizardry," he says. "Pull out the plugs and probably very few of these people could move you, because they can't play. They are dominated by the electricity. Guys like Elmore James played acoustically and used electricity so they could be heard in a crowded room. They weren't depending on electricity to hide talent they didn't have. I don't want a bunch of flaky sounds. It's a dead end."

Dylan was still sequencing *Time* tracks when he was stricken with chest pains in May. He was declared fit after an initial medical exam.

"I accepted that, but the pain didn't go away," he says. "It was intolerable pain, where it affects your breathing every waking moment."

He entered a hospital May 25 and was diagnosed with pericarditis, a swelling of the sac around the heart, brought on by a fungal infection called histoplasmosis. Dylan spent six weeks off his feet. His brush with death brought delirium and ennui but no spiritual revelations.

"I didn't have any philosophical, profound thoughts," he says. "The pain stopped me in my tracks and fried my mind. I was so sick my mind just blanked out. I'm getting better; that's all I can say right now."

The alignment of events this year—his health scare, broad acclaim for *Time Out of Mind*, the papal encounter—has magnified Dylan's star power and fed an ongoing deification that he finds perplexing. In 1990, he received France's highest cultural honor. The next year, he got Grammy's lifetime achievement award. And in 1992, an all-star concert, pay-per-view, and compilation album toasted his 30th anniversary as a recording artist.

Such honors "are unexpected and unsolicited, and I'm not nonchalant about it, because in some sense it really does matter," he says. "I'm very appreciative."

But he's leery of the hype. Dozens of books are devoted to the enigmatic troubadour. He doesn't read them.

"I'm not going to read a book about myself," he says with a chuckle. "I mean, why? I'm with myself enough. I wake up every day and I'm still me. It would be torture to read about myself. I would rather read about anybody else but me."

BIBLIOGRAPHY

The selections used in this anthology were taken from the periodicals and editions listed below. In some cases, other editions may be easier to find. Hard-to-find or out-of-print titles often are available through inter-library loan services or through Internet booksellers.

Allen, Lynne. "Interview with an Icon." Originally appeared in *Trouser Press*, December 12, 1978.

Brown, Mick. "Jesus, Who's Got Time to Keep Up with the Times?" Originally appeared in *The Sunday Times*, July 1, 1984.

Cohen, Scott. "Bob Dylan Not Like a Rolling Stone Interview." Originally appeared as "Don't Ask Me Nothin' About Nothin' I Might Just Tell You the Truth: Bob Dylan Revisited" in *SPIN Magazine*, December 1985.

Creswell, Toby. "Gates of Eden Revisited: A Conversation with Bob Dylan." Originally appeared in *Rolling Stone Australia*, January 16, 1986.

De Yong, Jenny and Peter Roche. "Bob Dylan." Originally appeared in the *Sheffield University Paper*, May 1965.

Dolen, John. "A Midnight Chat with Bob Dylan." Originally appeared in the *Fort Lauderdale Sun-Sentinel*, September 29, 1995.

Ephron, Nora and Susan Edmiston. "Bob Dylan Interview." Originally appeared in *Positively Tie Dream*, August 1965.

Fariña, Richard. "Baez and Dylan: A Generation Singing Out." Originally appeared in *Mademoiselle*, August 1964.

Godard, J.R. "Dylan Meets the Press." Originally appeared in *The Village Voice*, March 3, 1965.

Gunderson, Edna. "At the Heart of Dylan." Originally appeared in *USA Today*, September 28, 1997.

Henshaw, Laurie. "Mr. Send Up." Originally appeared in *Disc Weekly*, May 12, 1965.

Hentoff, Nat. "The Crackin', Shakin', Breakin' Sounds." Originally appeared in *The New Yorker*, October 24, 1964.

Hickey, Neil. "The TV Guide Interview." Originally appeared in *TV Guide*, September 11, 1976.

Hilburn, Robert. "Bob Dylan: Still A-Changin'." Originally appeared in the *Los Angeles Times*, November 17, 1985.

Jerome, Jim. "Bob Dylan: A Myth Materializes with a New Protest Record and a New Tour." Originally appeared in *People Magazine*, November 10, 1975.

Jones Jr., Malcolm. "A Primitive's Portfolio." Originally appeared in *Newsweek*, March 20, 1995.

Robbins, Paul J. "The Paul J. Robbins Interview." From the *L.A. Free Press*, March 1965.

Rockwell, John. "Tour's Roaring Ovations Leave Dylan Quietly Pleased." Originally appeared in the *New York Times*, January 7, 1974.

Rosenbaum, Ron. "The Playboy Interview." Originally appeared in *Playboy*, March 1978.

Shelton, Robert. "One Foot on the Highway" from *No Direction Home: The Life and Music of Bob Dylan*. New York: HarperCollins, 1986.

Spencer, Neil. "The Diamond Voice from Within." Originally appeared in *New Musical Express*, August 15, 1981.

Vox, Bono. "The Bono Vox Interview." originally appeared as "Bono, Bob and Van" in *Hot Press*, August 10, 1984.

Young, Izzy. "What Was It You Wanted" originally titled "Folklore Center Interview." From the *Izzy Young Journals*, October 20, 1961.

Zollo, Paul. "Bob Dylan: The SongTalk Interview." Originally appeared in *SongTalk*, Winter 1991.